The Tasman Map
A Biography of a Map

The Mitchell Library vestibule and the Tasman Map Mosaic

The Tasman Map

A Biography of a Map

Abel Tasman, the Dutch East India Company
and the First Dutch Discoveries of Australia

IAN BURNET

ROSENBERG

DEDICATION

This book is dedicated to all those members of the Duyfken Foundation and their supporters who had the foresight to build the *Duyfken* replica ship and through their continued involvement keep the history of the first Dutch voyages to Australia alive.

First published in Australia in 2019
by Rosenberg Publishing Pty Ltd
PO Box 6125, Dural Delivery Centre NSW 2158
Phone: 61 2 9654 1502 Fax: 61 2 9654 1338
Email: sales@rosenbergpub.com.au
Web: www.rosenbergpub.com.au

ISBN 978-0-6484466-5-1 paperback
ISBN978-9-6484466-7-5 ebook

Printed in China by Prolong Press Limited

Contents

Acknowledgments

I would like to thank my wife Yusra Zahari and my daughters Miranda and Melissa who have supported me in all of my writing ventures.

Thanks go to Toni Pollard who provided invaluable comments and corrections on the drafts of this work. Thanks to Nick Birmingham who commented on the chapter relating to the voyages of the *Duyfken* and the *Pera*.

Thanks also to Simon Fieldhouse, Robert Garvey, Jeffrey Mellefont, Natali Pearson and Juna Rice who provided images or photographs for the book. My thanks as well to all those who work at the State Library of New South Wales for their assistance.

Prologue

Over time the names of the continent of Australia were to change from the 'known but unknown continent' of *Terra Australis Incognita*, to the land of *Locach* or *Boeach (Beach)* as described by Marco Polo, to *Java le Grande* as imagined by the Dieppe mapmakers, to *Nuca Antara* as drawn by Manuel Godhino de Erédia, to *Nova Guinea* as charted by Willem Janszoon, to *'t Zuyd landt* or *Terra del Zud* as named by the Dutch, to *Hollandia Nova* and then *Compagnis Niew Nederland* (the Company's New Netherland), as recorded on the Tasman Map.

The Tasman Map is an icon of early Dutch cartography and shows the first European discoveries of Australia. Over a period of only forty years from 1606 to 1644 and based on sixteen separate discoveries, the first map of Australia took shape and it shows a recognisable outline of the north, west and south coasts of Australia that was not to change for another 125 years until the arrival of the British explorer James Cook.

The version of the map held by the Mitchell Library in Sydney, Australia, is hand drawn on delicate Japanese paper and is thought to have been especially prepared for presentation to the Amsterdam Chamber of the Dutch East India Company. Every visitor who passes through the vestibule of the Mitchell Library stops to admire the magnificent marble mosaic of the Tasman Map which fills the entire vestibule floor and shows Abel Tasman's voyages of exploration around Australia in 1642/43 and 1644.

The history of the first Dutch discoveries of Australia is linked to spices since the Europeans considered that spices were worth their weight in gold. It was this search for the Spice Islands that drove the European 'Age of Discovery' and first brought their explorers and traders to South-East Asia. Thus we cannot talk about the first European discoveries of Australia without first talking about spices.

Medieval Europe could not grow enough feed to keep all their cattle alive during the winter and most of the herd were slaughtered and eaten during the autumn harvest festivals. Spices such as pepper, cloves, nutmeg and cinnamon not only helped disguise the flavour of salted or rancid meat, but their antibacterial properties preserved meats that were slowly putrefying. After the Crusades, demand for spices increased even more as the Knights returning home from their occupation of the Holy Lands had acquired a taste for the exotic flavours and aromatic scents of the East.

From early times Indonesian seafarers brought these spices to China and India from where they were traded across the Silk Road and along the Spice Route before they reached Europe. History's earliest written record of cloves dates from the third century BC in China where the annals of the Han Dynasty describe how the Emperor would not allow his courtiers to approach him without first chewing a clove bud to sweeten their breath. Considering the lack of hygiene in early times, cloves were invaluable as their properties killed oral bacteria and at the same time acted as a breath freshener. The Chinese also valued the analgesic effects of clove oil as a small amount of it applied to a toothache deadened a nagging pain, while rubbed into the temples it relieved a throbbing headache. India's traditional Ayurveda healers used cloves to treat respiratory and digestive ailments, clove tea was a useful household remedy for all sorts of stomach ailments and ground cloves mixed into a paste and applied to the skin helped to heal wounds and skin infections.

The Spice Route began at the regional trading port of Malacca on the Malay Peninsula and it was to here that Indonesian traders shipped pepper, cloves, nutmeg and cinnamon from all across the archipelago. From Malacca, Indian Gujarati traders shipped them to Calicut in India. From Calicut, Arabs and Persians traded these spices along the great geographic highways of the Red Sea and the Persian Gulf from where they were then carried on recalcitrant camels across the deserts of the Arabian Peninsula to the Mediterranean Sea.

It was the Venetians who eventually controlled the spice trade across the Mediterranean from the ports of Alexandria, Gaza and Antioch. On the Iberian Peninsula the Portuguese and the Spanish were envious of the wealth and power of Venice and from the fifteenth century both sought a maritime route that would take them directly to the Spice Islands and break the stranglehold that the Venetians and Middle Eastern merchants had on the trade. The Portuguese succeeded in rounding the Cape of Good Hope and the capture of Goa and Malacca allowed them to bring ships loaded with spices back to Lisbon. With great daring the Spanish found a route around South America through the Strait of Magellan and were able to bring back spices from the Spice Islands after completing that greatest voyage in maritime history – the first circumnavigation of the world.

The other factor that brought European explorers into the southern seas was the concept of a large southern land mass needed to balance the lands of the northern hemisphere. Aristotle speculated 'that there must be a region bearing the same relation to the southern pole as the place we live in bears to our pole'. Early globemakers were able to place the land mass of the known world in the upper part of their globe, but what lay in the southern part? Since the earth was spinning regularly around its axis it was easy for these early philosophers to conclude there had to be a land mass of equal size spread around the lower part of the globe in order to achieve balance. They believed this was absolutely vital – 'for otherwise, the stability of the world in its central position could not last'.

The 1570 world map by Abraham Ortelius shows the known world of Afro–Eurasia while below in the southern hemisphere and separated by ocean is a large Antarctic continent labelled Terra Australis Nondum Cognita – 'The South Land Not Yet Known', which he shows as having a northern peninsula extending to New Guinea and to an area near the south of Java. There were also those who wanted to believe this unknown land was fabulously wealthy, containing mountains of gold and silver similar to those found in Peru and it was this quest for gold that lured European explorers into the southern oceans.

World map by Abraham Ortelius, 1570 (National Library of Australia)

This book begins with the formation of the Dutch State, the rise of the Dutch East India Company (VOC), its struggle for trade supremacy over the Portuguese, Spanish and English trading houses and its resulting domination of the valuable spice trade from the East Indies. The Dutch East India Company became the world's first joint-stock company and the world's first multinational company. From their headquarters in Batavia (Jakarta) the Dutch developed a trading monopoly that spread from Indonesia across the Far East to India, Malaya, China and Japan, bringing huge wealth to the Netherlands during what became known as the Dutch Golden Age.

The book follows the first Dutch voyage towards the South Land and the landing on Cape York by Willem Janszoon in the *Duyfken* in 1606. In the next 40 years there were eleven accidental Dutch discoveries of the west coast of Australia, beginning with Dirk Hartog's landing in 1616 and five planned voyages of discovery including the voyages of exploration by Abel Tasman when he discovered Tasmania and New Zealand in 1642 and when he charted the north and north-west coasts of Australia in 1644.

The book will follow these early voyages and show how the maps they produced began to define a continent until the Tasman Map shows a recognisable chart of the north, west and south coasts of Australia. As a trading company the Dutch East India Company was looking for commercial opportunities to reward its shareholders. Unfortunately the South Land they discovered had no spice trees, no obvious mountains containing gold or silver and only desolate coasts occupied by near-naked Aborigines. Consequently, it was after the last Tasman voyage of 1644 that the Company lost interest in the land they had named Hollandia Nova.

The Tasman Map remained unchanged for the next century and a quarter until James Cook on the *Endeavour* charted the east coast of Australia, claiming it for King George III in 1770 and naming it New South Wales. On his return to England, Cook was able to follow the route that the Spaniard Luis Vaz de Torres had followed through the Torres Strait in 1606, a route which despite two attempts had eluded Dutch discovery and which perhaps would have allowed them to explore the east coast of Australia.

It was in 1925 and 1933 that the Mitchell Library in Sydney acquired the Tasman Huydecoper Journal and the Tasman Bonaparte Map, which show the results of the early Dutch mapping of Australia and Tasman's voyages of discovery. The story of how these treasures of Dutch exploration and cartography were acquired will bring new recognition to these icons of both Dutch and Australian history

While it is true that a picture is worth a thousand words, a map can tell a thousand stories – including the excitement, apprehension and dread as passengers and crew leave the Netherlands for the East Indies, the deprivations of eight months at sea on a voyage halfway around the world, the lives lost to scurvy, pneumonia and shipwreck, the tragedy of the wreck of the Batavia, the desperate voyages of a few survivors to safety in an open boat, the discoveries of unknown lands, and deaths at the hands of cannibals. These are all stories which are part of the Tasman Map.

1   *The Low Countries, the United Provinces and the Dutch Republic*

This story begins in the low lands of north-western Europe. Who would have believed that these coastal estuaries, swamps and marshes at the margins of the North Sea would become an economic powerhouse and the epicentre of global trade?

The physical location of the Low Countries is different from anywhere else in Europe and its low-lying location between land and sea defines its history until the present day. Much of its land had to be reclaimed from the marshes and the sea by people who worked together to build dams, dykes and windmills to pump out its water. Elsewhere in Europe most of the lands were controlled by lords and the nobles who allowed peasants to work their land and pay rent in the form of labour and produce. However, in the Low Countries the people, by reclaiming the lands with their own hands, owned more than half of it. Hence the popular saying that 'God made the earth, but the Dutch made Holland'.

Consequently these people who had reclaimed their own land had no allegiance to any lord of the manor. In contrast to the feudal kingdoms of the rest of Europe where this lord would have his own allegiance to both a duke and to the bishops of the Roman Catholic Church, and this duke would have his own allegiance to a king and to the Holy Roman Empire.

Offshore, the North Sea was brimming with herring and the fishermen in these ports learned how to go further out to sea to net more fish, and to preserve them by certain methods of filleting and then by packing them in casks with salt. It is said that the early economy of Amsterdam was based on both herring and beer, because the city was given the exclusive right to import beer from Hamburg, while herring were an essential element of the people's diet and the export economy.

Located on the margins of the North Sea, the Low Countries saw the development of ports which depended on trade, manufacturing and the free flow of goods. Since this was not a feudal society most of these towns and ports were governed by guilds and councils, along with a figurehead ruler whose interaction with the citizens was regulated by a set of rules describing his authority.

By the thirteenth century, ports in the Low Countries profited by joining the Hanseatic

League, a group of powerful trading ports developed around the Baltic Sea, including Lubeck, Hamburg and Rostock. Its member ports quickly grew rich by the importing and exporting of goods including herring, salt, grain, iron ore, honey, textiles, timber and flax.

By the fifteenth century the ports of the Low Countries had already established themselves as one of Europe's greatest seafaring localities. The Dutch were accomplished shipbuilders, navigators and mapmakers who, located between the powerhouse economies of England and Germany, were at the crossroads of major trade routes. Its merchants made handsome profits exporting items such as clothing, salted herring, soap and tapestries, by shipping grain south from the Baltic and by bringing goods like salt, wine and olive oil north from the Mediterranean.

Amsterdam, surrounded by marsh, lakes and riddled by waterways is located near the mouth of the Amstel River before it drains into the Zuiderzee, providing a safe inland port with access to the interior. It became an important trading centre where goods from the North Sea, the Baltic and the Mediterranean could be stored, processed, refined and then distributed along rivers and canals across Northern Europe. This bird's-eye view of Amsterdam from as early as 1544 shows the number of ships anchored in its harbour and how its canals allow the access of goods directly into the city and its warehouses.

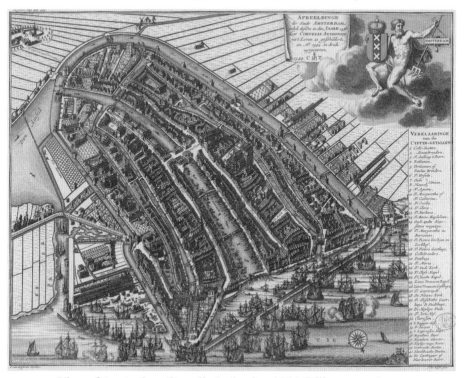

View of Amsterdam, Cornelis Anthonisz, 1544 (Rijksmuseum)

From 1506 the Low Countries were ruled by Charles V of Spain after he inherited the Duchy of Burgundy, and since he was born and lived in the Flemish city of Ghent he had a personal attachment to these lands. He became the King of Spain in 1516 and then the Spanish–Habsburg monarch and Holy Roman Emperor in 1519, making him the most powerful ruler in all of Europe.

However, the Holy Roman Empire was about to face a defining challenge. The German priest, Martin Luther, objecting to the sale of indulgences which combined the forgiving of sin with fundraising for the building of Saint Peter's Basilica in Rome, nailed his Ninety-Five Theses to the door of the Catholic Church in the German city of Wittenberg in 1517. Convinced of the need to reform an autocratic and venal church, he refused to recant his protests against the Catholic Church as demanded by the Pope. Called before a general assembly of the estates of the Holy Roman Empire that took place in Worms, a town on the Rhine, Charles V as Holy Roman Emperor placed Martin Luther under an imperial ban, resulting in his excommunication by the Pope and condemnation as an outlaw which meant he could be killed without any legal consequence.

Aided by the translation of the Bible into German and the invention of the printing press, the distribution of religious books and pamphlets in support of Martin Luther quickly spread the ideas of the Protestant Reformation across Europe. The seeds of the Reformation fell on fertile ground among the peasants, seafarers, craftsmen, guildsmen and merchants of the Low Countries whose sense of independence meant they had a long history of opposing any arbitrary authority. The Protestant movement in the Low Countries was soon reinforced by the arrival of Protestant refugees fleeing from persecution in Germany and France. As support for traditional Catholicism crumbled, different religious denominations proliferated in the Low Countries, but it was Calvinism, a moderate branch of Protestantism that followed the teachings of the French theologian John Calvin, that became the most significant.

Charles V sought to zealously suppress the Reformation by banning the Protestant Bible and using the methods of the Spanish Inquisition such as the burning of martyrs at the stake and the execution of thousands of people for their religious beliefs. In 1556 Charles abdicated the throne and granted rule of the Spanish Empire including the Low Countries where he was Lord of the Seventeen Provinces, to his son Philip II. After assuming the throne Philip II discovered that his father had left behind huge debts incurred for the military costs of defending the empire against the French, the Italians and the Turks. Phillip II then decreed that the merchants of the industrious cities of the Low Countries would have to pay an additional and unpopular tax just so that he could meet the interest on these debts.

The persecution of Protestants, the increased taxes and resentment against being ruled by Catholic Spain soon became the seeds of an anti-Spanish republican movement in the Low Countries. Willem, Prince of Orange, who was the nearest thing to Dutch aristocracy, remained loyal to the Spanish court even though sympathetic to the republican cause, which earned him the nickname of 'Willem the Silent'. When King Philip II prepared to leave the Low Countries in 1559 and board the ship which was to take him to Spain, he blamed Willem for all that had gone wrong during his rule. Willem replied that all which had taken place had been a result of the natural aspirations of the states and its peoples. Upon hearing this the King, boiling with rage, pointed at the Prince, then seizing him by the wrist and shaking it violently, exclaimed in Spanish, 'No los estados, ma vos, vos, vos' – 'Not the States, but you, you, you!' – repeating three times the word 'vos', which is disrespectful in Spanish.

In 1566 the Protestant populations, embittered by Spanish persecution, the additional taxes and the harsh winter famine, began ransacking Catholic churches and destroying the 'papal idolatry' which they considered an insult to God. The revolt began in Flanders in the south and within three days more than 400 churches were ravaged, paintings burned, statues smashed and priceless religious objects turned to rubble. In response Phillip II sent in 10,000 Spanish soldiers led by the battle-hardened Duke of Alba to quash the rebellion. Alba's reputation was so forbidding that people began to flee the southern provinces even before his troops had arrived. On arrival in Brussels, the Duke established what became known as the 'Court of Blood' where thousands were executed or banished, and thousands more fled to Amsterdam and the northern provinces.

King Philip II reproaches Willem the Silent upon his departure from the Netherlands, Cornelis Kruseman, 1832 (Rijksmuseum)

Prince Willem was no longer able to remain silent and as the Spanish repression increased he switched sides. Forced to flee to Germany, his landholdings were confiscated and his eldest son taken in irons to Spain. Willem, while living in exile, decided to abandon his Catholic faith, he joined the Reformed Church and in 1568 led a ragtag Protestant army into the Low Countries, pledging that in areas he controlled people would be free to worship how they pleased. Amsterdam had continued to support the Spanish king but the turning point came in 1578 when Willem succeeded in winning the city over to his cause and the protests there became so intense that the Catholic leaders were forced to leave.

The following year the seven northern provinces of Holland, Zeeland, Friesland, Utrecht, Groningen, Overijssel and Guelders broke with their southern and mainly Catholic neighbours to form the Union of Utrecht, declaring they no longer recognised the Spanish King and creating the anti-Spanish alliance known as the United Provinces. Known retrospectively as the Dutch Republic, it was in reality a loose association of medieval cities, represented by a States General whose answerability was never precisely or legally defined. Nominally above the States General, but also appointed by them, stood the Stadtholder, Willem of Orange. The map of the Low Countries on the next page shows the seventeen provinces and the boundary between the northern seven provinces and the ten southern provinces, which is now the boundary between Holland and Belgium.

In response Philip II offered a reward of 25,000 crowns to anyone who killed Prince-Willem, calling him a 'pest on the whole of Christianity and the enemy of the human race', and in 1584 the Prince was assassinated by a young fanatic from Burgundy named Balthasar Gerard. However, the United Provinces continued to oppose the Spanish under the leadership of his son Prince Maurits of Nassau.

According to the Union of Utrecht every province had the freedom to regulate the religious question as it wished; however, Catholic services in the northern provinces were quickly forbidden and the Reformed Church soon became the 'official' church. With Catholicism now effectively banned in the north, the ruling nobles in the southern provinces of Walloon, Flanders, Hinaut and Artois turned to the Spanish for support through the creation of the Union of Arras. Philip II responded by sending in more troops and in 1585 Antwerp, the largest city in the Low Countries at the time, was captured by Spanish forces. The capture of the city was made easier by the Duke of Parma's offer to allow the Calvinists two years to remove their capital and possessions. This led to many of its bankers, merchants and artisans fleeing north where their knowledge, experience and capital helped transform Amsterdam into one of the most important ports and commercial centres in the world.

The war which had started out as a religious conflict between Catholics and Protestants had evolved into a conflict between the Spanish Empire and the fledgling Dutch Republic. Intermittent conflict with Spain would continue for the next 80 years until 1648 when there was a comprehensive peace settlement between Spain and the United Provinces. With their independence now secure, there were years of huge economic growth for the Dutch Republic as new companies were formed, the world's first stockmarket provided investor funds, voyages of discovery were made, ships filled its harbours and goods flowed in from around the world.

Map of the Low Countries showing the northern and southern provinces

2 Francisco Serrão and the Portuguese in the East Indies

On the Iberian Peninsula, both the Spanish and the Portuguese were envious of the wealth and power of Venice and contemplated a sea route to India and the Spice Islands that would break the stranglehold that the Venetians and the Middle Eastern merchants had on the spice trade. This required a great deal of imaginative thinking and the risk of sailing into uncharted waters, or as some still believed, even off the edge of the world. Relying on Atlantic fishing for a large part of their livelihood, the Portuguese were skilful and self-reliant sailors, experienced in the rigours of the Atlantic Ocean. They sailed far out into the Atlantic, where they colonised the island of Madeira, discovered the islands of the Azores in the mid-Atlantic and began exploring down the coast of West Africa.

In 1454 Prince Henry and his nephew, Affonso, now King of Portugal, lobbied the Pope for the right to claim all lands discovered as far as India. The Portuguese hoped to outflank the Muslim power that extended across the Middle East and establish a new trade route connecting Europe directly with India and the Spice Islands. Incredibly, the Papal Decree gave the Portuguese exclusive rights to the islands, ports and seas of India, a region of the world of which they had almost no knowledge. They were also given the responsibility of finding the Christians the Pope expected to be in India and enlisting their support against the enemies of the faith:

> Our joy is immense to know that our dear son, Henry, Prince of Portugal, following the footsteps of his father of illustrious memory, King John, inspired with a zeal for souls like an intrepid soldier of Christ, has carried into the most distant and unknown countries the name of God … If by his effort the Ocean can be made navigable as far as India, which it is said is already subject to Christ and if he enters into relations with these people, he will induce them to come to the help of the Christians of the West against the enemies of the faith … By our apostolic letter we wish the same King Affonso, the Prince, and all their successors, occupy and possess in exclusive rights the said islands, ports and seas undermentioned, and all faithful Christians are prohibited without the permission of the said Affonso and his successors to encroach on their sovereignty.

Vasco da Gama and his tiny fleet of two carracks, a caravel and a supply boat rounded the Cape of Good Hope and reached India in 1498, 'In search of Christians and spices'. When they arrived at the port of Calicut, da Gama and his men were the first Europeans to reach the south coast of India since the Greeks and Romans traded for pepper on the Malabar Coast in the first century AD. It was a long journey home, made more difficult by the delay in the onset of the monsoonal winds and an outbreak of scurvy amongst the crew. Scurvy is an affliction caused by a diet lacking fresh fruit or vegetables and the vitamin C they contain. After three months' sailing, the armada reached the coast of East Africa and was able to resupply with fresh food and water at Malindi. Vasco da Gama wrote of the Arab traders of Malindi offering oranges to his afflicted sailors and of their miraculous recovery.

Lisbon greeted the return of the armada with enormous excitement in September 1499. The sea route to India was now open. Despite the loss of almost half the crew, the voyage had been a success and their small but precious cargo of spices repaid the expenses of the voyage six times over. King Manuel granted da Gama the title of 'Admiral of the Sea of India', with the full honours, benefits, freedoms, powers, stipends, rights and collection of rents that accrue to an Admiral of the Realm. In a letter to the Catholic monarchs in Rome, the King triumphantly announced:

> We sent Vasco da Gama, our noble servant and his brother Paulo da Gama with him, on a quest of discovery. They set off with ships to cross the seas and were gone for two years. They entered and sailed the sea there to find great cities, buildings, riches, and large settlements. There they found an extensive trade in spices and precious stones from Mecca to Cairo via sailing ships. Our discoverers actually saw them and consider them a large well-equipped fleet. From Cairo the trade spreads itself out all over the world and we have the following products of it: cinnamon, cloves, ginger, nutmeg, pepper and other spices. We also have the wood and leaves of the same. We also have many fine stones such as rubies, among others.

The Portuguese might have been interested in legitimate trade, but their naval and military superiority soon led them to capture the trade in spices and oriental goods by force of arms from the Arab and Indian traders, and Lisbon replaced Venice as the main distribution point for spices into Europe. Having established their hegemony over the seas, the Portuguese needed to establish a permanent land base in India. After their capture of Goa, Alfonso de Albuquerque and his soldiers went about rebuilding the fortress and establishing a city that was to become the capital of the Portuguese empire in the East. The friendly relations between the Hindu empire of Vijayanagar and the Portuguese authorities in Goa, united in their enmity against Islam, enabled the Portuguese to retain their presence in Goa with little or no military presence for hundreds of years. In fact, Goa remained a Portuguese colony for 450 years until annexed by India in 1961. A description by the French traveller Francois Pyrard in 1620 paints a fascinating picture of the city:

It is about a hundred and ten years since the Portuguese made themselves masters of the island of Goa, and I have often wondered at the rapidity with which the Portuguese have been able to erect stately edifices, so many churches, convents, palaces, fortresses, and other buildings after the European fashion … Thus whoever has been in Goa may say that he has seen the choicest of rarities in India, for it is the famous and most celebrated city, on account of its commercial intercourse with people of all nationalities of the East, who bring them products of their respective countries, articles of merchandise, necessaries of life, and other commodities in great abundance, because every year more than a thousand ships touch there laden with cargo.

For the Portuguese, a further prize lay to the east. This was the port of Malacca on the Malay Peninsula. Because of its location, Malacca had become the main trading port of the region, frequented by ships from India, Persia, Arabia and Egypt in the west, from China and Japan in the east, and by archipelago traders from Sumatra, Java and the Moluccas. To become the Lords of Malacca would allow the Portuguese to control trade all the way from China and the Spice Islands to Goa and Lisbon.

The first Portuguese ships reached Malacca in 1509 and the contemporary Portuguese chronicler Tomé Pires wrote:

When Diego Lopes de Sequeira arrived before the port of Malacca, there were at that time … according to what is truly stated … a thousand Gujarati merchants in Malacca, among whom there were a great many rich ones with a great deal of capital, and some who were representatives of others; and with the Parsees[Persians], Bengalese and Arabs there were more than four thousand men here, including rich merchants and some who were factors for others.

Alfonso de Albuquerque needed time to muster a fighting force able to take Malacca by storm, and in 1511 he arrived off the city with a fleet of fifteen vessels and a force of 700 Portuguese, including Ferdinand Magellan, Antonio de Abreu and Francisco Serrão as his captains, and 300 Malabari soldiers. After a six-week siege and an all-out assault, the Sultan of Malacca fled and the city surrendered.

Determined to stop spices from Malacca reaching Venice through the traditional Middle Eastern trade routes, the Portuguese were now the Lords of Malacca and Tome Pires, the Portuguese Controller of Spices in Malacca, wrote in his Suma Oriental in 1515 that:

Whoever is Lord of Malacca has his hand on the throat of Venice. As far as from Malacca, and from Malacca to China, and from China to the Moluccas, and from the Moluccas to Java, and from Java to Malacca and Sumatra, all is in our power.

Only a few months after the capture of Malacca, three Portuguese ships under the command of Antonio de Abreu sailed eastwards towards the Spice Islands. They were a crew of 120 including 60 Malays and Javanese, their Malay pilot Nahkoda Ishmael, who was familiar with the trading route to the Spice Islands, and Francisco Rodrigues, the Portuguese pilot who chronicled their journey. The expedition had been given explicit orders from Alfonso de Albuquerque to honour local customs and law as this was to be a mission of exploration and trade, not conquest and plunder.

Taking advantage of the monsoonal winds, the small fleet travelled south-east through the narrow straits between Sumatra and the island of Bangka before entering the Java Sea. Sailing along the north coast of Java, the local pilots would have used the numerous volcanoes rising above the green, terraced rice fields as their landmarks before stopping to resupply at the port of Gresik in East Java. They continued sailing eastwards past the islands of Bali, Lombok and Sumbawa with their towering volcanoes to a cape they named Cabo de Flores, or the Cape of Flowers, after the vivid red flamboyant trees that grow in profusion along this peninsula on the eastern end of the island now called Flores. From here they sailed north, setting their course towards a volcano which was a bright beacon on the horizon and is described by Francisco Rodrigues:

> Antonio de Abreu and those who went with them set their course toward the north of the small island called Gunung Api [Fire Mountain] because from its highest point streams of fire run continuously to the sea, which is a wonderful thing to behold.

The nutmeg tree is indigenous only to the tiny islands of the Banda Archipelago, all of which are mere specks in the Banda Sea. The largest is Lontor, a remnant rim of an older volcano that erupted catastrophically some time in the distant past. In the centre of the old crater the almost perfectly symmetrical cone of an active new volcano rises out of the sea to a height of 656 metres. Anchored in its lee, the Portuguese could see the slopes covered with the evergreen nutmeg trees they had come so far to find. The nutmeg is a fleshy apricot-like fruit and the aromatic spice comes from the grated nut, as well as from the bright red outer covering of the seed known as mace. Nutmeg was not without purported medical properties as it was said to cure 'stinking breath, clear the eyes, comfort the stomach, liver and spleen, and digest meat'.

The arrival of Antonio de Abreu and his two ships at Banda in 1512 was the culmination of a 1500-year quest by Europeans to reach the fabled Spice Islands. This quest began with the early Greek traders in the Arabian Sea, followed by the Romans in the Indian Ocean, the Portuguese voyages down the west coast of Africa inspired by Prince Henry the Navigator, and the westward voyage of Christopher Columbus across the Atlantic. There is no record of how Antonio de Abreu and his captains and crew celebrated this historic event, or if they ever made any fine speeches on their arrival in Banda.

Fully laden, the returning fleet ran into a storm in the middle of the Banda Sea. A junk captained by Francisco Serrão was separated from the other vessels and started breaking up in the heavy seas. Serrão and his crew of Portuguese and Malay sailors saved their lives by running the vessel onto a small islet in the Lucipara Shoals. According to legend, the Portuguese then ambushed some local fishermen as they came ashore to plunder their vessel and forced them to take the shipwrecked crew north to the island of Ambon.

The Portuguese had kept their swords, armour and muskets and were able to impress their Ambonese hosts with their use of modern weaponry. News of their military prowess quickly spread throughout the islands. Curious to meet these fair-skinned foreigners, Sultan Bolief of Ternate sent his brother to persuade the shipwrecked Portuguese to return with him to Ternate. They travelled north in large outrigger canoes known as kora-kora, each manned by up to 100 rower-warriors and flying colourful flags and banners. The crew rowed to the steady beat of drums and cymbals as they made their way up the Patinti Strait with the mainland of Halmahera on one side and a chain of volcanic islands rising out of the sea on the other.

The clove tree is indigenous only to these tiny islands and Francisco Serrão and his comrades could smell the sweet fragrance of clove even before they reached their destination. When the fair-skinned strangers landed on the island of Ternate the Sultan embraced every man. Beaming with pleasure and admiration, he lifted his hands to heaven. The contemporary Spanish historian Bartolomé de Argensola quotes him as saying:

> These my people, are the warriors you have so longed for on account of my prophecy. Honour them, and let us all vie in entertaining them, since the grandeur of our country depends on their arms.

In 1518 the Portuguese reached an agreement with Sultan Bolief to establish a permanent trading post on Ternate, to supply him with arms and build a fortress on the island in exchange for what the Portuguese expected would be a monopoly on the clove trade. So it was that almost one hundred years from the days and dreams of Prince Henry the Navigator and their first forays down the west coast of Africa, the Portuguese had not only reached the Spice Islands but were about to establish a permanent presence there.

Every year the Royal Clove Ship departed Goa in April, arriving in Ternate after the clove harvest had finished in October. Following the loading of cloves in Ternate and nutmeg in Banda, the ship sheltered in the Bay of Ambon until the trade winds changed in favour of the return voyage. Leaving Ambon in May, the vessel returned to Goa in time to rendezvous with the large Portuguese carracks leaving for Portugal. Ambon had one of the best harbours in the archipelago and eventually the Portuguese decided to build a fort there to store and protect the cloves they were bringing from Ternate and the nutmegs they were bringing from Banda until the next trading vessel arrived from Goa or Malacca.

King Manuel of Portugal became known throughout Europe as 'Manuel the Fortunate' or the 'Grocer King' and began to live in the luxury and style of a Roman Emperor. New buildings and monuments were erected in Lisbon reflecting the city's new-found wealth and the architectural influences of both Africa and India. The ruling class decorated their homes with oriental carpets, bedspreads of colourful Indian cotton and cushions of silk. Spices such as pepper, cinnamon, cloves and nutmeg were on every dining table.

The City of Lisbon, Braun and Hogenberg, Civitas Orbit Terrarum, 1572 (Beinecke Rare Book and Manuscript Library, Yale University)

Below the royal coat of arms of the Kingdom of Portugal, the 1572 image of the City of Lisbon shows trading vessels and large East Indiamen anchored in the River Tagus, with smaller vessels bringing their goods ashore to the large open area of the Praça do Comércio and the royal warehouses. To the west of the square are the naval shipyards busy building the vessels that would carry these goods from India and the East Indies. The streets behind the Praça do Comércio are still the commercial hub of Lisbon, housing banks, insurance companies and business offices.

Today this huge open space is commonly known as Palace Square because the square is lined on three sides by the buildings and graceful arcades of the former Royal Palaces, glorious in their royal yellow. As the commercial docks and warehouses moved downstream, the Praça do Comércio became the gateway to Lisbon and from here Royalty and Ambassadors would alight from their vessels and be escorted up the marble steps to the King's Palace.

Over the next 100 years Portuguese maritime trade grew to extend more than halfway around the world – from Lisbon to Goa, to Malacca, to Ternate, to Solor, Macau and Nagasaki. The value of the Portuguese trade is shown by the capture of the Portuguese galleon *Madre de Deus* off the Azores in 1592 by the English. An inventory of its cargo showed she carried 425 tonnes of pepper, 45 tonnes of cloves, 35 tonnes of cinnamon, 3 tonnes of mace, 3 tonnes of nutmeg, 25 tonnes of cochineal and 2.5 tonnes of benjamin (an aromatic resin), as well as ebony, ivory, pearls, silks, and precious jewels. The cargo value of this single ship was estimated at half a million pounds, almost half of England's treasury at the time.

However, unlike in Venice, Antwerp, Amsterdam or London, a large and successful mercantile community did not develop in Lisbon. Disdain of the merchant was deeply ingrained in Portuguese society and they were often seen as parasitic and profiteering middlemen. This longstanding prejudice is demonstrated by a letter the mercers of Lisbon sent to the King in 1689:

> Without trade there is not a kingdom which is not poor, nor a republic which is not famished. Yet in this capital city of your Majesty, the merchants are so little favoured and commerce is despised to such a degree, that not only are men discouraged from becoming traders, but all those of spirit decline to have anything to do with it, since they see with their own eyes that in the conceit of the Portuguese, a merchant is no better than a fish-porter. This is the reason why there are so few merchants in this Kingdom, and why so many foreigners of all nations swarm here, who are the bloodsuckers of all your Majesty's money.

On the contrary, in the Low Countries the merchants of Antwerp and Amsterdam were extremely adept at market-related commercial practices and had made their cities the main centres for the storage and distribution across northern Europe of the spices and other goods imported by the Portuguese.

The 1575 map by Abraham Ortelius on the next page shows the extent of the Portuguese trading empire which extended all the way from Goa in India, to Malacca, to the Moluccas, to Chinese Macau, and then to Nagasaki in Japan. The map also shows land south of Java named Beach (of the continent of Australis) and is a part of Terra Australis Nondum Cognito shown on the Ortelius world map of 1570.

This land was described by Marco Polo while on his return from China in 1295 with a fleet of fourteen Chinese vessels sailing with a young Mogul princess betrothed to the Arghun Khan of Persia. The Chinese fleet had stopped in Champa in Central Vietnam before sailing on to North Sumatra. It was from Champa that he describes a land south of Java known as Luca Veach, Locach or Boeach. Scholars have pointed out that he may been referring to a place south of Champa and there was a transcription error when Champa was replaced with Java in his text. If this is correct then the land he described

The East Indies, Abraham Ortelius, 1575, Theatrum Orbis Terrarum (National Library of Australia)

as south of Java was in fact Java itself.

The important question is that, since the Portuguese had been trading for 100 years across the eastern archipelago and especially in its trade for sandalwood on the island of Timor, did they ever reach Australia?

Much has been written about the maps originating from the French port of Dieppe, which are thought by some to be evidence of an early Portuguese discovery of Australia and various historians have twisted and contorted these maps to fit the coasts of Australia. A number have argued that Jave La Grande as shown on the Dieppe maps was an artefact of sixteenth-century cosmography and does not represent an Australia discovered by unknown and unrecorded Portuguese voyagers. However, it should be remembered that the lack of recorded Portuguese discoveries can also be attributed to the great Lisbon earthquake of 1755 when the Casa da India and all its records, manuscripts maps and charts were destroyed by earthquake, fire and the resultant tidal wave that swept up the River Tagus.

Manuel Godhino de Erédia, the son of a Portuguese captain and a Macassan princess, was born in Malacca and educated by the Jesuits in both Malacca and Goa. Erédia worked in Goa as a cosmographer, taught mathematics and prepared new maps of Asian countries for the King of Spain. He returned to Malacca in 1600 on a mission to explore further the Indonesian archipelago as he had read from the Marco Polo texts of a land to the south of Java called Nuca Antara and was interested in its exploration. However, because of local wars and the growing incursion of the Dutch East India Company his services were required in Malacca as a soldier and military engineer. His map of 1601 shows the land of Nuca Antara directly south of Java, while the only land due south of Java is Christmas Island. It is not thought that Erédia personally voyaged there but based his map on reports of Indonesian fishermen who had ventured further south.

Since Manuel Godhino de Erédia was of Macassan origin he may have been familiar with the voyages of Macassan seafarers to Northern Australia or the land they described as Marege to collect, boil, dry and smoke trepang for the China market. Such voyages are believed to have commenced before the 1600s, but these seafarers would have told him that Marege was south of Timor and not south of Java.

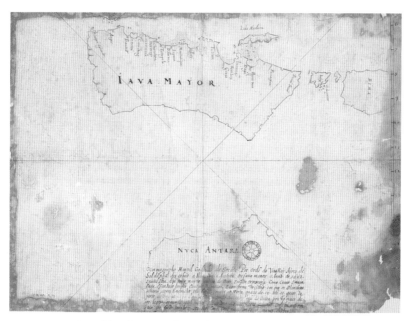

Map of land south of Java known as Nuca Antara, Manuel
Godhino de Erédia, 1601 (National Library of Brazil)

The Portuguese cartographer, João Teixeira Albernaz, received his license as a master for nautical charts in 1602 having been examined by the royal chief-cosmographer. Three years later he was appointed as cartographer for the Casa da India where he produced hundreds of maps, mainly of Brazil. His 1630 map of the Indian Ocean shows the land of Nuca Antara due south of Java which he attributes to having been discovered by Manuel Godhino de Erédia in 1601. It is interesting that his map mislocates the Dutch discoveries of Eendrachtlandt by Dirk Hartog, Frederik de Houtman and others to fit below the Nuca Antara as mapped by Erédia. It is important to note that his map shows no other Portuguese discoveries of Australia and especially none of those indicated by the Dieppe Maps.

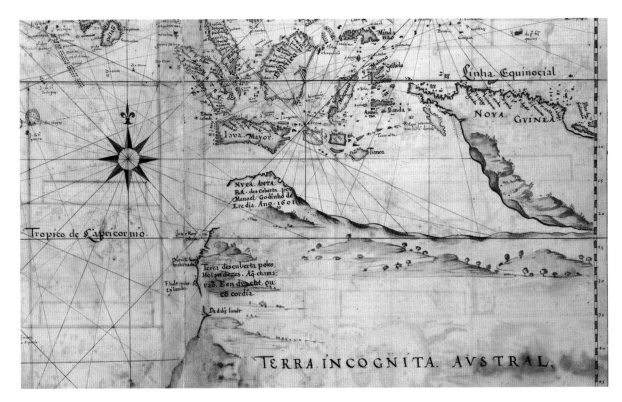

Map of the Indian Ocean, João Teixeira Albernaz, 1630 (Library of Congress)

3 Ferdinand Magellan and the Spanish in the East Indies

The marriage of King Ferdinand of Aragón and Queen Isabella of Castile in 1469 united Spain against the Muslims who still occupied Al-Andalus, including the cities of Seville, Córdoba and Granada. Almost immediately after the Moors surrendered Granada in January 1492, Ferdinand and Isabella agreed to finance the voyage that Columbus proposed to sail west across the Atlantic to reach India and the Spice Islands.

Having reconquered their lands and united Spain, the Crown could no longer resist the temptation of capturing their share of the market in spices, silks, jewels and other exotic products from India and the Orient. The Crown appointed Columbus viceroy and governor-general of any land discovered, giving him rights to one-tenth of all merchandise shipped, including pearls, precious stones, gold, silver and spices. There was also a religious aspect to this voyage, and in the prologue to his journal Columbus wrote:

> Your Highnesses, as Catholic Christians and as princes devoted to the holy Christian faith and propagators thereof, and enemies of the sect of Mahomet and all idolatries and heresies, took thought to send me, Christopher Columbus, to the said parts of India, to see those princes and peoples and lands … and to bring about their conversion to our holy faith.

The return of Christopher Columbus from his discovery of the Americas caused a diplomatic storm in Europe as the Portuguese accused the Spanish of breaking the Papal Decree issued to Prince Henry and King Affonso in 1454 that guaranteed a Portuguese monopoly on all discoveries beyond Guinea. The confrontation between the two Iberian kingdoms obliged Pope Alexander Borgia to play an active part in the negotiations that led to the signing of the Treaty of Tordesillas in 1494.

In what today might seem to be the height of arrogance, Spain and Portugal, with the blessing of the Pope, divided the world in half along a pole to pole meridian in the middle of the Atlantic Ocean close to longitude 46 degrees 30 minutes west. This was halfway between the Portuguese claimed islands of the Azores, and the Spanish-claimed island of Hispaniola. Spain could claim any new territory discovered to the west of the line of demarcation and Portugal could claim any new territory discovered to the east.

Spain got the territories discovered by Columbus and what they hoped was a western route to the Indies, while the Portuguese protected their African discoveries and an eastern route to the Indies. The decision to position the line in the mid-Atlantic was intended to reduce any further disputes over territory, conveniently forgetting that a line cannot be drawn on water and that neither country had the ability to accurately measure longitude. The Spice Islands were the prize they both wanted to claim as their own and an even bigger problem was trying to determine where this line lay on the other side of the globe and whether the islands could be claimed by either Portugal or Spain.

The result of the Treaty of Tordesillas is shown on the Portuguese map known as the 1502 Cantino Planisphere which shows the islands discovered by Columbus in the Caribbean or 'Western Ocean' and the line of demarcation drawn in the central part of the North Atlantic. This map was smuggled out of Lisbon in 1502 by an Italian spy named Alberto Cantino, masquerading as a dealer in purebred horses. Cantino had acquired the map on behalf of his client, the Duke of Ferrara, who wanted the latest map of the world for his personal collection.

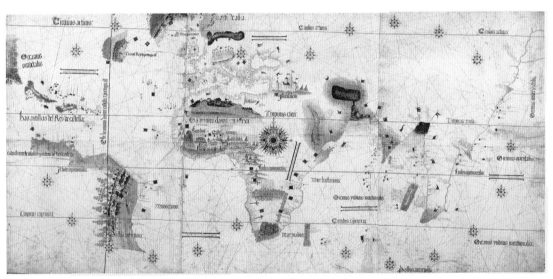

The Cantino Planisphere, 1502 (Biblioteca Estense, Modena)

The Spanish now had to reach the Spice Islands. Spain needed somebody to lead an expedition around South America and that person came in the form of Ferdinand Magellan. He was a captain in the first Portuguese expedition to Malacca and then fought in the battle when the second expedition commanded by Admiral Alfonso de Albuquerque captured Malacca. Ordered to return to Lisbon, Magellan was denied any chance of joining Francisco Serrão in Ternate and learned the Portuguese Viceroy now considered his friend a renegade, since he had refused orders to return to Malacca.

It is a measure of Magellan's determination to reach the Spice Islands that he made the decision to go into exile and bring his knowledge, experience and ambition to the rival court of Spain. He arrived in Seville in October 1517 bringing valuable information for the Spanish; this included letters from Francisco Serrão describing Ternate and the Moluccas, as well as charts of the Java and Banda Seas he had obtained from the de Abreu expedition. However, what really caught the attention of the Spanish was a globe constructed by the Portuguese cartographers Pedro and Jorge Reinel, which showed that the Spice Islands could lie within Spain's half of the world as determined by the Treaty of Tordesillas. The Portuguese considered all this information a state secret, the penalty for its disclosure was execution, but Magellan had made his decision and there was no turning back.

Just as Christopher Columbus had convinced King Ferdinand before him, Ferdinand Magellan convinced King Charles V that there was an alternative route to the Indies by sailing west around the world, and that the riches of the Spice Islands rightfully belonged to Spain. Of course he was telling the King exactly what he wanted to hear, for if the voyage were successful the Spanish would be able to seize the trade in spices from both the Venetians and the Portuguese.

King Charles V was not only enthusiastic about what Magellan showed him; he already had the financial backing to put his plan into action. Events moved quickly. It took only two months of deliberation for the King to award Magellan's commission in March 1518. Magellan must have found it hard to believe his good fortune, for the king appointed him captain-general of the expedition as well as granting him one-twentieth of the profits and the right of governorship of any new lands he might discover.

The *Trinidad*, *Victoria*, *San Antonio*, *Concepción* and *Santiago*, all painted black and named the Armada de Moluccas, left the Castilian port of San Lucar de Barrameda in August 1519 heading into the South Atlantic. Their orders were to find a western route to India and the Spice Islands, a route that Columbus had ventured to find almost 30 years earlier until he found his voyage blocked by a then unknown continent. After the discovery of the Americas, the Spanish explorer Vasco Balboa had crossed the Isthmus of Panama in 1513 and saw the great expanse of the Pacific Ocean laid out before him. Sailing far into the south Atlantic, Magellan discovered what is now called the Strait of Magellan, a series of interlinking waterways extending for 660 kilometres between the Atlantic and the Pacific Oceans. The frigid waters of the strait are surrounded by bleak, windswept prairies in the east, and deep fiords lined by dark forests of Antarctic beech in the west. Glaciers spawned off the Southern Andes flow into the strait, creating walls of solid ice that rise above its waters. The Strait of Magellan separates Patagonia from Tierra del Fuego and sailing through the narrow waterway against the prevailing westerly winds and with little room for tacking can be extremely difficult.

Once they had navigated the straits and entered the Pacific Ocean, Magellan and his pilots felt sure that they were now within striking distance of the Spice Islands. The armada, now reduced to three vessels and 200 men decided to proceed across the Pacific, not knowing the enormous breadth of the ocean and how much misery and suffering lay ahead. They lost 29 men to scurvy during a voyage of three months and twenty days before they finally reached the island of Guam, where the fruit and vegetables they obtained began to restore the surviving crew to health. In April 1521 the Armada de Moluccas entered the port of Cebu in the Philippines and, after an exchange of emissaries, Magellan went ashore with his entourage to meet Humabon, the King of Cebu.

Magellan probably planned to establish his governorship of Cebu and his right to one-twentieth of the ensuing profits according to the Royal charter. Whatever Magellan's plan, it ran into a problem when Lapulapu, a chief on the island of Mactan, refused to pay tribute and submit to Humabon's and consequently Magellan's rule, daring the Spanish to attack.

Magellan had no reason to believe that his superior arms would not prevail in the ensuing battle. On that fateful day Magellan was forced to lead a small party of 49 of his most faithful followers against Lapulapu. Eleven of them prudently decided to stay and guard their small boats while the remaining 38 men waded ashore to be faced by 1000 armed warriors. Magellan and eight others were killed in the ensuing battle and their bodies floated unrecovered in the sea. Magellan's vision and determination against all odds to find a western route to the Spice Islands came to this sorry end in Mactan harbour, and Antonio Pigafetta, the chronicler of the voyage, wrote an epitaph for his captain-general:

> So noble a captain … he was more constant than anyone else in adversity. He endured hunger better than all the others, and better than any man in the world did he understand sea charts and navigation.

Without Magellan's determined leadership the remnants of the Armada spent eight months wandering the Sulu Sea, sailing as far south and east as the island of Borneo and committing acts of piracy against Chinese junks, before reaching the Spice Islands. The *Victoria* and *Trinidad* arrived in the Moluccas just before sunset on 8 November 1521. Casting anchor off the island of Tidore, the two remaining vessels of the Armada de Molucca discharged their artillery in celebration, for their 27 month-voyage had brought them halfway around the world before finally reaching the Spice Islands.

Rising directly out of the sea before them lay the volcanic island of Tidore. As the setting sun coloured the sky, the sailors could see before them forests of clove trees covering the slopes of the volcano and smell the scent of exotic spices that filled the air. The following day the armada had a royal visitor. The description by Antonio Pigafetta clearly demonstrates the wealth the Sultan of Tidore had derived from the clove trade:

Next day the King came to the ships in a prahu, and went around them. We met him in a boat to show him honour, and he made us enter his prahu and sit near him. He was sitting under a silk umbrella, which sheltered him. In front of him was his son with the royal sceptre, there was also two men with gold vases to give him water for his hands, and two others with gilt caskets full of betel. The King gave us a welcome, and said that from a long time back he had dreamed that some ships were coming to Molucca from distant countries and that to assure himself with respect to this he had examined the moon, and that he had seen that they were really coming, and that they indeed were our ships.

The Spanish traded for cloves until they had nothing left to exchange. The scent of the precious cargo loaded onto their ships permeated the air and, to the sailors' delight, masked the usual shipboard smells of bilge water, stale sweat and rotting food. After a month on the island, the ships and their precious cargo of cloves were ready to leave for Spain. The northerly monsoon had started to blow and the two captains decided that the *Victoria* captained by Juan Sebastian Elcano should immediately depart westwards for the Cape of Good Hope and that, after repairs, the *Trinidad* would sail eastwards across the Pacific. Crew members were free to choose which vessel and captain they thought most likely to survive the hazards of the voyage and deliver them safely back to Seville. Sixty of the crew decided to sail immediately aboard the *Victoria*; the remaining 54 decided to wait for the repairs to the *Trinidad* before sailing east.

The last few months of their voyage back to Spain must have been a nightmare, for the *Victoria* was little more than a floating wreck and her crew the living dead. The survivors were forced to man the pumps 24 hours a day to keep the vessel afloat, working the sails to keep her on course drained any remaining energy, and more men died of hunger and fatigue. It is impossible to describe how the survivors must have felt as they approached Spain for all would have despaired many times during their voyage around the world of ever sighting their homeland again. History has described their return as triumphant, but the condition of the *Victoria* and her wretched crew must have been a pitiful sight. Pigafetta wrote:

> On Saturday the sixth of September, 1522, we entered the Bay of San Lucar, and we were only eighteen men, the most part sick, of the sixty remaining who had left Molucca, some of whom died of hunger, others deserted at the island of Timor, and others had been put to death for their crimes. From the time that we departed from that Bay until the present day we had sailed fourteen thousand four hundred and sixty leagues, and completed the circuit of the world from east to west. On Monday the eighth of September we cast anchor near the Mole of Seville, and there we discharged all the artillery. And on Tuesday we all went, in our shirts and barefoot, and each with a torch in his hand, to visit the shrine of Santa Maria de la Victoria and that of Santa Maria de Antigua.

Of the five ships and 237 men of the Armada de Moluccas that had departed Spain three years earlier, the *Victoria* and only eighteen survivors had achieved the greatest voyage in maritime history – the first circumnavigation of the world. These thin and ragged sailors had measured the true dimensions of our planet and turned the concept of a spherical earth by the Greek philosophers and geographers such as Aristotle and Ptolemy into a hard-won reality. The skill of their captain, Juan Sebastian Elcano, had brought them home, but they would have wished that Ferdinand Magellan were still with them, for without his vision and determination the *Victoria* would never have found the Strait of Magellan or crossed the Pacific. Only a few pages of Pigafetta's journal describe their return journey. Sick from hunger and fatigue, his only priority was survival. The map by Battista Agnese shows not just the route of the *Victoria* but also the route of the Spanish silver and gold from Peru crossing the Isthmus of Panama and then across what became known as the Spanish Main on its way back to Europe. The map did not show any Spanish extension of the concept of Terra Australis except for land south of the Strait of Magellan.

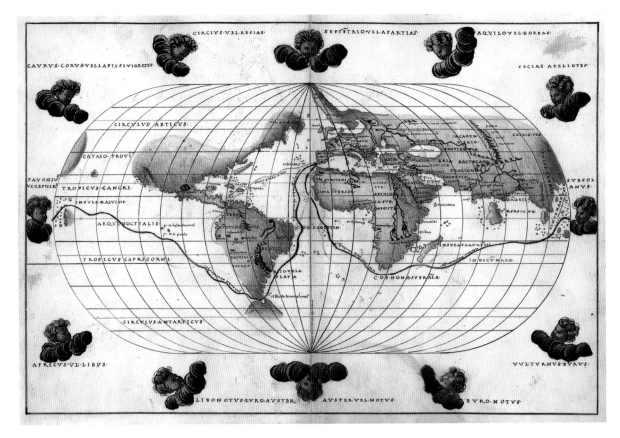

The route of the first circumnavigation of the world, Battista Agnese, 1544 (Library of Congress)

Importantly for both King Charles V and the financiers of the Armada de Moluccas, the *Victoria* had returned with a full cargo of cloves, nutmeg, and sandalwood on board. The cloves weighed in at 25 tonnes and were of first-grade quality. Valuable proof of the new trade route they had discovered, these were quickly sold in the spice markets of Europe and made enough money to cover several times the entire cost of the Armada de Moluccas.

4 Spain and Portugal Struggle for Supremacy in the Moluccas

The return of the *Victoria* to Spain caused another diplomatic storm. The question was, did the Spice Islands lay in the Portuguese or Spanish half of the world? King John III of Portugal lodged a protest with King Charles V, claiming that the Spanish had encroached on his territory as defined by the Treaty of Tordesillas. In response, King Charles V cleverly offered to submit the dispute to arbitration. The Portuguese made a strategic mistake by agreeing to this process, since it implied that Spain might have a claim to the Spice Islands.

Both sides gathered experts to support their claim. However, by the time the two sides sat down to negotiate, Pedro Reinel and his son Jorge who had provided maps to Magellan, were firmly back in the Portuguese camp. On the other hand, another Portuguese mapmaker Diego Ribeiro, who had made the maps for the Armada de Moluccas, stayed on the Spanish side. Pietro Martire d'Anghiera, Secretary to the King of Spain, described the Spanish delegation:

> Nunno Garcia and Diego Ribeiro, being all expert pilots and clever in the making of sea charts, should be present, and bring forth their globes and maps with other instruments necessary to declare the location of the Islands of the Moluccas about which was all the contention and strife.

Their first meeting was held on a bridge spanning the Portuguese–Spanish border. Both sides were represented by nine members as well as their mapmakers and cosmographers. Neither the Portuguese nor the Spanish were able to accurately measure longitude, so neither could determine the position of the Spice Islands with any degree of accuracy. Each side had its respective cosmographers make persuasive arguments with charts and globes but there could be no resolution to their differences and the talks ended in a stalemate. In fact, another two centuries were to pass before the invention of the shipboard chronometer by the English watchmaker John Harrison allowed for the accurate measurement of longitude.

The Spanish decided to take advantage of the stalemate by sending an armada across the Pacific to capture the Spice Islands by force. The armada left in 1525 under the command of Frei Garcia de Loayasa, with Juan Sebastian Elcano as his second-in-command. Sailing through the narrows of the Strait of Magellan against the prevailing winds was never easy and of the seven vessels only four were able to battle their way through the straits and the rest were either smashed to pieces or retreated to the Atlantic. A huge gale then scattered the armada across the Pacific and the vessels were never to see each other again. Only the flagship *Santa Maria* continued the mission to seize the Moluccas for the Spanish King. In mid-Pacific Frei Garcia de Loayasa died of scurvy and Juan Sebastian Elcano assumed command but tragically the former captain of the *Victoria* and hero of the world's first circumnavigation also died of scurvy.

Finally the *Santa Maria* reached the Moluccas and anchored off Tidore, its rigging reduced to mere rudiments, the ship barnacled and worm-eaten, its surviving crew exhausted and starving. The Portuguese immediately engaged the Spanish ship in combat, and after firing off its cannon the *Santa Maria* proceeded to sink out of sheer decrepitude with the crew swimming ashore to be welcomed by the Sultan of Tidore. Assured of the arrival of more Spanish vessels, the Sultan switched his allegiance back to the Spanish and they set about building Fort Mariaco on the west coast of the island. Detail from this map of the Spice Islands shows the locations of Fort Gamalama built by the Portuguese on Ternate and Fort Mariaco built by the Spanish on Tidore and only separated by a few kilometres of water.

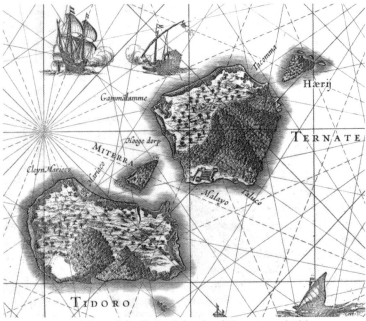

Map of the Spice Islands of Ternate and Tidore,
Willem Blaeu, 1647 (National Library of Australia)

The next Spanish armada left from Acapulco on the Pacific coast of Mexico in 1527, shortening the length of the voyage and avoiding the hazards of the Strait of Magellan. The three ships, commanded by Alvaro de Saavedra Cerón, also ran into a Pacific storm which sank two of the ships leaving only the flagship *Florida* to reach the Moluccas to reinforce the Spanish fort. When still more reinforcements were needed, the captain of the *Florida* twice attempted to sail back across the Pacific but was thwarted by the prevailing easterly winds and had to return to Tidore. It was on this voyage along the north coast of New Guinea that he named a large island, possibly Biak, as Isla del Oro or the Island of Gold.

Only the narrow strait between the two islands separated the Portuguese on Ternate from the Spanish on Tidore, and both sides were determined to rule the Moluccas with the support of their local allies. They both knew this struggle would decide not only who would control the clove and nutmeg trade from the Spice Islands, but also the fate of the Portuguese and Spanish Empires in the Far East. Eventually King Charles V came to realise that because of the difficulties of crossing the Pacific, his claim to the Spice Islands was commercially impractical. Heavily indebted to the Habsburg bankers who had financed his wars with the Dutch Republic, the French, the Italians and the Turks, he decided to give up his claim in return for compensation from the Portuguese.

In 1529 the two crowns signed the Treaty of Saragossa which ceded the Spice Islands to the Portuguese. By the use of clever diplomacy, together with his cunning cosmographers, King Charles had turned a dubious claim to the Spice Islands into 350,000 solid gold ducats. He even had a clause inserted into the treaty allowing him to reclaim his rights if new geographical evidence on the location of the Spice Islands emerged in his favour. The two crowns agreed that the line of demarcation should lie 17 degrees east of the Spice Islands, placing them within Portugal's hemisphere of influence. Legalese has not changed in almost 500 years and the text reads as follows:

> In order that it may be known where the said line falls, a model map shall at once be made on which the said line shall be drawn in the manner aforesaid, and it will thus be agreed to as a declaration of the point and place through which the line passes. This map shall be signed by the said Charles V, Lord Emperor and King of Castile, and by the said Lord King of Portugal, and sealed with their seals. In the same manner, and in accordance with the said model map, the said line shall be drawn on all the navigation charts whereby the subjects and natives of the kingdoms shall navigate.

The news of the Treaty of Saragossa had to be rushed to the Moluccas to stop any more killing between the two Iberian rivals. Too late. For in 1527 a fleet commanded by Jorge Menesez reinforced the Portuguese on Ternate, and in early 1528 a force of 100 Portuguese and 1000 local fighters crossed the narrow channel between the two islands, capturing the royal town of Mariaco and besieging the Spanish fort. The Sultan of Tidore had to accept the terms of the peace, which meant submission again to the Portuguese and his old enemies from Ternate. The Spanish captain agreed to surrender the fort in return for safe conduct for his men to Jailolo on Halmahera, where they remained for several years until news of the Treaty of Saragossa finally reached them and the Spice Islands fell completely under Portuguese domination.

Today we know the Spice Islands lie between 127 and 128 degrees east, well within the Portuguese hemisphere of influence as originally defined by the Treaty of Tordesillas. The final comment is from the Spanish historian Bartolomé de Argensola, who wrote in 1609 of the diplomatic controversy over the Moluccas:

> The most bloody Theatre of continual Tragedies was Ternate and all the Moluccas. There both Nations of Castile and Portugal decided their Quarrel by the Sword, whilst their Kings in Europe only contended by Dint of Cunning, and Cosmography.

After the Treaty of Saragossa, the Spanish decided to base their Pacific trade in the Philippine Islands, themselves named after King Philip II. In 1564 the Spanish admiral Miguel Lopez de Lagazpi sailed from Acapulco and occupied Cebu. In 1571 he captured the city of Manila. From this time, the Spanish used Manila as their base but they still had to learn how to best use the trade winds to return across the Pacific Ocean.

An Augustinian friar, Brother Andrés de Urdaneta, had first crossed the Pacific at the age of seventeen with the ill-fated Loayasa/Elcano expedition. During this voyage he had risen from the position of Elcano's pageboy to become an officer. In subsequent years, Urdaneta had formed a theory that the winds and currents in the northern Pacific circulated in a clockwise direction, while in the southern hemisphere they circulated in an anticlockwise direction. This made it impossible to sail across the Pacific in the equatorial regions, against the winds that blew incessantly from the east

The Spanish King asked Urdanata, now 52 and in poor health, to help organise a new expedition to the Philippines. On the return voyage from Manila he attempted to prove his theory by sailing as far north as possible before turning eastwards across the Pacific. The powerful winds of the North Pacific allowed Andrés de Urdaneta to reach the coast of California in three months. From there they sailed south to Acapulco, where the Augustine friar was hailed as a hero.

Soon, a galleon was sailing annually from Manila to Acapulco with a cargo of spices traded from the Moluccas as well as Chinese silks, porcelains and lacquer ware. The Spanish transported these cargoes, together with gold and silver from Peru, across the Isthmus of Panama to the Caribbean ports, where they were loaded onto the treasure fleets bound for Spain.

One hundred years after the first voyage of Christopher Columbus towards the Indies, the annual voyage of the Manila galleons was the fulfilment of his dream of sailing west to bring the riches of the Indies to Spain. A flourishing trade developed and the Manila galleons sailed to Acapulco with spices and silks and returned across the Pacific loaded with Spanish silver dollars minted in Peru. Worth eight reales and known as 'pieces of eight', these became the preferred trade currency throughout the Orient and the Indies. The route of the Manila galleons was the final connection in a trading network that now encircled the world and was the beginning of the modern global economy. Along the Indian Ocean and Pacific Ocean trade routes, silver and gold flowed to the Indies and the Orient, while spices, silks, porcelain, lacquer ware and other exotic oriental trade goods flowed back to Europe.

In 1580 King Henry of Portugal died leaving no direct heirs. Through his mother, the former Princess Isabella of Portugal, King Philip II of Spain was able to lay a claim to the Portuguese throne and then sent his army into Portugal to enforce his rights. He was crowned King of Portugal in 1581 and a 60-year union gave the Spanish control over Portugal.

The United Provinces were now at war with both Spain and Portugal. Hoping to cripple the economy of the rebellious Protestant provinces and force an end to their revolt, King Philip II of Spain and Portugal now stopped Lisbon from trading their spices with the merchants of Amsterdam. However, the effect was the opposite since these merchants sought to bypass Lisbon and make their own voyages to the East Indies.

5 Cornelis de Houtman and the Dutch in the East Indies

The entry of the Dutch into the trade for spices in the East Indies would be important because while the Portuguese and the Spanish had not made any recorded discoveries of Terra Australis it was the Dutch who would significantly map what they would call 't Zuyd Landt or Terra del Zud.

The decision by the Dutch merchants of Amsterdam to make their own voyages to the East Indies was aided by Jan Huygen van Linschoten who published his book *Itinerario* in 1596. The introduction to the English translation of his work reads:

> Being young and living idelye in my native Countrie, sometimes applying myself to the reading of Histories and some straunge adventurers wherein I tooke no small delight, I found myself so much addicted to see and travaile into straunge countries, thereby to seeke some adventure, that in the end to satisfy myself, I determined … to take the matter upon me, trusting in God that he would further my intent.

The young van Linschoten left Holland at the age of sixteen and travelled to Spain to stay with his half-brother. Living in Seville, he quickly learnt Spanish and later moved with his brother to Lisbon. In 1583 he sailed from Lisbon to India to take up a position as secretary to the Archbishop of Goa, an important position that gave him access to an enormous amount of privileged information. Van Linschoten never ventured further east than Goa but kept his eyes and ears open for the next five years, assiduously collecting information on every facet of the Indies, the spice trade and Portugal's Estado da India.

After his return to Holland in 1592 he began writing his famous *Itinerario* or 'Travel account of the voyage of the sailor Jan Huygen van Linschoten to the Portuguese East Indies'. His book revealed a marvellous world to his readers. No one had extensively described the Indies to a wide audience since Marco Polo. He wrote of exotic peoples and places, of different customs and dress, of the treasure and wealth that would come to those willing to risk the dangers and sail to the eastern seas.

Van Linschoten gives a frank account of the Portuguese, their greed and divisiveness and their lack of organisation. He undermined the myth of Portuguese invincibility in the region, showing that enterprising competitors could gain a share of the wealth of the Indies. He also published the 'Travel account of the Navigations of the Portuguese', which included vital navigational and cartographic information he had secretly compiled from Portuguese maps and pilots' logbooks during his stay in Goa.

In 1593 three Amsterdam merchants began meeting in secret to plan an expedition to the East Indies. One of the first things these men did was to send Cornelis de Houtman to Lisbon. Posing as a merchant, his job was to obtain information about the Portuguese spice trade, the East Indies, and to confirm the writings of van Linschoten. In 1594 this group, now consisting of nine wealthy merchants, gathered in a wine tavern in Amsterdam to discuss plans for a joint trading voyage to the East Indies and declared themselves directors of a company they named the 'Company for Far Distant Lands'. To help raise the necessary capital they commissioned a map which acted as a prospectus because it depicted the East Indies and showed in botanical detail the valuable commodities grown in the Spice Islands, such as nutmeg, cloves and three different types of sandalwood. Engraved on copper plate, it represents a breakthrough in mapmaking, showing a much sharper image than previously achieved by using woodcuts and is a masterpiece of cartographic art.

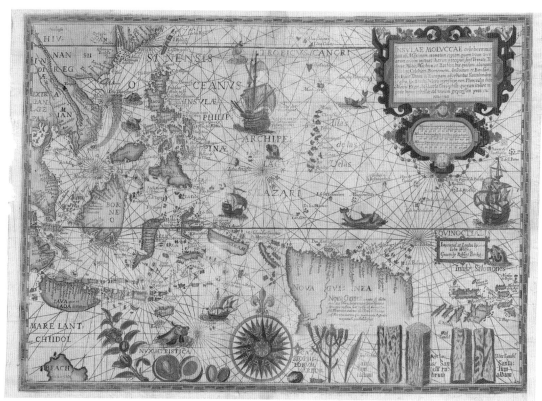

Map of the East Indies and the Spice Islands, Petrus Plancius, 1594 (Maritime Museum, Rotterdam)

Frontispiece of van Linschoten's *Itinerario*, 1596 (Royal Library, Netherlands)

In 1594 the keels of four ships, the *Hollandia* and the *Mauritius* (both 460 tons), the *Amsterdam* (260 tons) and the yacht *Duyfken* (Little Dove, 50 tons) were laid near Amsterdam. The *Duyfken*, which measured only twenty metres from stem to stern, was smaller, faster and able to sail into shallower water and would act as a scout boat for the expedition. Prince Maurits agreed to christen his namesake *Mauritius*, which was a great honour for the nine Amsterdam merchants and a source of pride for the recently declared United Provinces.

Cornelis de Houtman was appointed commander of the expedition and the fleet left Amsterdam in April 1595 carrying trade merchandise plus 100,000 Spanish silver dollars which the Dutch purchased in Europe and packed into chests to form ballast for their ships sailing to the East Indies.

Van Linschoten had advised the expedition to avoid the Portuguese-controlled ports of East Africa, India and the Strait of Malacca by sailing directly across the Indian Ocean to the Sunda Strait between the islands of Sumatra and Java and then to the pepper port of Bantam. Van Linschoten believed the Portuguese were not yet trading in Bantam, which is located on the north coast of Java and near the northern entrance to the Sunda Strait, but when the Dutch expedition arrived there in June 1596 a boat carrying six Portuguese merchants came out from the town to greet them. The Portuguese told them that five Chinese junks had just sailed fully loaded with pepper and there was another junk in the harbour trying to buy up all the remaining spices in the port.

The Dutch describe Bantam as being shaded by coconut trees, encompassed on both sides by a river, and being almost as large as the old town of Amsterdam. The houses were made of bamboo and stood upon four wooden poles, their rooms hung with silk or cotton curtains. There were no ordered streets, the town was surrounded by foul low-lying water, but the marketplace was full of merchants from Malacca, Bengal, Malabar, Gujarat, Canton and the Moluccas, with the Chinese being the most active traders in the town.

The initial Dutch encounter with a representative of the Sultan of Bantam went well. They were told not to trust the Portuguese for they were two-faced, that the harbour was free for all merchants, while at the same time promising the Dutch they would have preference over all others. De Houtman presented the Regent, who was acting on behalf of the boy Sultan, with a gift of beautiful crystal glasses, a gilded mirror and some scarlet cloth. In return they were entertained to a banquet and offered a warehouse ashore from which to begin trading. The chronicler of their voyage, Willem Lodewijcks, wrote: 'Many Gentlemen, Merchants, Chinese and Arabians came to our warehouse and into our ships offering us pepper, but our factor offered them too little a price'.

The factor (or merchant) was Cornelis de Houtman. Arrogant and intemperate, he was a poor choice as commander. When the town's traders were unwilling to sell their spices at the prices he was offering, he captured some junks bringing cloves and nutmeg from the Spice Islands. The Javanese then seized his merchants ashore, holding them hostage until he paid reparations for the stolen spices. Frustrated, he took revenge by bombarding the town with cannon fire.

No longer welcome in Bantam, the Dutch fleet sailed along the north coast of Java looking for another port where they could trade for spices. After they dropped anchor off Tuban, vengeful Javanese boarded the *Amsterdam* and hacked twelve of its crew to death including its captain Jan Jacobs Schelinger. De Houtman was then involved in a senseless massacre off the island of Madura in East Java where, suspicious of the welcoming motives of a flotilla of small craft circling his ship, he took pre-emptive action and blew them out of the water with a fusillade of cannon fire.

Unable to trade anywhere in Java, Cornelis Houtman wanted to sail on to the Moluccas but his captains and crew would go no further. The fleet was in complete disarray and Willem Lodewijcks recorded:

> The 12 January we set sail again, some desiring to sail Eastward, others Westward, but in time we set Westward to sail once again to Bantam, werewith the flagship *Mauritius* sailed Southeastward, to get about the island of Java, and we followed her.

After reprovisioning in Bali, the three remaining vessels of the fleet departed for their long voyage home and after being away for three years reached the Dutch Republic at the beginning of 1597. By the time of their return to Amsterdam only 89 of the original 249 crew members were still alive and seven more men died after having to be carried ashore.

The first Dutch voyage to the East Indies had been a disaster and its cargo of spices barely covered the cost of the voyage. However, it had been a success in that the Company for Far Distant Lands had pioneered a new sailing route to the East Indies and had reached Java and the spice markets at Bantam. The 1599 map by Theodore de Bry shows the four vessels of this first Dutch voyage sailing in the South Atlantic before rounding the Cape of Good Hope, on to Madagascar and then sailing directly across the southern Indian Ocean to Bantam and the return voyage of three vessels from Bali back to the Netherlands. The de Bry map also shows a northern peninsula of Terra Australis Incognita, the still unknown south-land, extending to an area south of Java as also seen on the maps of Abraham Ortelius.

In 1598 the Company for Far Distant Lands sent another fleet to the East Indies, consisting of eight ships commanded by Admiral Wybrand van Wawijck and with Jacob

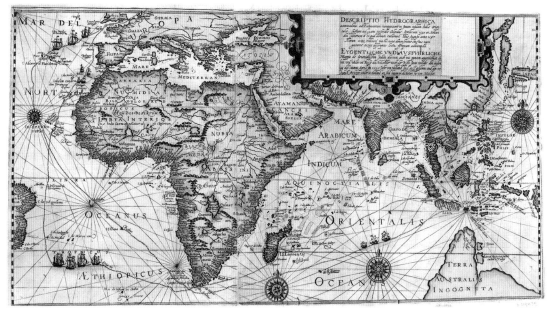

Map of the first Dutch voyage to the East Indies, 1595, Theodore de Bry (Bartele Gallery, Jakarta)

van Neck as the chief merchant. Six of the ships were named after the United Provinces of the Netherlands: *Hollandia, Zeeland, Utrecht, Gelderland, Friesland* and *Overijssel*. The seventh won the name *Mauritius* after the Statholder and the eighth was named *Amsterdam*. For this voyage the *Duyfken* had been renamed since a list of the ships along with their captains and merchants ended with a clarification – 'a pinnace which in the former voyage, called *Duyfken*, is now named *Overijssel* of fifty tons'.

Trading in Bantam, the shrewd van Neck was able to undo some of the ill will created by Cornelis de Houtman by agreeing to pay more than the market rate for spices. A brisk trade followed and within weeks four of the ships were filled with pepper. They returned to Amsterdam in July 1599, the voyage having taken only fifteen months, which was half as long as the first expedition.

Church bells rang out in celebration all over Amsterdam as Jacob van Neck and his crew paraded in triumph through the streets of the city behind a troupe of trumpeters. A painting by Andries van Eertveldt shows the four ships – the *Hollandia, Mauritius, Friesland* and the small yacht *Overijssel* – being welcomed by smaller ships on their triumphant return to Amsterdam in 1599. The fleet had returned laden with 300,000 kilograms of pepper, 120,000 kilograms of cloves, as well as nutmeg and mace and this second voyage was a legendary success for the Company for Far Distant Lands, yielding a profit of 400 percent for its investors.

Commanded by Wybrand van Wawijck, two of the vessels of the second voyage, the *Amsterdam* and the *Utrecht*, continued on to the Spice Islands of Ternate and Banda to trade for cloves and nutmeg. After the *Amsterdam* cast anchor off Fort Gamalama on Ternate, Sultan Said came out to greet the ships although he prudently refused to go aboard. As a leader of his people, the Sultan was a great warrior and a devout follower of Islam. Van Wawijck described him as a strong man about 36 years of age, with a pleasant disposition and an intense curiosity to learn anything new. He took a special interest in the ship's cannon which he had the Dutch fire against his own small vessels to observe the effects. The *Utrecht*, commanded by Heemskerck, received a cool welcome when it reached the Banda Islands in mid-March 1599. The Bandanese were unhappy to trade because of their past bad experiences with the Portuguese, however Heemskerk eventually succeeded in winning their confidence and left behind 22 men to stockpile nutmeg so that future Dutch fleets would be able to purchase it on their return.

The next Dutch fleet under the command of Admiral Wolfert Harmenz sailed in 1601 and was the first to challenge the Portuguese. Reaching the Sunda Strait the five ships of the Dutch fleet the *Gelderland*, *Zeelandia*, *Utrecht*, *Wachter* and the yacht *Duyfken*, received warning from a Chinese vessel of a fleet of Portuguese ships waiting in Bantam: 'Saying that before the town of Bantam lay a Portuguese armada of 30 sail, as he said, so many ships, galleys, fusten and frigates that it made a great fright amongst us'. The Hollanders used the superior accuracy and range of their cannon to drive off the Portuguese vessels which tried to stop them reaching the port. The Battle of Bantam is depicted heroically in the painting by Claesz Jansz Visscher which shows not only the size and strength of the Dutch ships but also includes a map, which looking from the perspective of the northern hemisphere, shows the Malay Peninsula, Sumatra and Java. The Hollanders rejoiced in their victory as they wrote:

> The Almighty Lord cannot be praised and thanked enough for the triumphal victory told above, of which the fruits shall be revealed more and more in time to come, having in no small way diminished the arrogance, reputation and airs and graces of the Portuguese and exalted the bravery of the East Indiamen.

This victory was by vessels equipped as a merchant fleet, but the Dutch realised that if they were to capture the spice trade from the Portuguese and the Spanish they would eventually need to send war fleets to the East Indies. From Bantam the *Gelderland*, *Zeelandia* and the *Duyfken* sailed to Ternate to trade for cloves while the *Wachter* and

Utrecht sailed to the Banda Islands to trade for nutmeg. After their vessels returned fully loaded to Bantam the Dutch received permission from the Sultan to leave two merchants or factors, Claes Gaef and Jan Lodewyckz Roosenjin, in Bantam to purchase pepper and other spices coming from across the archipelago and store them in 'factories' in preparation for the arrival of the next fleet.

Sea battle between Dutch and Portuguese ships in the Bay of Bantam, 1601, Claes Jansz Visscher
(Atlas van Stolk, Rotterdam)

After the success of the Amsterdam merchants, their competitors in Rotterdam and Zeeland decided to send their own fleets to the Indies, hoping to gain their share of the hugely profitable spice trade. The Amsterdam merchants responded to this competition by sending these instructions to the commanders of their fleets:

> You know as well as we do what losses it would cause us if the Zeeland ships were to arrive before ours are fully loaded. Therefore, buy. Buy everything you can lay your hands on, and load it as quickly as possible. Even if you have no more room for it, keep on buying and bind it to yourselves for future delivery.

As strange as it may seem, the merchants from Zeeland appointed Cornelis de Houtman to command their fleet. His two ships stopped in Aceh in North Sumatra to trade for pepper. Here the arrogant and intemperate Cornelius de Houtman was killed and his brother Frederick taken prisoner by the forces of the Sultan of Aceh. The Sultan offered Frederick de Houtman the post of king's agent if he could confirm his loyalty by converting to Islam. De Houtman heroically refused this offer, using the next eighteen months he spent in prison to learn Malay. He published the first Dutch-Malay dictionary and phrase book on his return to the United Provinces. He also had an interest in astronomy and used his time in Aceh to map the southern skies, later publishing a catalogue of 303 southern stars.

Between 1595 and 1601 merchants from the cities of Amsterdam, Rotterdam, Hoorn, Enkhuizen, Middleberg, Rotterdam, Veere and Delft sent 65 vessels in fourteen separate fleets to the East Indies, most of them completing successful voyages and returning with cargoes of spices that brought their owners immense wealth. Each voyage was financed separately, with the goods sold and profits distributed at the end of each voyage. During almost the same period only 46 Portuguese vessels sailed from Lisbon, indicating how rapidly the Dutch were overtaking the Portuguese in the Asian trade.

6 The United Dutch East India Company

The United Provinces realised that to challenge the vice-regal power of the Portuguese in the East Indies they needed an organisation working in the national interest rather than individual commercial interests. In this atmosphere of increasing trade rivalry a commission was formed by Johan van Oldenbarnevelt which recommended the merging of the trading companies from Amsterdam, Delft, Rotterdam, Hoorn, Middelburg and Enkhuizen into one major company.

Competition over trade with the east was fierce and the United Provinces not only had to challenge the Portuguese and Spanish, but also a rising threat from the English East India Company. Queen Elizabeth I signed the charter of 'The Company of Merchants Trading to the East Indies' in 1600 and in 1601 a fleet of five ships left London commanded by James Lancaster. The vessels carried £21,742 in Spanish silver dollars and £6860 in trade goods and they returned from Bantam fully laden with pepper, making the voyage hugely profitable for its investors.

Despite the opposition of the different trading companies and after a period of bitter political infighting, Johan van Oldenbarnevelt and Prince Maurits brought enough pressure to bear on the parties for them to agree to amalgamate. In January 1602, van Oldenbarnevelt called a meeting of all the business and political leaders of the major Dutch cities trading with the East Indies. A single company with a monopoly on trade, he argued, could combine its members' existing capital, property and accumulated experience and thereby increase profits, and it was van Oldenbarnevelt who drafted the company structure and its charter.

In 1602 the States General joined the six companies together into the Vereenigde Oost-Indische Compagnie (VOC) or the United East India Company with a founding capital of 6.5 million guilders and a monopoly on all trade east of the Cape of Good Hope and west of the Strait of Magellan. Significantly, rather than finance each voyage separately, the Company would have permanent capital and the VOC was the founding company of the Amsterdam stock exchange. Its shareholders were from all levels of society as only 84 of the 1000 investors could be described as large investors and the rest were small merchants, craftsmen, labourers and all those citizens willing to invest some capital for a period of at least ten years. This permanent trading capital made the Dutch East India Company the first modern corporate enterprise as well as the first multinational corporation, and it even designed the first corporate logo which is still recognised today.

The VOC flag

This revolution in commercial financing gave the VOC an enormous advantage over its main commercial competitor, the English East India Company. To finance the growing trade the Bank of Amsterdam was established in 1609, the precursor to, if not the first true central bank. The VOC received a monopoly over Asian trade which it would keep for the next two centuries, and became the world's largest commercial enterprise of the period. It could maintain its own armed forces, coin its own money, manufacture its own weapons and enact its own laws. It could establish ports and territories, appoint governors, dispense justice and make treaties or declare war on those who opposed it. This was a private for-profit company with all the powers of a sovereign state.

The directors of the Dutch East India Company, known as the Gentlemen Seventeen (Heeren XVII), representing the VOC chambers of Middelberg (Zeeland), Amsterdam, Enkhuizen (North Holland), Hoorn (West Friesland), Delft and Rotterdam (South Holland), were responsible for the building, equipping and manning of the fleets that departed annually for the East Indies as well as organising the auctions of the commodities brought back by the returning fleets. Spices were initially the most important trading commodity of the VOC, with pepper, cloves, nutmeg, mace and cinnamon making up the majority of ships' cargoes bound for Europe. However, over time these cargoes changed to include Indian textiles, Chinese porcelain, Chinese tea and other valuable Asian commodities.

East India House in Amsterdam, especially built for the Company, was the centre of all its business activities and it was here that the directors of the joint company gathered for their twice-yearly meetings. East India House is now part of the buildings of the University of Amsterdam and in 1997 the Directors' Room was restored to its original glory, including paintings of the VOC ports at Ambon, Canton (China), Cochin (India), Judea (Thailand), with that of Kasteel Batavia hanging in its central position over the gilded decorative woodwork of the fireplace. In 1663 Olfert Dapper described the Directors' Room of East India House:

> Hanging in the hall is the great city of Batavia, with its terrifying and invincible castle … hanging all around are the islands of the Moluccas, fortresses, orchards filled with spice trees, cities, harbours, capes that we occupy at the other end of the world.

Spices brought huge profits because of the seemingly insatiable demand and the Dutch word peperduur (as expensive as pepper) reflects the prices of spices at the time. Industries related to the VOC such as shipbuilding, sailmaking, ropemaking, navigation, cartography, printing, banking and insurance all flourished. The growth of the Dutch East India Company was closely supported by the Dutch state and we have a description by one of its governors-general, van Imhoff, who wrote that the VOC was:

> No mere Merchant, but also represents the Power of the Dutch Nation, and that whereas it journeys and trades in the former capacity, it is in the latter capacity that it is established there; to achieve its true goals the Company must assure its existence in both capacities and on the strength of both capacities, so tightly is the political interwoven with the mercantile, and vice versa.

As the profits flowed to the shareholders, a large and increasingly wealthy middle class drove a growing art market. The arts flourished, for those who had money wanted to show off their new-found wealth. There was plenty of artistic talent drawn into the city of Amsterdam and the Golden Age of Dutch Art had begun. Painters in the United Provinces no longer worked only for the church and the aristocracy as elsewhere in Europe. Their clients now were the bourgeoisie who wanted new subjects – subjects from daily life that had never been pictured before such as the merchants and their ships.

Although a proportion of the two million inhabitants of the United Provinces continued to adhere to Roman Catholicism, the Dutch business world and all the organs of state were dominated by Protestants. The seventeen directors of the Company all

The VOC Directors' Room at East India House (Ian Burnet)

belonged to the Dutch Reformed Church and stipulated that no religion other than the Calvinist version of Protestantism was to be permitted in the Company's fortresses, towns and settlements in the Far East. It goes without saying that being a Protestant was an important qualification for anyone seeking to make a career with the Dutch East India Company.

For one hundred years the Portuguese were rarely challenged in the Eastern Seas and had an almost complete monopoly of the trade into Europe. This led to complacency and an inability to adjust to the challenges that were to come from the rival Dutch company. The Portuguese Estado da India was described as 'rigid, orthodox, decaying, and mouldering like an ancient ruin in the tropical jungle'. Portugal was a small country with only limited manpower. Whereas the Dutch could call upon the services of German, French and Scandinavians to serve and fight for them, all the Portuguese could do was empty their jails, as according to the Bishop of Evora:

> Nothing better can be expected from the bad choice which is made in Portugal of the soldiers we send to India, by emptying the prisons of all the ruffians who are jailed there because they do not know how to keep faith with God or Man. And therefore it is hardly surprising that those who misbehave in this way at home should act the same way abroad.

In one of their first actions, three ships of the Dutch East India Company under the command of Jacob van Heemskerk captured a Portuguese Royal carrack, the *Santa Catarina*, near the entrance of the Strait of Singapore in 1603. The Portuguese vessel was returning from its annual trading voyage to Macau and had lain overnight at anchor as it could only navigate the shoal-ridden strait in daylight. Aided by vessels from the Sultan of Johor the struggle to capture the carrack lasted all day until the Portuguese captain and crew surrendered. As described by the Hollanders:

> Meanwhile the young King of Johor had been informed about our intention to intercept the Macau carrack … he argued that his river was the best place to await it, as all carracks must pass through the Strait of Singapore. Even if they should try to pass the Strait by night, which was impossible, they could never do so without being observed from the river … After we had carefully prepared ourselves, we hauled anchor at approximately 8 am and approached the carrack, which set sail as well. All day long we pounded the carrack with both our ships, though we tried to aim for the mainsail, lest we destroy our booty by means of our own cannonades.

The booty was immense, as the carrack was laden with valuable goods from China and Japan, including gold, silks, lacquer ware, and 100,000 pieces of Chinese porcelain. The captured cargo was auctioned in Amsterdam for 3.5 million guilders, a profit which was equal to half the paid-up capital of newly formed Company. This action was viewed by many, including some of the shareholders of the VOC as an act of piracy but the issue was resolved a year later when the Amsterdam Admiralty Court ruled that the vessel had been lawfully seized and its cargo confiscated as an act of war.

The Hollanders were now ready to directly challenge the Portuguese and their crown monopoly of the spice trade. The VOC prepared a war fleet of fourteen vessels to sail to the East Indies which included 6 ships provided by the Amsterdam Chamber: *Geunieerde Provincien* (United Provinces), *Amsterdam, Gelderland, Hof van Holland* (Garden of Holland), 4 ships provided by the Zeeland Chamber: *Delft, Duyfken, Dordrecht* and *Zeelandia*, with 4 ships provided by the Chambers of Horn and Enkhuysen: *Hoorn, Medembilik, West Friesland* and *Enkhuysen*. In December 1603 these heavily armed warships under the command of Admiral Steven van der Haghen and carrying a total of 1200 soldiers, sailors and crew sailed for the East Indies. This was the first war fleet to be fully equipped by the Dutch East India Company and was under orders to attack the Portuguese strongholds in the Spice Islands. Most of the fleet reached Bantam at the end of December 1604. From here the war fleet then sailed to Ambon where the commander of the Portuguese fortress sent an emissary to the Dutch warships saying that if they came in friendship they would be welcome. The Dutch responded by saying they were prepared to capture the fortress by force, unless perchance the Portuguese were willing to hand over the keys. The Portuguese replied that, even though outnumbered, they would defend the fortress and the honour of Portugal to the last man. The Dutch were triumphant when after a short bombardment the Portuguese commander committed suicide and his men surrendered.

Jan Huygen van Linschoten's assessment of the weakness of the Portuguese had proved to be correct and the loss of their fortress in Ambon was the beginning of the decline of the Portuguese Estado da India. After this success, Stephen van de Haghen split his fleet, sending five vessels to capture the Portuguese fort on the clove island of Tidore and another seven to capture the Portuguese fort on the nutmeg island of Banda.

Fresh from their victory over the Portuguese in Ambon, the Dutch arrived in Ternate with a fleet of five vessels. Captain Sebastiaanszoon told Sultan Said that he had come in response to his repeated requests for Dutch assistance to expel the Portuguese and the Sultan should now join him in an attack on their fort on Tidore. The Dutch and the Portuguese began to exchange cannon fire, resulting in the destruction of one of the Dutch ships. Next, Captain Sebastiaanszoon landed a strike force of about 150 soldiers on the rocky coast. Climbing an adjacent mount, they set up a cannon to fire from high ground and sent a force to attempt to scale the walls of the fort. After the Portuguese gained the military advantage and just when the Dutch were in full flight, a fire spread to the gunpowder magazine and the resulting explosion destroyed the fort and buried the Portuguese within its walls. This was a stunning victory for the Dutch. A lithograph by the artist de Bry shows in detail the VOC war fleet, the attack on the Portuguese fort, the explosion of the gunpowder magazine and soldiers fleeing from the burning fortress. After their victory, Captain Sebastiaanszoon and his fleet returned to reinforce the fortress in Ambon, leaving behind only one merchant and four soldiers on Tidore to defend the considerable gains they had made.

Alarmed at these attacks by the 'Dutch thieves, liars and pirates' who were now challenging Portuguese trade, the new Captain of Malacca, André Furtado de Mendoça, offered protection to the Sultan of Johor if he would break his ties with the Dutch and expel their representatives from his capital at Johor Lama. The Sultan replied that he

The VOC attack on the Portuguese fort at Tidore, de Bry, 1606 (Beinecke Rare
Book and Manuscript Library, Yale University)

would rather lose his entire kingdom than give in to such demands from the 'Enemies of
Islam'. Francisco Silveira writing in his recommendation for reforms in the governance
of the Estado da India provided a warning of what was to come:

> Seeing that, today, these individuals from Zeeland have come right under the nose of the
> viceroys, plundering and upsetting the trade and commerce in spices: then tomorrow, due to
> our own lack of order, they will try and evict us from our own houses. This should certainly
> be enough to rouse our Portuguese from their slumber.

As he predicted, in April 1606 a Dutch fleet of eleven ships under the command of
Admiral Cornelis Matelieff de Jong arrived in the East Indies. The Admiral had been
ordered to keep the purpose of his mission secret – for it was the capture of Malacca
and the impregnable fortress of 'A Famosa' from the Portuguese. The fleet first visited
Johor, where the admiral concluded a treaty with the Sultan. Their written agreement
called for cooperation between the Dutch East India Company and the Sultanate of
Johor for the conquest of Malacca and the removal of their common enemy, the Portuguese. It was also agreed that upon the successful capture of Malacca, its town and
fortress would be controlled by the Dutch, while all the surrounding territory would be

controlled by the Sultan. Importantly, the treaty required both parties to respect each other's religion, a condition inserted by the Sultan whose predecessors had endured the Portuguese intolerance of Islam.

The attack on Malacca could now begin. Dutch ships blockaded the city from the sea and commenced a bombardment of the Portuguese fort; with the assistance of forces from Johor they landed 700 soldiers to attack the city from the north and south. Unable to breach the fort's defences, many residents of Malacca were killed or died from hunger and disease during the next four months of the siege. At the same time, a powerful Portuguese armada raised at considerable expense and commanded by the Viceroy, was sailing from Goa in a determined effort to expel the Dutch from the East Indies. A letter from the Portuguese King reads:

> I have decided that the Viceroy, Dom Martin Afonso de Castro, go from Goa to Malacca with the greatest and most powerful armada of oared ships and large ships that it is possible to assemble, and take as many men of war, munitions, provisions and other necessary things that can be obtained from that Estado, and that they leave without fail during the month of April 1606 … to proceed with the war against the said rebels, provide their customary assistance to the city of Malacca, and sending the armada divided into fleets from there to the Straits of Singapore, Sabang and Sunda, and to wherever else it be necessary to secure those seas, and to cleanse them of the said rebels.

Stopping in Aceh, the Portuguese armada received news of the Dutch attack on Malacca and immediately sailed to relieve the embattled citadel. Warned of their imminent arrival, the Dutch abandoned their siege and hurriedly re-embarked their soldiers and artillery. On the evening of 17 August 1606 the Dutch and Portuguese fleets came face to face off Cape Rochado and the scene was set for one of the greatest sea battles in the Eastern Seas. The Portuguese fleet consisted of 17 ships and over 2000 men while the Dutch fleet consisted of 11 ships and 1200 men. At dawn the following day the two fleets engaged in battle, resulting in the destruction of two Portuguese and two Dutch ships, with many dead and wounded. At noon they broke off the fight and drew apart.

The Dutch were outnumbered and after his losses Cornelis Matelieff ordered his fleet to withdraw to Johor and prepare to attack the Portuguese under more favourable circumstances. Malacca was saved, but the Portuguese lacked the leadership necessary to take advantage of their numerical superiority to pursue and defeat the Dutch fleet and an opportunity to inflict a decisive victory against the VOC was lost.

In 1606 the burgher masters of the city of Amsterdam commissioned the artist Pieter Isaacsz to paint the lid of a clavichord which was to be placed in the City Hall. The painting shows an allegory of Amsterdam as the centre of world trade and on the left we see the maid of Amsterdam seated on a throne with the arms of the city above her head. Two women offer her a ship model and pearls, sea gods and river gods form her entourage, her right hand holds a bouquet of tropical fruit and her left hand points to a globe and navigation instruments which lie on the ground. In the centre of the painting we see three ships, the largest which is displaying the arms of Prince Maurits of Nassau, is the *Mauritius*. On the right are depictions of Asian sculptures, temples and a temple procession. The key to understanding this symbolic narrative is in the Latin verse written on a tablet leaning against the obelisk which reads:

> Did you really believe that I, Amsterdam, barred from the Spanish West, would be lost? Wrong, because with God's help I opened the sea route to Africa and India, to where exotic China stretches out, and to a part of the world that even the Ancients did not know of. Continue to favour us, Dear God, and pray that they learn of Christ.

The purpose of this painting was to make clear to all those attending receptions at the City Hall that Amsterdam would be the new centre of world trade. An extraordinary and presumptuous message, since it was only 30 years earlier that the United Provinces had started their revolt against the Spanish Empire and the VOC had failed to capture the centre of eastern trade at Malacca.

Painting on the clavichord in Amsterdam City Hall, 1606, Pieter Isaacsz (Rijksmuseum)

After his occupation of Portugal in 1581, King Phillip II of Spain and Portugal promised to keep the empires of Portugal and Spain separate in the Eastern Seas. But if the Portuguese in Malacca and the Spanish in Manila could combine operations, there was still the possibility of a conclusive defeat of the ships from the Dutch East India Company. Phillip II ordered Juan de Silva, the Spanish Governor of Manila, to prepare an armada to sail to Malacca and that the Portuguese Viceroy of India should do the same. In December 1615 the largest armada the Philippines had seen, consisting of ten galleons, four galleys and three frigates set sail for Malacca where it was planned for the Spanish and Portuguese armadas to join forces and attack the VOC at Bantam in Java and then reconquer the Portuguese forts on the islands of Ambon, Ternate and Banda.

The Viceroy in Goa prepared four galleons to sail to Malacca. Although considerably fewer than the number promised to the Spanish, this armada departed in May 1615. However, one vessel was sunk in a battle off North Sumatra with the Acehnese, and the other three vessels were attacked in the Strait of Malacca by a superior Dutch fleet commanded by Steven van der Haghen. In a battle which lasted three days, the Portuguese vessels were doomed and the fate of their flagship is described by those ashore in Malacca:

> It began to burn, to our very great sorrow, for it was an unusually fine vessel; it carried thirty six pieces of artillery and a quantity of ammunition. When the fire reached the powder magazine, so great was the noise made that the land of Malacca trembled and the houses shook. A cloud of smoke arose to the heavens which hid the clouds, and in that instant we lost sight of the galleon.

Unaware of the fate of the Portuguese ships, the Spanish armada arrived in the Strait of Singapore from Manila on 25 February 1616 where they fortuitously met a Portuguese galleon and carrack returning fully loaded from Macau. Juan de Silva escorted the vessels to Malacca, whose citizens had given up any hope that the returning vessels from Macau could escape attack from the Dutch fleet. Their arrival escorted by the Spanish was seen as a miracle. Governor De Silva received a huge welcome and the people of the city showed him their gratitude:

> It was a most fortunate event, and was worthily celebrated by the public acclamations of the inhabitants of Malacca who called Governor Don Juan de Silva their redeemer. They received him in their city with demonstrations of joy and honours as if he were a Viceroy, for as such did they regard him; and they assured themselves that with his valour and powerful fleet, they were able to deliver India from the inopportune war and the continuous pillaging of the Dutch.

Unfortunately, after these celebrations Juan de Silva contracted a malignant fever and died only eleven days later. With their commander now dead, and many of his crew also dying of fevers, the armada turned to sail back to Manila without any glorious victory over the Dutch at Bantam, or the islands of Ambon, Ternate or Banda.

Dutch attacks on Portuguese shipping gradually demolished much of the Portuguese trade, such that Malacca and Macau no longer contributed to the finances of the Estado da India based in Goa. The Portuguese desperately needed ships to protect their maritime trade and their far-flung seaborne empire. However, many of the ships that arrived in Goa to fight off the Dutch challenge never got as far as Malacca or Macau. Goa was virtually bankrupt and many of these ships rotted away on the Mandovi River, their unpaid sailors forced to seek other means of support often in private trade or as mercenaries for Asian rulers. One of the Portuguese commanders described the outcome in no uncertain terms:

> What we lost were galleons and cities, poorly provided with supplies, munitions and weapons, badly provided with captains, badly provided with men of valour and experience, and which above all were misgoverned.

7 *Willem Janszoon and the Voyage of the Duyfken, 1606*

In 1528 the Spaniard Alvaro de Saavedra Cerón commanding the *Santiago* attempted to sail from the spice island of Tidore directly east across the Pacific and charted the north coast of Papua New Guinea where he named an island as Isola Del Oro or 'Island of Gold'. This island of gold captured many people's attention including those at the Dutch East India Company. Spain had huge quantities of silver and gold coming from their colony in Peru to finance their military activities against the United Provinces and Spanish silver dollars or pieces of eight had become the standard European trade item in Asia. The VOC was forced to buy these silver dollars in the European money exchanges and ship them in their vessels sailing to the East Indies. Visions of mountains of silver and gold in Papua New Guinea or Terra Australis filled the dreams of the directors of the Company and they were keen to make a voyage of exploration as soon as possible.

Willem Janszoon began his seafaring career with the Company for Far Distant Lands as a steersman aboard the ship *Hollandia* which was part of the second fleet the VOC sent to the East Indies in 1598. This fleet consisted of eight ships under the command of Admiral Wybrand van Wawijck which were patriotically named after the Seven United Provinces, and for the purposes of this voyage the yacht *Duyfken* was renamed the *Overijssel* after the province of that name.

The *Duyfken* measured twenty metres in length, her rig comprised three masts and six sails and as many as twenty crew were packed into this tiny vessel. On her return to the Netherlands the *Duyfken* was overhauled, provided with new ropes, sails and anchors in preparation to sail to the East Indies for the third time with the Dutch fleet of 1601 under the command of Admiral Wolfert Harmenz. It was this fleet of five ships, the *Gelderland, Zeelandia, Utrecht, Wachter* and the *Duyfken*, which had been the first to challenge the Portuguese in what became known as the Battle of Bantam.

The sturdy little *Duyfken* sailed again in December 1603 captained by Willem Janszoon together with twelve heavily armed warships commanded by Admiral Steven van der Haghen. This was the first war fleet sent to the East Indies by the Dutch East India Company and it was under orders to capture the Portuguese forts in Ambon, Tidore and Banda.

After the capture of these forts the *Duyfken* sailed from Bantam at the end of 1605 with special orders to explore Nova Guinea. There are no surviving ships' logs or original charts of this voyage in the VOC files but the English East India Company records a report from their trade representative in Bantam, Captain John Saris: 'The eighteenth here departed a small pinnasse of the Flemings, for the discovery of the island called Nova Ginnea, which, as it is said, affordeth great store of Gold.'

The *Duyfken* first sailed to the Banda Islands and the newly established Dutch trading post there before setting off on its historic voyage along the south coast of New Guinea. After calling at the islands of Kai and Aru, Willem Janszoon followed a south-easterly course before reaching the estuary of the Digul River. From here they sailed along False Cape before turning south and then east to become the first European explorers to reach Australia when in March 1606 they sighted the low-lying west coast of the Cape York Peninsula. Climbing the rigging to get a better view of what was beyond the low sweep of coast they could not see any gold-bearing mountains in the interior, although there may have been columns of smoke indicating that the land was inhabited. Their first landing was at a river which they described on the map as Rivier met het busch (River with bush). A sandy spit covers part of the entrance into the Pennefather River which then broadens into a large estuary that extends a few kilometres inland. The *Duyfken* would have needed fresh water and firewood for the cook's stove so they lowered the ship's boat and started to row ashore. They carried arms in case of trouble but the local Aborigines, astounded to see a boat this size, filled with strange white people, had probably kept out of sight.

From here the *Duyfken* headed south and entered a wide bay that earned the name Vliege Bay or Fly Bay, after these most ubiquitous of Australian insects. Further down the coast they charted Dubbel Rivier or Double River at the confluence of the Watson and Archer Rivers. Here they sent their longboat upriver, where they obviously caught some good fish, as they named it Rivier Vis or Fish River.

Finally the *Duyfken* reached a point which they marked on their chart as Cabo Keer-weer or Cape Turnabout. When they encountered native peoples the crew had been instructed to show them samples of precious minerals and different spices to see if these were recognised. On their voyage down the coast and his landings ashore the chief merchant, Jan van Roosenjin, had only seen a dry desolate land inhabited by a primitive people. There were no spice trees, no mountains that might contain silver or gold, nothing that could be of value to Dutch merchants. Here at Cape Turnabout the crew of the *Duyfken* decided they had seen enough and the decision was made to turn around. Willem Janszoon assumed that this coast was a southern extension of Papua New Guinea and on his map it is named as Nova Guinea.

Willem Janszoon and more importantly Jan van Roosenjin would have been aston-

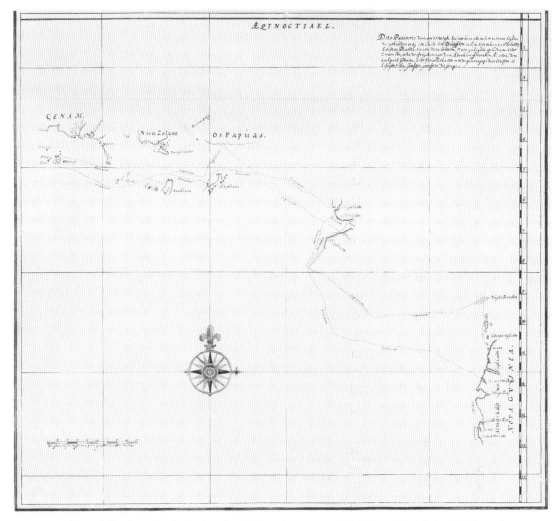

Chart of the Cape York Peninsula, Willem Janszoon, 1606 (Austrian National Library)

ished to learn that the dry red earth of this coast which they considered useless contains huge quantities of bauxite, the mineral that can be smelted into aluminium. In fact in the more than 400 years since their discovery of Australia this remote coastline has hardly changed except for the development of the world's biggest bauxite mine at Weipa.

Somewhere along this coast there was the first encounter between the Dutch explorers and the Australian Aborigines. The Aboriginal people had already lived there for thousands of years, their intimate knowledge of the land and sea developed over millennia meant that they lived in harmony with their environment. The first contact was therefore a meeting between two very different worlds, the beginning of which was marred by clashes.

Sailing north past their first landfall the crew of the *Duyfken* entered a very large river in the ship's boat. Although left unnamed on their chart it is now called the Batavia or the Wenlock River. In a later voyage by Carstensz he observed that the Aborigines had knowledge of muskets, whose terrible effects they presumably learned from the Dutch as he recorded in his log:

> In the afternoon we sailed past a large river which the men of the *Duyfken* went up with a boat in 1606, and where one of them was killed by the spears of the blacks.

Continuing northwards, the *Duyfken* passed a series of islands including Wallis Island which is marked on their chart as Hooge Eylandt (High Island), until they found their course barred by shoals which they named Vuijle Bancken (vile banks). Turning west they rounded False Cape returning again to the estuary of the Digul River and a village marked on their map as Tyuri. From here they sailed north-west on a straight course until they reached a part of the Papuan coast they marked as Os Papuas before turning away from the coast towards the Aru and Kai islands and then returning to Banda to report on their voyage. John Saris in Bantam heard of the return of the *Duyfken* from a local trader who had arrived from Banda as he reported:

> The fifteenth of June [1607] here arrived Nockhoda Tingall a Kling man from Banda in a Java Junke, laden with mace and nutmegs which he sold to the Guzerats. He told me that the Flemmings Pinnasse, which went upon the discovery for Nova Ginny, was returned to Banda, having found the island: but in sending their men on shoare to intreate of trade, there were nine of them killed by the heathens, which are man-eaters: so they were constrained to return, finding no good to be done there.

There has been speculation about where the nine men were killed. From the report of Jan Carstensz there was only one crew member of the *Duyfken* killed on the Cape York Peninsula and the Australian Aborigines are certainly not cannibals. Another possible location is at the village they named Tiuri near the mouth of the Digul River; however, if Willem Janszoon had lost almost half of its crew there it seems unlikely that he would sail north-east to reach the coast of Papua again at the point marked Os Papua rather than return directly to Banda. We may never know the answer but there is some reason why this part of the Papuan coast and the *Duyfken* should be remembered, for on the 1630 map by Jan Janssonion it is named Duyfken Island.

Near the beginning of this chapter, I stated that there are no surviving ships' logs or original charts of the *Duyfken* voyage in the VOC files. So if the original charts have disappeared, then how do we know the details of this first voyage to Australia?

The VOC sought to keep this voyage secret in order to prevent other nations from exploring the region and the *Duyfken*'s log and chart were filed in what became known as 'The Secret Atlas of the VOC', which over time has been lost, stolen or just vanished into the archives. However, in 1930 a copy of a map from the 'Secret Atlas' was found

Chart of the voyage of the *Duyfken,* 1606 (Austrian National Library)

in the Austrian National Library by Dr F.C. Weider. This chart, copied from the original made on board the *Duyfken,* provides a source of valuable information regarding the voyage and the inscription on the top right-hand corner of the chart reads:

This sea chart shows the way, in sailing both outbound and return of the voyage of the yacht *Duyfken* when visiting the lands east of Banda unto Nova Guinea.

That the VOC wanted to keep this voyage secret is demonstrated by the 1630 map by Jan Janssonius which shows parts of the Papuan coast discovered by the *Duyfken* including Duyfken Island and the estuary of the Digul River with the village marked as Tyuri, but nothing of the discovery of the Cape York Peninsula.

Insulularum Indiae orientalis, detail, after Jan Janssonius, 1630

Containing almost 600 maps covering the entire known world, Blaeu's *Atlas Maior* was the largest and most expensive book published in the seventeenth century and is considered a masterpiece of the Golden Age of Dutch Cartography. For over a hundred years the *Atlas Maior* remained the most prestigious atlas in the world and the premier product of the Dutch publishing industry.

One of the most enterprising map collectors of the seventeenth century was the Amsterdam lawyer Laurens van der Hem (1621–78). When the Latin edition of Blaeu's *Atlas Maior* was published in 1662 he acquired a copy which he used as the base for an even more ambitious collection of maps and topographical drawings and prints.

Among the most impressive of van der Hem's additions to the *Atlas Maior* is a set of four volumes of manuscript maps and topographical drawings which were originally made for the VOC. Van der Hem arranged the sheets in his Blaeu's Atlas according to his own ideas, amplifying the volumes with more than 1800 maps, charts, townscapes, architectural prints and portraits, many of them beautifully coloured to enhance the harmony and unity of the whole. It is believed that around 1670 van der Hem acquired copies made of the original charts of both the *Duyfken* and *Pera/Arnhem* expeditions which were part of the VOC's 'Secret Atlas' and he became one of the few private citizens to possess this confidential material.

More than 50 years after the death of Laurens van der Hem his map collection including the Blaeu Atlas was sold at public auction at The Hague in November 1730 and acquired by Prince Eugene of Savoy. Apart from collecting paintings, antiquities and other objects of art, the Prince had built up a library of international standing, containing some 15,000 volumes. The acquisition of the van der Hem map collection greatly enhanced his library and the Blaeu Atlas was considered one of the showpieces of his collection.

After the death of Prince Eugene his heiress sold the library to the Hofbibliothek in Vienna, which is now the Austrian National Library, and the *Duyfken* charts were forgotten for the next 200 years until rediscovered in 1930 by Dr Wieder when he was examining this collection of 46 volumes and found copies of the original maps from 'The Secret Atlas of the VOC' including the charts of the voyage of the *Duyfken* to Australia in 1606.

In June 1608 a Dutch fleet including the *Duyfken* sailed from Ambon and succeeded in capturing the Spanish fort on the island of Makian. Shortly after this engagement the *Duyfken* seems to have met her fate after she was damaged by what must have been a tsunami, as the accident causing the loss of two Dutch ships is described as the result of the swell and surf of a terrific high sea while they were at anchor. Captain Saris, the English Company's agent at Bantam, makes another entry in his diary:

1608. The first of September arrived a small pinnasse of the Flemmings from Makian, by whom we understood of two ships called the *China* and the *Duyfken* were cast away, while riding at anchor afore Makian.

After years of faithful service the brave little *Duyfken* was considered damaged beyond repair. But the *Duyfken* and Willem Janszoon will always be remembered for their historic voyage to Cape York, the first European discovery of the Australian continent, and the first segment of Australia to become part of the Tasman Map.

The founder of the Duyfken Replica Project was Dutch-born Australian historian Michael Young who lobbied extensively for a new replica project after the launch of the *Endeavour* replica at Fremantle in the mid-1990s. The Duyfken Replica committee was established in 1995 consisting of Michael Young, Dr Kees de Heer, Peter Becu and journalist James Henderson. This led to the establishment of the Friends of the Duyfken group and then with John Longley's support the Duyfken 1606 Replica Foundation. The foundation was initially chaired by the dynamic entrepreneur Michael G. Kailis of Perth, who led the charge in raising the $3.9 million building budget by raising significant donations from governments and private industry. On 27 March 1997, Dutch Crown Prince Willem-Alexander laid the *Duyfken* replica's keel at the construction shipyard in front of the Fremantle Maritime Museum in Fremantle.

When the original *Duyfken* was built, ships were not built according to plans but evolved with the skill of a master shipwright according to his instructions and the material at hand. The aim was to build the replica in the same way as the original, which is by building it plank-first with no frames to predetermine the shape of the hull. This of course was a huge leap for the twentieth-century shipwrights who were used to building a ship frame first. *Duyfken*'s hull is built from European oak imported from Latvia and her sails and rigging are made of natural flax and hemp. Oak planks, some of them more than 100 mm thick, were bent to shape by heating them over open fires until the timber became malleable and could be fastened to each other to form the shell of the hull. The inside frames or ribbing were added afterwards in the same manner as similar ships are still built in Indonesia.

The hull of the *Duyfken* replica was launched in January 1999 and the ship was ready for sea trials the following July. In April 2000 it sailed from Fremantle on what would be a re-enactment of the original *Duyfken* voyage from Banda to Cape York. The crew had to learn new sailing skills, those needed to sail the equivalent of a 400-year-old ship and it is believed to be the only ship operating in the world using a traditional Dutch whipstaff or 'Kolderstok' for steering. The *Duyfken* replica followed Willem Janszoon's original route from Banda to the Queensland coast, but unlike the voyage of 1606 they

The *Duyfken* replica ship at Banda (Robert Garvey)

came ashore with the permission of the Aboriginal people of the Cape York Peninsula. This time, message sticks and handshakes were exchanged – not musket balls and spears.

In May 2013 a memorial was erected near the small community of Mapoon and on the land of the Tjungundji people to commemorate the first recorded contact between Indigenous Australians and Europeans. Unveiling the memorial with the elders and the traditional owners of the land were the Mayor of Mapoon and representatives from the Queensland Government and the government of the Kingdom of the Netherlands.

Surrounded by the trees of this casuarina-fringed coast and flanking the entrance pathway are six ironstone boulders placed within a landscaped enclosure representing the main tribes of the area. The memorial is surmounted by a silhouette of the *Duyfken* which has been laser-cut from a plate of aluminium, the end product of the bauxite that gives this landscape its distinctive red hue. The outline of the *Duyfken* features a bird cut into its mizzen sail, representing both the 'Little Dove' of the ship's name and the Torresian Imperial Pigeon which is the hero bird of the local peoples.

Looking out to sea from a certain angle, the silhouette of the *Duyfken* can be placed on the horizon, reminding viewers of the extraordinary vision that once greeted the ancestors of today's Mapoon community, a vision heralding unimaginable change.

1606 was a remarkable year in Australian history because after this first sighting of the continent in March by Willem Janszoon there was another sighting in October.

Community members at the First Contact Memorial in Mapoon, Jeffrey Mellefont (Australian National Maritime Museum)

8 Luis Vaz de Torres and the Voyage of the San Pedrico, 1606

The philosophic commitment to the concept of Terra Australis as a geographical necessity to maintain the balance of the Earth's distribution of land masses dates back two thousand years to the ancient Greeks, including Aristotle and Ptolemy. The 1592 map by Abraham Ortelius showing the *Victoria* crossing the Pacific depicts the land south of the Strait of Magellan as stretching across the entire South Pacific Ocean and is named Terra Australis Magellica Non Dum Detecta or 'The South Land of Magellan Not Yet Detected'. It is also of interest that his map shows Terra Australis reaching all the way to New Guinea, which is depicted as an island although he notes that this is not proven.

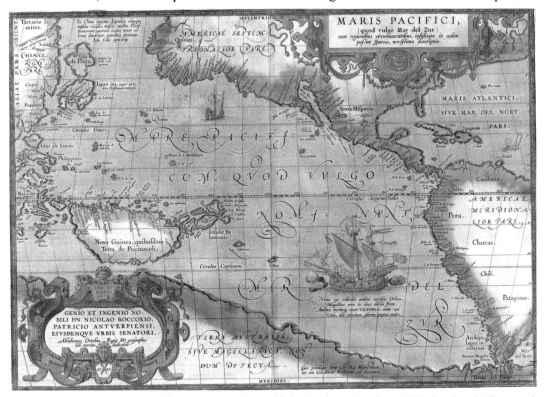

The *Victoria* crossing the Pacific Ocean, Maris Pacifici, Abraham Ortelius, 1592 (National Library of Australia)

Bounded by four continents, the Pacific Ocean is Earth's largest feature and was unknown to Europeans until Spanish explorer Vasco Nuñez de Balboa sighted it in 1513 from a peak in Darién, Panama. According to the Treaty of Tordesillas (1494) and the Treaty of Saragossa (1529) papal bulls had granted Spain rights to all lands discovered in the western hemisphere up to the Indonesian Spice Islands. The Spanish believed they 'owned' the Pacific Ocean and all its undiscovered lands and islands, the more so after Vasco Nuñez de Balboa crossed the Isthmus of Panama and waded into its waters.

Spain's major exploratory expeditions of the Pacific were launched from its colonial bases on the west coast of South America and were motivated by a combination of Christian fervour and gold fever. Pedro Sarmiento de Gamboa (1532–92), a Spanish soldier and navigator, arrived in Peru in the 1550s and became the leading authority on Inca legends and history. He theorised that such a highly developed and rich society was not indigenous to South America and had come from a land to the west, possibly from the Terra Australis, the still unknown south-land. Others had speculated that perhaps the Inca had brought their gold with them from Ophir, the biblical region where the stones are made of gold and from where King Solomon received cargoes of gold to build his temple in Jerusalem. If this is the case, then Terra Australis and Ophir must be located out there, somewhere in the vastness of the Pacific Ocean!

A new Spanish viceroy arriving in Peru in 1564 found Sarmiento's ideas persuasive and supported the idea of a voyage of discovery, but he wanted his nephew, 25-year-old Alvaro de Mendaña de Neira, to lead it. Sarmiento would be second in charge and Hernán Gallego, an older experienced mariner, would be the chief pilot. The two-ship expedition left Callao near Lima, Peru, in November 1567 and the ships finally sighted land on the eighty-first day of their voyage and more than 6000 miles from Peru. In the hope of finding gold they named these islands the Solomon Islands and they are shown on the Ortelius 1592 map to the east of New Guinea. During their three-month stay on Santa Isabel an uneasy peace prevailed between the Spanish and the islanders as food was scarce and somehow King Solomon's gold was always over the next ridge or on the next island. The Spaniards moved to the island of Guadalcanal where bloody encounters with the natives ensued and it was the same on San Christobal. It was obvious they had not reached a southern continent, nor had they discovered the source of King Solomon's gold. The majority of the men voted to return across the Pacific and the ships weighed anchor in August 1568. However, the chief pilot, Hernán Gallego, was still a believer in the gold to be discovered as he wrote:

> I consider it certain that, if they had let me go ahead, we should have found a land very prosperous and rich … And we were not very far from it, and of its goodness I did not wish to speak at this time, because all, being despondent, desired to return to Peru.

Mendaña later commented critically on Gallego's statement by saying that 'the land he did not see was reported to be very good, but he certainly did not see it'.

After their two-year ordeal Mendaña received little praise back in Peru for what was perceived as a failed voyage. He returned to Spain to plead the case for another voyage and after a delay of almost 30 years he was finally granted funds for a second voyage to colonise the islands he had discovered. Spain's territorial claim to some undiscovered continent with untold riches of gold and silver was still a mesmerising idea and the settlement of the Solomon Islands would confirm the Spanish claim to the Pacific and expand their empire.

In 1595 Mendaña sailed from Peru in the *San Geronimo* and the Santa *Ysabel* to establish a Spanish colony in the Solomon Islands with Pedro Ferdinand de Queirós as his chief pilot. With food and water running low, they reached a group of high volcanic islands somewhere south-east of the Solomon Islands. Mendaña named the largest island Santa Cruz and decided to colonise them for Spain. A settlement was established but hardly lasted more than a month due to disputes with the islanders and amongst the settlers themselves. As Queirós wrote:

> Some were saying: Where have you brought us to? What place is this where no man goes? … People would only come take gold, silver, pearls, or other things of value, and these are not here. Others said: We did not come to sow, for that purpose there is plenty of land in Peru … take us to seek those other islands or take us back to Peru.

After two months on Santa Cruz people were dying every day and Mendaña, himself already seriously ill then dies. One of the priests, officially representing the soldiers, drew up a petition listing reasons for abandoning the moribund settlement. Queirós then took command and sailed the fleet to Manila, passing east of the Solomon Islands but not sighting them, before crossing the Pacific and returning to Peru. Queirós is seemingly undeterred by the dangers and privations he had encountered on this abortive voyage and petitions the Viceroy of Peru for a ship and sailors to find Terra Australis and the gold that must still lie somewhere in the Pacific:

> I offered that, if he would give me a vessel of 70 tons and 40 sailors I would return to discover those lands and many others which I suspect to exist, and even felt certain that I should find in those seas.

The new Viceroy of Peru encouraged Queirós to return to Spain to seek financial support. After his arrival he then petitioned Pope Clement VIII to support the continuation of the discoveries the Spanish had made in the Pacific. Queirós told the Pope of the 'infinity of souls' that were waiting to be saved for Christianity and the great lands and riches that were waiting to be discovered in southern latitudes, lands that were already designated as being in the Spanish half of the world. The concept was of course magnificent – vast dominions to be added to the Spanish Empire, millions of souls to be saved and brought into the Catholic faith and more riches in gold and silver.

With the Pontiff's blessing, Queirós then approached King Philip III of Spain who after two more years of the claimant's pestering agreed to sponsor a third voyage of discovery. The King's orders declared that he took particular inclination and pleasure in the prospect that the discovery would bring the holy faith among those remote peoples for the glory of God and he signed a letter ordering the Peruvian Viceroy to give all necessary aid to Queirós. The Viceroy provided three ships, the flagship *San Pedro and San Pablo* commanded by Queirós, a second vessel named *San Pedrico* commanded by Luis Vaz de Torres and the launch named *Los Tres Reyes* commanded by Pedro Bernal Cermeño, all with 159 soldiers and sailors and a number of Franciscan friars onboard. He also appointed a young gentleman named Don Diego de Prado y Tovar to accompany the expedition. The small fleet left Callao in December 1605 to search for Terra Australis Incognita in the vast vastness of the Pacific Ocean and Queirós described their departure:

> The sails were set, and the men on their knees prayed for a good voyage … All the artillery, muskets and arquebuses were fired off. The ships passed near the royal ships, which were saluting with their cannon, with many people on their decks and galleries.

On 30 April 1606 they reached not the Solomon Islands or Santa Cruz, but the islands of the New Hebrides. Arriving from the north the Queirós fleet entered a large bay backed by the mountains of Vanuatu, which certainly appeared large enough to be the gateway to a continent. Queirós named the land Austrialia del Espiritu Santo in honour of King Phillip III's Austrian royal house declaring:

> I take possession … of all this region of the south as far as the pole, which from this time shall be called Austrialia del Espiritu Santo, with all its dependencies and belongings; and this forever, and so as right exists, in the name of the King, Don Philip III.

The bay was named for St Phillip and St James, its port was to be called Vera Cruz and the city to be erected nearby was named New Jerusalem, with its gates and its church to be built of marble. Such a grand declaration had to be followed by a grand act and Queirós elevated his officers to become Knights of the Holy Ghost and other senior crew members to be magistrates of the city of New Jerusalem. They spent a month in the bay, but where was the gold? Prado y Tovar, a genuine Knight of Calatrava, was scornful and later wrote:

> It was all wind, both walls and foundations, for he sought to cover up thus what he had promised on the way and was mistaken … I said to him before his friends … God has given you

Indians, not only two but thousands as in the islands ... and now this land which you call the great Austrialia of the Holy Ghost. We have only found the black devils with poisoned arrows; what have become of the riches? We quite understand that all your affairs are imaginary and as such have gone off with the wind.

It would seem that others on board the flagship were of the same opinion because as Queirós lay ill in his cabin, too weak to assert his authority, his crew decided they would leave the bay and return to Acapulco. As described by Luis Vaz de Torres in his account to the King of Spain:

From within this bay and from the most sheltered part of it, the Capitana departed at one hour past midnight, without any notice given to us, and without making any signal. This happened on the 11th of June 1606.

Torres waited at Espiritu Santo for fifteen days for his commander and the flagship to return. He then opened the sailing orders given him in case of separation from Queirós and according to Prado:

Torres summoned the council and produced a closed and sealed paper and said it was from the Viceroy of Peru. It said that in case the ships should separate they should make every effort to go to 20 degrees of south latitude to see if there was land in the region and if not they should go to the city of Manila.

The galleon *San Pedrico* and the tender *Los Tres Reyes* then sailed south-west looking for Terra Australis. Facing difficult weather and an equally difficult crew, Torres gave up the search at 21 degrees South, an estimated 190 miles from the mainland of Australia when a few more days sailing would have brought them to the Queensland coast, or worse, the hazards of the Great Barrier Reef.

After turning north they reached the Louisade Archipelago off the east coast of New Guinea. Unable to make the north coast of New Guinea due to the prevailing winds, the *San Pedrico* turned west to follow the south coast of New Guinea, hoping that the 1592 map of Abraham Ortelius was correct and that it was in fact an island. As described by Torres:

From hence I stood back to the NW to 11 ½ degrees south: there we fell in with the beginning of New Guinea ... I could not weather the east point, so I coasted along to the westward on the south side.

The vessels sailed a north-westerly course along the south coast of New Guinea until they reached the Gulf of Papua and the mouth of the Fly River, where they were blocked by the coast and shallow water. Torres was in trouble. The trade winds were blowing from the south-east, so to turn back and sail directly into the prevailing wind would have been almost impossible. Hence they were forced to turn south and encountered a multi-tude of reefs and shoals in three to four fathoms of water. The last thing that the captain of any vessel wants to do is run aground at high tide, so Torres and his crew invented a new method of sailing. The vessels would wait until the tide was receding and then let their ship drift with currents that led to the deepest channels. Once the tide appeared to be rising again they would anchor and wait for the next receding tide to be able to make further progress. Prado describes this method as coming from divine revelation:

> Seeing that we could not get clear of these shoals we took counsel as to what was to be done, and decided not to weigh anchor until ebb water and go with the foresail only to steer the ship, because the stream would carry the ships through the trough of the water, and to anchor at the flow of the tide. The opinion was as if it had come from heaven, for in this way we secured the ships and saved our lives.

They were amongst reefs and shoals for the next 34 days until in October 1606 they reached the channel immediately north of Cape York, now known as the Endeavour Strait. For many years it was assumed that Torres took a route closer to the New Guinea coast to navigate the strait that now bears his name, but in 1980 the Queensland mas-ter mariner Captain Brett Hilder demonstrated from the ships' logs that Torres took a southerly route through the strait past High Island and would have sighted the mainland of Australia. Torres became the first European to navigate the strait and by doing so proved that New Guinea was an island. Diego Prado y Tovar in his chronicle states: 'We were amongst reefs and shoals for 34 days … there were many large islands and they appeared more on the southern side'.

Without realising it, the large island on the southern side would have been the Terra Australis they had been sent to discover. Detail from the map by the Portuguese car-tographer João Teixeira Albernaz in 1628 shows New Guinea, the Solomon Islands and Vanuatu (Austrialia del Espiritu Santo) but does not delineate any of 'the many large islands that appeared more on the southern side' as described by Prado, which would of course be Australia. This meant that Torres sailed far north of High Island and did not find the Endeavour Strait as discovered later by James Cook.

Unsure of exactly where they were, the vessels followed the south coast of Papua and the north coast of Ceram until somewhere near the island of Batanta they encountered a local trading vessel and a Portuguese-speaking Moor who told them they were five days sail from the island of Bachan in the North Moluccas, where there was a Jesuit priest. As Prado wrote in his chronicle:

> It is impossible to exaggerate the pleasure we all felt at such good news, and certainly for us he was like an angel, for we had already gave ourselves up for lost … we thought it was so

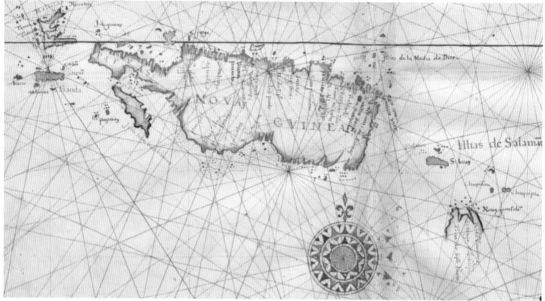

Map of New Guinea, João Teixeira Albernaz, 1628 (Bibliotheque national de France)

until this man told us where we were. We gave thanks to God.

When they reached Bachan in November 1606 Torres learnt from the Sultan, himself allied with the Spanish, that in response to the Dutch capture of the Portuguese forts in Ambon and Tidore, the Spanish had sent a fleet from Manila to Ternate where they captured Fort Gamalama from the Sultan of Ternate and were now in control of the islands of Ternate and Tidore. On reaching Ternate they anchored off Fort Gamalama and remained on the island for three months to recover their health. Before Torres left for Manila the Captain of Fort Gamalama commandeered the *Los Tres Reyes* and requested him to leave twenty men to reinforce the fort from an expected Dutch attack. The VOC must have later heard verbal reports from the Ternate that Torres had sailed along the south coast of New Guinea to reach the Spice Islands but there was no way to confirm this information.

To their great relief, Torres, Prado and the *San Pedrico* eventually reached Manila in May 1607. The following month Torres sent his report to the Spanish King and to Queirós his former commander, stating that he would report in person as soon as the colonial authorities obeyed the royal order to assist his return voyage to Spain. The next we hear from Torres is in a letter complaining that the Manila administration would not expedite his voyage home:

> Being in the city of Manila at the end of a year and a half of navigation and discovery among the lands and seas in the unknown southern part, and seeing that in this Royal City of Manila they have not hitherto thought fit to give me dispatch for completing the voyage Your Majesty commanded … I have thought proper to send a person to give an account to Your Majesty.

The person chosen to deliver his letter was one of the Franciscan monks who had sailed with them. Unfortunately this is the last we hear from Luis Vaz de Torres and it is not known if he ever left Manila or survived the voyage back to Mexico and then Spain. Torres' report that New Guinea was an island was considered to be a state secret and his report and the map of their voyage were buried in the files and never seen again. However, a copy of Torres' report of his voyage was deposited in the archives in Manila, where it remained unknown and untouched until the British East India Company captured Manila in 1792 and it was the British Admiralty that gave the Torres Strait its name almost 200 years after Torres had made his historic voyage.

From Manila, Diego de Prado y Tovar was able to travel on a Chinese vessel to Macao and then return to Spain on a Portuguese ship via Malacca, Goa and Lisbon. Prado wrote his *Relacion Sumaria de Capitan Don Diego de Prado* after his return to Madrid in 1608 and when he became a monk in the order of Saint Basil in Madrid. A copy of Prado's report, now in the Mitchell Library, was accidently found 300 years later in a collection of old documents held by a London bookseller.

The voyages of discovery by Sarmiento, Mendaña, Queirós and Torres were Spain's last major attempts to explore the South Pacific. The expectations of vast dominions to be added to the Spanish empire, the millions of souls to be saved and brought into the Catholic faith and the discovery of riches in gold and silver did not happen and a government severely strapped for funds had to cut its losses.

Eventually the Spanish authorities in Manila lost interest in supporting their base in the Moluccas and decided to abandon the fortress on Ternate altogether. In 1663 the last Spanish captain of Fort Gamalama loaded his men, trade goods and cloves onto twelve junks and sailed for Manila, ending the turbulent 140-year Spanish presence in the Spice Islands that had begun with the arrival of the Armada de Moluccas in 1521. Once the Spanish departed the remainder of the Ternatean court returned from Jailolo and began to build their settlements around the Dutch fort at Melayo, now renamed Fort Oranje. The Ternateans continued their informal alliance with the Dutch, believing them to be only interested in trade and that they would not interfere in local affairs or their religion. This may have been the policy of the early Dutch commanders trying to win local support against a common enemy but would certainly not be the policy of the future Dutch governor-general, Jan Pieterszoon Coen, something the Moluccans came to learn to their lasting regret.

Mar del Sur, Hessel Gerritsz, 1622 (Bibliothéque national de France)

In 1617 the Dutch East India Company appointed Hessel Gerritsz as their exclusive cartographer. It was his task to provide charts for all ships of the VOC which sailed from the Dutch Republic, including those from chambers other than Amsterdam. The discoveries of the *Duyfken* appear on the 1622 map of the Pacific Ocean (Mar del Sur) by Hessel Gerritsz. The text written next to Cape York Peninsula recognises the possibility that this is the discovery of a new land, separate and different from the island of Nueva Guinea as it reads:

These parts were sailed into with the yacht of Torres about Nueva Guinea on 10 degrees westward through many islands and dry banks and over 2, 3, 4 fathoms for full 40 days. Presuming Nueva Guinea not to stretch over the 10 degrees south – if this were the case – then the land from 9 to 14 degrees must be separate and different from the other Nueva Guinea.

Separate and different from the other Nueva Guinea means it must be part of Australia. This map, held in the Bibliothéque nationale de France is hugely significant because this is the first time any actual part of the Australian continent appears on a world map.

Mar del Sur, detail, Hessel Gerritsz, 1622 (Bibliothéque nationale de France)

9 Jan Pieterzoon Coen and the Founding of Batavia

Ambon had the most protected harbour in all the archipelago and after its capture by Steven van de Haghen in 1605 the Dutch reinforced the Portuguese fort there and re-named it Fort Victoria. It was important they have the right man in charge and van de Haghen appointed Frederik de Houtman as the first VOC governor. He was experienced in the East Indies as he had taken part in the first Dutch voyage in 1595 with his brother Cornelis de Houtman as the commander. In their second voyage his brother was killed in Aceh and Frederik de Houtman was imprisoned by the Sultan of Aceh for eighteen months. He used his knowledge of the Malay language and its people to maintain good relations with the Ambonese leaders and served as governor for the next six years. Ambon was the first permanent settlement for the Company in the East Indies and it remained their headquarters for the next twenty years.

A painting of Ambon showing both Dutch ships and kora-kora in the harbour and a greatly exaggerated Castle Victoria now hangs in the Rijksmuseum in Amsterdam. The adjacent cartouche with an image of Frederik de Houtman apparently implied that he had captured Ambon for the VOC, but after protests from the ignored Steven van de Haghen it can be seen that the text in the two cartouches has been painted out.

Born in the prosperous Dutch seaport of Hoorn, Jan Pieterszoon Coen grew up sur-rounded by ships loading and unloading their goods and preparing for their next voyage to the Baltic, the Mediterranean or the East Indies. He spent his teenage years in Rome as an apprentice bookkeeper with an Italian merchant house and on his return to the Netherlands he signed up as a junior merchant with the Dutch East India Company, departing Amsterdam in 1607 on his first voyage to the East Indies on the fleet com-manded by Admiral Verhoef.

The tiny Banda Islands, located in South Maluku, are rimmed by coconut trees and covered in an evergreen forest of nutmeg trees and larger kenari trees that protect them from the harsh tropical sun. Jan Pieterszoon Coen was a member of the Dutch fleet that

Painting of Fort Victoria on Ambon, attributed to David de Meyne, 1670 (Rijksmuseum)

sailed in 1609 to the Banda Islands with orders to build a fort and consolidate Dutch control over the nutmeg trade. Ignoring the objections of the island chiefs, Admiral Verhoef had his men start their construction on the site of a previously abandoned Portuguese fort on Banda Neira. As the walls rose, opposition from the Bandanese increased until the admiral was forced to arrange a peace meeting with the local chiefs. The admiral and his men were then lured into a deadly ambush and Jan Pieterszoon Coen narrowly escaped death when the Bandanese surrounded and killed Admiral Verhoef along with 42 of his soldiers and senior officials.

Dedicated to the service of the Dutch East India Company, Jan Pieterszoon Coen rose rapidly through the ranks and was to become a legend. In 1613, he was promoted to director-general of East Indies trade, based in the pepper port of Bantam. Five years later and at only 31 years of age, he became the fourth governor-general of the East Indies and based in Ambon. However this location was too remote from the major sea lanes of the Malacca Strait and the Sunda Strait that carried trade around the Orient and the In-dies. The VOC needed a more central location to build and repair their ships, warehouse their spices and to be their military and administrative headquarters. The possibilities were Malacca, Johor or Bantam.

The Dutch attempt to capture Malacca from the Portuguese in 1606 had failed due to its impregnable defences. Jan Pieterszoon Coen had his doubts about a Dutch fort in Johor and he wrote to the Gentlemen Seventeen that the situation in Johor was un-stable because of attacks by the Acehnese. Coen had sought exclusive trading rights in Bantam, but the governing regent had no wish to grant any nation such rights in what was a successful international trading port and he was justifiably suspicious of Dutch ambitions. In 1608 Admiral Cornelis Matelieff de Jong in a letter to the Gentlemen Sev-enteen described another possible location for the planned headquarters:

> The city of Bantam, albeit well situated, is not only very unwholesome, but also has a very young king – fourteen years old – who is impossible to negotiate with; moreover, his council is so divided by factionalism that one cannot accomplish anything … We need a place where we can call, coming from the Cape of Good Hope, without being subjected to the monsoon … But then we can expect some inconveniences from the people of Bantam, for as soon as they learn that we want to establish our residency in Jacatra, they may well make common cause with the Portuguese and become our and Jacatra's enemies … If we choose Jacatra, they should give us a suitable location, be it big or small, close to Jacatra's river, where we could build our fortified headquarters to protect ourselves from Portuguese attacks.

Jan Pieterszoon Coen then entered into negotiations with the prince of the neigh-bouring province of Jayakarta, who was more than happy to use the Dutch to gain his independence from Bantam. In 1618 the prince signed an agreement with the VOC allowing the building of warehouses on the east bank of the Ciliwung River at Jacatra (subsequently named Batavia and then Jakarta) where it entered the harbour of Sunda Kelapa. The map of West Java shows Bantam is located in the first major bay east of the Sunda Strait and Batavia is located at the next major bay to the east and where the map shows a large river.

The ruler of Bantam and the English East India Company opposed the Dutch settle-ment and separately besieged the occupants of the fortified Dutch warehouses but were never allied. In 1619 an English fleet commanded by Sir Thomas Dale arrived off Sunda Kelapa with orders to protect English trade. The English had twice the number of ships as the Dutch and a concerted English attack could have ended Coen's plans to establish

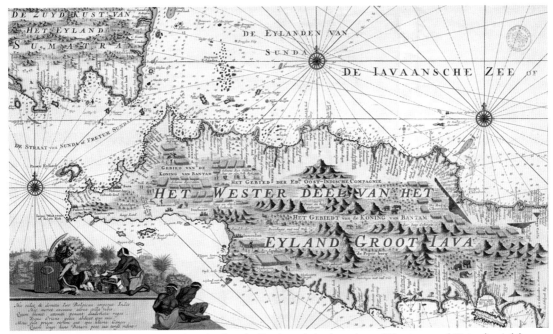

Map of West Java (detail) showing the Sunda Strait and the location of Bantam and Batavia, Adriaan Reland, 1718 (Dutch National Archives)

a base for the Dutch East India Company there. The Battle of Jacatra lasted three hours. The formidable English fleet fired their cannon from a discreet distance, only a single Dutch sloop was lost and at no time did the English try to board the Dutch ships. The only explanation is that there was no 'United' English East India Company. Dale's fleet represented three different commercial ventures and since each venture was separately financed, none of its commanders was willing to risk his own vessel for the common purpose. Coen was not to know this and unwilling to risk the destruction of his fleet he sailed that night for Ambon to obtain reinforcements, leaving a message to those in the fortified Dutch warehouse to hold out:

> In the meantime try to hold the fortress as best you can. If the time should come that you can no longer hold the place you should try to come to some understanding with either Jacatra or the English. It is our opinion that, if such an emergency should arise, you would be better by surrendering to the English.

The men in the Dutch warehouse were able to hold out against both English and Bantamese demands for surrender until Jan Pieterszoon Coen returned with enough men and materials to build Kasteel Batavia, a square fortress with four bastions lying at the mouth of the Ciliwung River.

The Dutch East India Company set about building a walled city, which they named Batavia after the tribe that had occupied Holland in Roman times. Modelled after a typical port city in the Netherlands, it lay at sea level so that small boats had direct access by river and canal to the city and the warehouses the VOC was building. A plan of Batavia from 1669, only 50 years after its founding, shows a walled city built around the mouth of the Ciliwung River with Fort Batavia guarding the entrance to the river. A bridge connects the fort to the city to the south and 175 huge sandstone blocks to build the massive six-metre-high entrance to Fort Batavia were shipped as ballast on the East Indiaman *Batavia* bound for that city in 1629. Unfortunately the *Batavia* foundered on the coast of West Australia and lay undiscovered until 1963. The blocks of the water gate have now been rebuilt and are displayed in the Shipwreck Galleries of the West Australian Maritime Museum.

Opposite Fort Batavia the Dutch built the warehouses which stored the spices they were gathering from across the archipelago and the trade goods they brought from Holland and India. Twice yearly these spices would be transferred to the ships of the 'home fleet' of East Indiamen bound for Amsterdam. Over time Batavia grew in the image of a Dutch city, with grand whitewashed buildings lining its canals built in the Dutch architectural style with hipped red-tiled roofs and wooden-shuttered windows. For the next 200 years Batavia would be the headquarters of the growing mercantile empire and as described by Jan de Marre in his epic poem *Batavia*:

> Whoever wishes to contemplate the Company in the possession of regal and princely power, must seek her in Asia, where she sits enthroned; is mistress of life and death; deposes and raises up kings; makes war and peace; has her own mint; and possesses all the attributes and signs pertaining to independent sovereigns.

Sometimes known as 'King Coen', Jan Pieterszoon Coen ruled his realm with an iron fist from 1618 until 1623, and then from 1627 until 1634, delivering the Gentlemen Seventeen on the Board of the VOC what they wanted, which was vast quantities of Asian commodities at low prices. One of his contemporaries describes his all-powerful position:

> As the Governor-General of the Dutch East Indies he had immense authority, which was an arbitrary and independent power in all matters: for there are few or no members of the council, who do not stand in need of his good offices, for example to obtain lucrative employments for their relations or favourites; and if this not be sufficient, to make them obey the nod of the governor, he is not destitute of the means of tormenting them, in every way and under

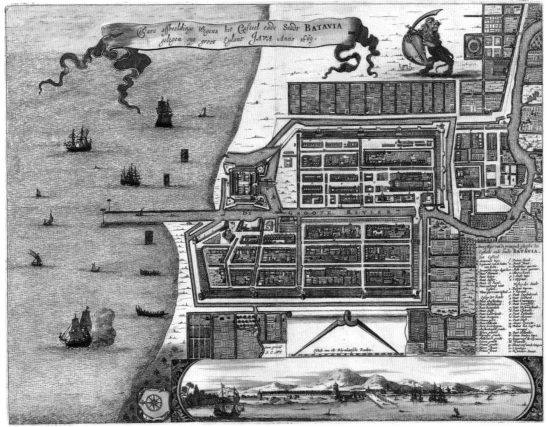

Plan of Batavia, 1669 (Princeton University Library)

various pretences, of even sending them prisoners to Europe.

A portrait of Coen as governor-general shows a stern and austere man with a long narrow face and deep-set eyes, leaving the lasting impression with the viewer that he was not a man to be crossed.

The Dutch East India Company became a mighty naval, military and trading organisation and looked upon the English East India Company as an impertinent intruder into a trade that it intended to develop as a monopoly for itself. In 1619 a treaty allied Protestant England and Holland against Catholic Spain and Portugal. Under the treaty, two-thirds of all the spices from the Spice Islands were to go to the Dutch and one third to the English. The directors of the VOC instructed Jan Pieterszoon Coen to cooperate with the English in the Indies. However, any concession to the English was totally against the nature of Coen and he wrote to the Gentlemen Seventeen in Amsterdam:

Portrait of Jan Pieterszoon Coen, Jacob Waben, 1629
(Westfries Museum, Hoorn)

I admit that the actions of the master are of no concern of the servant ... But under correction Your Honours have been too hasty. The English owe you a debt of gratitude, because after they have worked themselves out of the Indies, your Lordships put them right back again ... it is incomprehensible that the English should be allowed one third of the cloves, nutmegs and mace, for they cannot lay claim to a single grain of sand in the Moluccas, Amboyna or Banda.

Having witnessed the murder of Admiral Verhoeff and 42 of his comrades, Jan Pieterszoon Coen was always going to take his revenge against the people of Banda for their treachery. He requested instructions in writing from the Gentlemen Seventeen and they ordered him to subjugate the inhabitants of Banda and to drive their leaders out of the land.

By 1621 Coen had assembled a fleet of thirteen vessels and an army of over 1500 soldiers in Batavia. Reinforced by additional men and vessels in Ambon and 80 Japanese mercenaries, this formidable fighting force finally reached the Banda islands in 1621. Everything looked peaceful as they admired the beauty of the islands that lay before them, like green emeralds on an azure sea.

Coen was initially cautious and was looking for some sort of provocation from the Bandanese. Finally, after provocations on both sides, he unleashed the Banda massacre, attacking and burning villages all over the island and rounding up men, women and children. Jan Pieterszoon Coen set out to obliterate Bandanese society with as many as 15,000 islanders slaughtered, enslaved or shipped into exile, and the survivors hiding in the mountains. The Dutch blockaded their mountain hideouts, where most died of hunger. Coen described the obstinacy of these people as so great that they would rather all die together in misery than surrender to his men. With the entire population of the island now virtually eliminated, the VOC divided up the islands into 68 separate land holdings and established its own colony of Dutch plantation owners and enslaved or indentured workers to cultivate the nutmeg trees.

Jan Pieterszoon Coen knew that without provocation he could not repeat such brutalities against the islands of Ternate and Tidore. He needed a different strategy to gain a monopoly over the clove trade. This involved the transplantation of clove trees from the spice islands of Ternate and Tidore to Ambon and its surrounding islands in Central Maluku, which the Dutch now controlled. Here the VOC required the obligatory cultivation of clove trees by officially authorised villages. In these villages each Ambonese head or family had to plant and maintain 100 or more clove trees and any clove trees that were cultivated without consent were destroyed. The uprooting or burning of clove trees – known as extirpation – became a form of punishment for those villages that dared challenge the self-declared Dutch monopoly and trade their excess cloves with native traders from Java or Macassar.

Five years after his founding of Batavia and establishing the Dutch monopoly over the growth of nutmeg and cloves, Jan Pieterszoon Coen handed his post of Governor-General to Pieter de Carpentier in 1623 and returned to the Netherlands, where he received a hero's welcome in his hometown of Hoorn.

Having established an almost complete monopoly over the spice trade the VOC grew rapidly. By the mid-1600s it boasted 150 merchant ships, 40 warships, 50,000 employees, a private army of 10,000 soldiers and a network of trading posts that extended all the way from the Persian Gulf to the China Sea.

This was not just the Golden Age of the Dutch East India Company but also the Golden Age of Dutch Art. As wealth flowed back into the United Provinces, the extraordinary demand for paintings meant that almost every town and city had an active group of artists and thousands of paintings – landscapes, portraits, still lifes and scenes from daily life were created.

The Portuguese had been defeated and their forts captured in Ambon, Tidore and Banda. The Spanish had withdrawn from their fort in Ternate to Manila, so that the only commercial rival the Dutch had for the valuable spice trade was now the English East India Company.

10 Francis Drake and the English in the East Indies

In November 1577 Francis Drake departed Plymouth with a fleet of five ships and 164 men under mysterious circumstances. He had recruited the seamen for a voyage to Alexandria in Egypt, but most of them believed their real destination was to the Caribbean for another lucrative raid on the Spanish treasure ships. The fleet sailed down the Atlantic towards the coast of West Africa where Drake captured some Portuguese ships to supplement his supplies and a Portuguese navigator to guide them across the Atlantic. Before departing West Africa, Drake gathered his captains and crew and revealed they were on a voyage to discover new lands in the Southern Ocean, including Terra Australis. For now, Drake's plan to sail through the Strait of Magellan and raid the unsuspecting and unprotected Spanish treasure ships in the Pacific Ocean remained a closely held secret.

A portrait of Francis Drake shows a man of supreme confidence, a bon vivant who dined off the finest silver and delighted in regaling the ten 'gentlemen adventurers' who had joined his flagship with his exploits on the Spanish Main. As a natural leader he demanded complete loyalty from his men but was also a braggart and easily antagonised by anyone who dared oppose him.

By June 1578 the fleet reached Port St Julian on the South American coast where Magellan had wintered in 1520. Here Drake's fleet spent two months over the worst of the winter. The fleet scuttled one vessel on the voyage south and another had become unseaworthy so only three vessels departed their winter anchorage, the flagship *Golden Hind* with the *Elizabeth* and the *Marigold*. Sailing south they entered the Strait of Magellan and the chaplain Francis Fletcher eloquently describes their passage:

> The land on both sides is very high and mountainous, having on the north and the west side the continent of America, and on the south and east part nothing but islands, among which lie innumerable frets or passages into the South Sea. The mountains arise with such tops and spires into the air, and of so rare a height, as they may well be accounted amongst the wonders of the world; environed, as it were, with many regions of congealed clouds and frozen meteors.

In September 1578 the fleet cleared the strait only to encounter a fierce Pacific storm that raged for seven weeks, driving their vessels further and further south. The ships of the fleet struggled to stay afloat. Through the roar of the storm they heard desperate cries from the *Marigold* as she sunk with the loss of the entire crew and the *Elizabeth* was separated from the flagship, her fate unknown. After the storm abated Drake and his crew on the *Golden Hind* headed north to a pre-arranged meeting point off the coast of Chile. Unbeknown to them the *Elizabeth* had survived the storm and taken shelter in the Strait of Magellan. Here Captain Winter declared to his journal that it was his intention to join the *Golden Hind* but his crew would go no further, arguing forcefully that 'they had been hired by Drake for Alexandria and if this was Alexandria then they would rather be hanged in England'.

Reaching Valparaiso in Chile, Drake raided a Spanish ship for its treasure and more importantly its wine, bread and bacon. Refreshed and resupplied, the English marauders started their four-month reign of terror along the Pacific coast. In a raid on the port of Arica, Drake plundered two more Spanish vessels, off the vice-regal port of Callao de Lima in Peru they captured a vessel departing the harbour and learnt that a Spanish treasure ship had just left for Panama fully loaded with gold and silver. Unaware of the presence of English pirates in the Pacific and completely unprotected, the ship was an easy target for Drake and his crew. It was such a huge prize that Drake's men laboured four days in transferring its cargo of 80 pounds of gold, 26 tons of silver and 13 chests of silver reales, as well as precious stones, jewels and a golden crucifix, to the *Golden Hind.*

Drake had all the plunder and riches his vessel could carry, but he now had to find a way home. Staying well offshore to avoid Spanish shipping, the *Golden Hind* sailed to California then continued north past the Columbia River as far as the 48th parallel. Drake was searching for the postulated Northeast Passage that would allow his return to the Atlantic, but after describing freezing rain and the ship's ropes stiff with cold, they turned back to warmer climes near San Francisco Bay. Here the crew took time to rest, take on fresh food and make necessary repairs to the *Golden Hind.*

Drake saw only one course open to him. With no possibility of retracing his path south and risk being captured by the waiting Spanish, his only choice was to follow Magellan's route across the Pacific to the Spice Islands and then return to England around the Cape of Good Hope. As Francis Fletcher wrote in his journal:

> He thought it not good to return by the Straits, for two special causes: the one, lest the Spaniards should there wait and attend for him in great strength, from whose hands, he being left but one ship, he could not possibly escape. The other cause was the dangers of the mouth

of the Straits in the South Sea, where the continuous storms blustering, as he found by experience, besides the shoals and the sands upon the coast, he thought it not a good course to adventure that way: he resolved therefore to avoid these hazards, to go forward to the islands of the Moluccas, and hence to sail the course of the Portuguese by the Cape of Good Hope.

Departing California in July 1579, the crew of the *Golden Hind* set a south-westerly course to the middle latitudes and then turned due west to take advantage of the prevailing winds across the Pacific. They made a relatively easy crossing compared to the sufferings of Magellan's armada 60 years earlier, stopping in Guam and then Mindanao to resupply. By November 1579 they had reached the Spice Islands:

> These are four high piked islands; their names, Ternate, Tidore, Matchan, Batchan all of them very fruitful and yielding abundance of cloves, whereof we furnished ourselves of as much as we desired at a very cheap rate. At the east of them lies a very great island called Gillola. We directed our course to have gone to Tidore, but in coasting along a little island belonging to the King of Ternate, November 4, his deputy or viceroy with all expedition came off to our ship in a canoe, and without any fear or doubting of our good meaning came presently aboard. Who after some conference with our general, entreated him by any means to run with Ternate, not with Tidore, assuring him that his king would be wondrous glad of his coming, and be ready to do for him what he could, and what our general in reason should require.

Following a successful visit by his emissaries, Drake accepted the invitation to meet Sultan Baabullah. In their meeting, the Sultan proposed an alliance with the English to overthrow the Portuguese, who had returned from Malacca and rebuilt Fort Mariaco on Tidore. Drake promised he would send a major expedition to Ternate within two years, pledging his word as a gentleman to that effect. The two men then sealed the bargain with an exchange of gifts; Drake presented Baabullah with a jewelled ring, a coat of mail and a helmet. Baabullah for his part presented Drake with a ruby ring and a letter pledging his allegiance to Queen Elizabeth.

Drake added six tons of cloves to his already heavy cargo of Spanish gold and silver, and not wishing to further delay their return to England the *Golden Hind* prepared to leave Ternate. They eventually reached the port of Cilacap on the south coast of Java where they resupplied with food and water. In March 1580 the *Golden Hind* set a south-westerly course across the Indian Ocean for the Cape of Good Hope and the journey home. The voyage was uneventful except for the usual storms rounding the Cape of Good Hope and the *Golden Hind* entered Plymouth Harbour in September 1580 after having made the second circumnavigation of the world.

The nation hailed Drake as a hero. More than half the crew of the *Golden Hind* had survived the journey and his rich booty was secured in the Tower of London. The Queen's share of the riches was more than the Crown's income for an entire year and

Francis Drake coming ashore to meet the Sultan of Ternate, Levinus Hulsius, 1603
(Princeton University Library)

Queen Elizabeth herself boarded the ship on its return to Greenwich where Drake entertained her to a magnificent banquet. When the feasting was over Queen Elizabeth summoned Drake to kneel before her and told him 'Master Drake, the King of Spain has asked for your head, and we have here a weapon with which to remove it'. Taking a gilded sword in her hand, she dubbed her pirate – Sir Francis Drake.

An English translation of van Linschoten's *Itinerario* appeared in London in 1598, and Queen Elizabeth signed the charter of the Company of Merchants Trading to the East Indies two years later. This document gave the founding merchants a monopoly over trade to the East Indies for the next fifteen years. Each merchant paid in what he was willing to risk and the total sum was used to buy ships and fill them with cargo to trade in the Indies. At the end of each voyage the ship and its cargo of spices were sold and the profits shared in proportion to each contribution. Known as 'joint stock', it was the forerunner of the modern company, its investors not lords or 'gentlemen' but ordinary merchants and traders willing to make a speculative investment.

In 1601 a fleet of five ships left London commanded by James Lancaster, the vessels *Hector*, *Susan*, *Ascension*, *Guest* and *Red Dragon* carried almost 500 men and 100 cannon, as well as £21,742 in Spanish silver dollars and £6860 in trade goods. Eighteen months later the ships reached Aceh in North Sumatra where Lancaster was welcomed by the Sultan. Trading could commence but there was little interest in the woollen cloth, tin, lead and other items of English cargo. Lancaster solved this problem by capturing a Portuguese galleon and after looting its cargo of Indian textiles he was then able to send one of his own vessels back to London fully loaded with pepper.

The remaining fleet continued on to Bantam where James Lancaster presented himself to the boy Sultan and his Regent. After the customary exchange of gifts, trading could begin and five weeks later their vessels were filled with sackfuls of pepper, and they were ready to return to London. Lancaster obtained permission from the Regent to establish an English 'factory' in Bantam and left behind three factors and eight seamen to store their remaining goods and continue trading for spices. These ships of this first English fleet returned to London fully laden with pepper, making the voyage hugely profitable for its investors. James Lancaster was a hero and was knighted for his efforts. The Company of Merchants Trading to the East Indies was now ready to challenge the Spanish and the Portuguese, arguing:

> Let the Spaniards shewe any juste and lawful reasons … why they shoulde barre her Majestie and all the other Christian princes and states, of the use of the vaste, wyde and infinitely open ocean sea, and of access to the territories and dominions of so many free princes, Kings and potentates in the East.

Following the successful sale of pepper from its first voyage, the English East India Company sent a fleet of the same four vessels to the East Indies, departing in 1604 under the command of Henry Middleton. Arriving in Bantam after a two-year absence, the crew found that two of their factors had died, but were joyously welcomed by the surviving factor Edmund Scott who was then replaced with John Saris. Two of the English vessels were loaded with pepper as quickly as possible and returned to London with their valuable cargo.

After sailing from Bantam to the Spice Islands in 1605, Henry Middleton with the *Red Dragon* and the *Ascension* arrived in Ambon in time to witness the arrival of twelve heavily armed Dutch warships, complete with 1500 sailors and soldiers under the command of Steven van der Haghen. This was the first fleet to be fully equipped by the Dutch East India Company and was under orders to attack the Portuguese strongholds. Unable to conduct any trade in Ambon, Henry Middleton decided to sail north to Ternate to trade for cloves while his other vessel sailed south-east to Banda to trade for nutmeg. As the *Red Dragon* came within sight of Ternate, Middleton had the good fortune to rescue Sultan Said from an attack at sea from his Tidorean enemies and take him aboard the *Red Dragon.*

Safely delivered to Fort Gamalama, the Sultan professed his eternal gratitude by providing the English with a house in which to live ashore and trade for cloves. Sultan Said entertained Henry Middleton in the richly decorated Royal Baileu and they talked of the visit of Sir Francis Drake to Ternate almost 30 years earlier, and of Drake's pledge to his father to return with forces to support the Sultan in an attack against the Portuguese on Tidore. Unfortunately Henry Middleton had to voice his regret that an opportunity for the English to establish themselves in the Spice Islands had been lost.

In 1607 the third English expedition to the East Indies consisting of three ships commanded by William Keeling sailed with £17,600 of gold bullion and £7000 of merchandise for trade. Keeling found six Dutch ships in the harbour of Bantam but the English factors were in good health and had supplies of pepper ready to load on his ships for the return voyage to London. Keeling's orders were to proceed to Banda on the *Hector* in the hope of establishing an English factory there. Anchoring in the shelter of Gunung Api, the volcano that dominates the islands, he was greeted by a party of Dutchmen who were intrigued by the unexpected arrival of the English ship and rowed out from their factory. Keeling was able to trade for nutmeg with the Bandanese, but his efforts were cut short by the arrival of the Dutch fleet of Admiral Peter Verhoef, whose orders from the Gentlemen Seventeen were:

> We draw your special attention to the islands which grow cloves and nutmeg, and we instruct you to strive to win them for the Company, either by treaty or by force.

Keeling and the *Hector* with only 68 men were outnumbered by a Dutch war fleet of six heavily armed vessels and 1000 men. He decided to withdraw to the outer islands of Ai and Rhun and loaded as much nutmeg as possible there before being told by Admiral Verhoef to leave the Banda Islands and never return.

The English vessel *Expedition* commanded by David Middleton must have passed the *Hector* returning from Banda in 1609, for Keeling wrote that 'he passed us in the night or else we should have surely seen him'. The Dutch had been busy building their fort on Banda and refused the English any access to these islands. The only place Middleton could trade for nutmeg was the outlying islands of Ai and Rhun whose headmen had steadfastly refused to sign any agreement with the Dutch. Returning to London with his vessel fully loaded with nutmeg, he was congratulated on his success against the VOC by his directors:

> Seeking trade at Banda … he was, with many reproachful and insolent speeches, forcibly put from all trading in those parts, which he got with strong hand against their will, from other broken islands near adjoining, with extreme hazard and danger.

Twelve separate English fleets sailed to the East Indies in the next ten years, earning an average profit of 155 percent. Yet the Company remained vulnerable to challenges from the Dutch, who in the same period had sent many more fleets to the East Indies. The reason for the ratio of seven Dutch East India Company voyages to every three English East India Company voyages during this period lies in Dutch maritime strength, the permanent capital of the VOC and the trading network they had developed for the sale and distribution of spices across northern Europe.

The Dutch East India Company and the English East India Company both had their factories in Bantam to purchase pepper, cloves and nutmeg and have them bagged and ready to be loaded on the next Company ships to arrive from London or Amsterdam. A fragile peace existed between their factors who only had each other for company in this Asian trading port, as Edmund Scott the English factor in Bantam wrote: 'Though we were mortall enemies in our trade, yet in other matters we were friends and would have lived and died for each other'.

However, the escape of some Portuguese prisoners from a VOC ship, who then sought protection in the English Company's factory in Bantam, caused an open rift between the two groups and they began to skirmish in the streets. The pretence of peace between the two companies was shed and the then English factor in Bantam, John Jourdain, wrote:

> The Hollanders say we go aboute to reape the fruits of their labours. It is rather the contrarye for they seem to barre us our libertie to trade in a free countrye, having many times traded in these places, and nowe they seek to defraud us of that we have so long sought for.

Many of those inhabitants who survived the Banda massacre had taken refuge on the islands of Ai and Rhun under nominal English protection. Nathaniel Courthope had taken possession of the island of Rhun for the English East India Company in 1616 when the islanders signed a document accepting James I of England as sovereign of the island. This tiny island was the only place in the Spice Islands where the English Company was able to establish a settlement. It became the first English overseas possession and King James I was able to declare himself 'King of England, Scotland, Ireland and Pulo Rhun'.

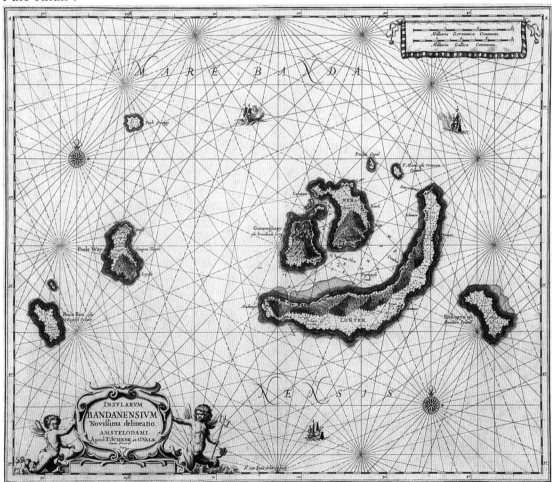

Map of the Banda Islands showing Ai and Rhun, Jan Janssonius, 1652 (David Parry)

The Dutch East India Company now had control over all the nutmeg trees grown in the Banda Islands except for Ai and Rhun, which were only ten kilometres away from Banda Neira and the last remaining outposts of the English East India Company in the Spice Islands. In 1615 the Dutch invaded Ai and the English retreated to Rhun where they regrouped. That same night, the English and their allies launched a surprise coun-ter-attack, retaking the island and killing 200 Dutchmen. A year later, a much stronger Dutch force attacked Ai. The defenders were able to hold off the attack with cannon fire, but after a month of siege they ran out of ammunition. The Dutch slaughtered those who remained and after strengthening the fort, appropriately renamed it Fort Revenge. A tiny band of 38 Englishmen led by Nathaniel Courthope defended Rhun against the Dutch for a further five years. Faced by overwhelming force they only surrendered after the capture and death of Courthope in 1620. The unfortunate inhabitants of Rhun were left defenceless after the departure of the English. The Dutch killed or enslaved every adult male, exiled the women and children, and then proceeded to chop down every nutmeg tree on the island, leaving behind a barren and uninhabited rock rising out of the Banda Sea.

11 Isaac Le Maire and the Voyage of the Eendracht, 1615

In 1578 the fleet of Francis Drake cleared the Magellan Strait only to encounter a fierce Pacific storm that raged for seven weeks, driving their vessels further and further south and into what they called Mare Furiosum instead of the Mare Pacifica. After the storm abated, Drake on the *Golden Hind* could see only open sea which meant that Tierra del Fuego was most likely an island and not connected to any southern land. Francis Fletcher wrote that they had:

> Plainly discovered that the same Terra Australis, left or set down to be Terra Incognita before we came here, to be no continent … but broken islands and large passages amongst them where the Atlantic Ocean and the Pacific Ocean meet in a most large and free scope.

The Dutch cartographer Jodocus Hondius put the true implication of Drake's discovery on his world map of 1595 with Tierra del Fuego drawn as a group of islands independent any southern continent.

When the Dutch East India Company was formed in 1602, Isaac Le Maire was one of its largest shareholders and a trustee. But he fell into conflict with the VOC as a result of perceived malpractice. The details of the offence were held secret but he was forced to resign in 1605 leading to his continuing resentment and opposition to the VOC. It seems that Isaac Le Maire may have invented forward selling for he found investors willing to buy VOC shares at a pre-arranged price and date in the future. Since his Groote Compagnie was also the largest shareholder he could cause the value of the shares to fall by suddenly selling off a significant percentage of the stock and then buying them back at a lower price. By way of justification he wrote to the directors of the VOC and forthrightly declared:

> Whatever I have done and what I do now is strictly in accordance with the law. You know that, but I will explain it just once more. The Groote Compagnie sold shares in the VOC to people who themselves elected to do so, they put their signatures under it freely. These

95

citizens were given security in exchange. You are saying that they lost money because of illegal means and I am telling you there is no question of loss because those involved knew that they were assured of having stocks and shares with a fixed value for a number of years. The Groote Compagnie guaranteed stability and security. As for succeeding in buying these shares for much less in the meantime, I'd say, too bad, that is the nature of all business. Business has no morality other than what is allowed and no law has been trespassed.

According to its charter the Dutch East India Company held a monopoly over the rights to trade in the region east of the Cape of Good Hope and west of the Strait of Magellan, thus preventing any other private trade in almost half of the world. Based on the discoveries of Francis Drake and the 1595 map of Jodocus Hondius, Isaac Le Maire saw an opportunity to break the VOC trading monopoly over this large and wealthy part of the world and founded the Australische Zuid Compagnie (The Australia South Company). This enterprise arose out of his resentment of the VOC and his desire to break its monopoly over trade with all of India, the East Indies and the Orient.

Isaac Le Maire then reached an agreement with Willem Schouten that they would each raise half the capital for the Australische Zuid Compagnie. Schouten was an experienced mariner who had already sailed three times to the East Indies in the position of supercargo, then as master of the *Duyfken* when it sailed to Java in 1601 and as captain of the *Delft* in 1603. Schouten helped raise his share of the capital from other merchants and probably acted as a front man for investors with the VOC who saw another opportunity for private trade in this huge region. Le Maire and Schouten also raised capital from the residents of their home port of Hoorn and induced:

> Messieurs Pieter Clemensz Brouwer, formerly burgemeester of the town of Hoorn, Jan Jansz Molenwerf, alderman, Jan Clemensz Kies, secretary of the town, and Cornelis Segertsz, citizen there, to become chief participants and to allow themselves to be used moreover as directors together with the aforesaid Willem Schouten, Isaac Le Maire and Jacob Le Maire.

In 1614 Isaac Le Maire won from the Netherlands States General a decree that anyone who found new passages to the south seas would have the right to the first four voyages exploiting them, and he secured a special charter authorising his Australia South Company to visit 'Tartary, China, Japan, East India, Terra Australis and the islands of the South Sea'. The Stadhoulder, Prince Maurits, also signed a letter giving Jacob Le Maire and Willem Schouten the right to trade and make treaties with 'Emperors, kings, counts, princes, republics and governors'.

The key to the success of this new enterprise would be the discovery of a new passage into the Pacific other than the Strait of Magellan for this was the only way Isaac Le Maire could circumvent the VOC monopoly. In June 1615 two vessels, the 220 ton

Endraacht (named the *Unity* after the union of the seven United Provinces) and the 110 ton *Hoorn*, sailed from the port of Hoorn in search of a new route to the Pacific, to find the 'known but undiscovered' Terra Australis and establish trade relations with its the inhabitants. Too old for voyaging himself, Isaac Le Maire appointed his 29-year-old son Jacob as supercargo and commander of the fleet, the 47-year-old Willem Schouten as captain of the *Eendracht* and Schouten's brother Jan as the captain of the *Hoorn.*

The purpose of their voyage was kept secret from the crew, who had been paid extra to sign on to go wherever their captains should require. After passing the equator the fleet changed course towards the Strait of Magellan and Jacob Le Maire informed his crew that their expedition would attempt to discover a new southern passage around South America and their objective was a voyage to the Solomon Islands and the discovery of the continent of Terra Australis, writing:

> We have declared to our Steersmen, Assistants and Officers that we mean to sail to Terra Australis and in the cabin read out to them the memorandum book of Quiros by Claes Jansoon, to inspire, so that they developed great desire and courage for it.

The seamen knew the stories of the undiscovered southern continent and the riches of King Solomon's gold so they soon contracted gold fever and named their expedition the 'goldfinders'. The vessels stopped at Point Desire in Patagonia to find wood, water and defoul their vessels. It was here that tragedy struck when a fire of dry reeds being burnt under the *Hoorn* in order to clean her bottom suddenly spread to the rest of the vessel. Unable to do anything to stop the fire, her crew were forced to stand by and watch in anguish as the second ship of their tiny fleet was consumed by the flames.

Sailing south past the Strait of Magellan the *Eendracht* followed the unchartered east coast of Tierra del Fuego and battling extreme tidal currents they passed through what they named the Le Maire Strait which separated Tierra del Fuego and what they named as Staten Land:

> On the 24 … keeping our course to the end along the shore we saw an opening or a channel from which a great stream issued and shot out towards the sea with great strength, so that it surged and boiled … and the ship came under water up to the anchor, indeed even nearly the whole bowsprit.

The strong westerly winds of the Southern Ocean give rise to large waves and the area of shallow water south of Tierra del Fuego makes them shorter, steeper and extremely hazardous to shipping. Battling against the wind and the waves, the *Eendracht* finally rounded the southernmost point of Tierra del Fuego, which Schouten named Caep Hoorn after his birthplace:

> In the evening 25 January 1616 the wind was south-west, and that night we went south-with

great waves out of the southwest, and very blue water, whereby we judged, and held for certain that … it was the great South Sea, whereat we were exceeding glad to think that we had discovered a way, which until that time, was unknown to men … on 29 January 1616 we saw land again lying north west and north northwest from us, which was the land that lay south from the straights of Magellan which reached southward, all high land covered over with snow, ending with a sharp point which we called Caep Hoorn.

There must have been tremendous excitement on board the *Eendracht* because Le Maire and Schouten knew the discovery of this new route into the Pacific would allow the Australia South Company to break the monopoly that the Dutch East India Company had on all trade between the Cape of Good Hope and the Strait of Magellan. At the same time the 'goldfinders' knew they were en route to the Solomon Islands and the gold mines.

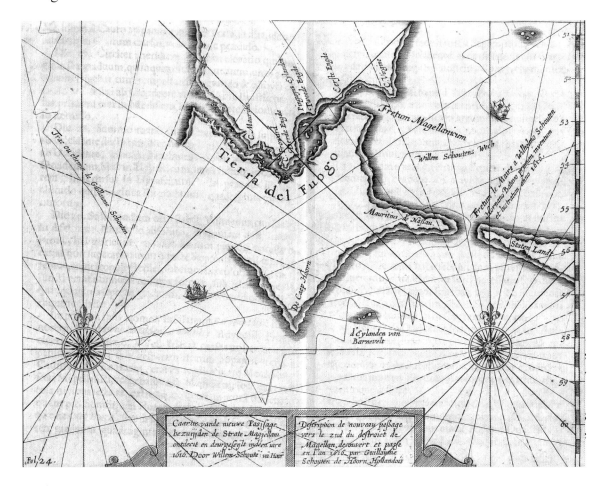

Map of the voyage of Willem Schouten around Cape Hoorn, 1619 (Biblioteca Nacional de Chile)

To counter the aims of the Australia South Company, the directors of the Dutch East India Company decided to send its own fleet to the East Indies via the Strait of Magellan. The first VOC fleet to take this route, it would enforce their right of passage through the Strait and ensure that the Australia South Company did not try to use the same route.

Commanded by Admiral Joris van Spilbergen on the *Morgenster*, the six vessels of this fleet had been given orders to attack Spanish towns until near Calao Lima in Peru they encountered a fleet of eight ships sent out in search of the Hollanders. The Spanish admiral boasted that he only needed two ships to capture these 'Hens of Holland' who must be wasted by so long a voyage from Europe and would yield at first sight. For his part Admiral Spilbergen ordered his gunners to prepare for battle, established rules of military discipline, and each ship and its crew was resolved to victory or death.

The two fleets drew near on the evening of 17 July, when the Spanish admiral sent a message to postpone battle till next morning. However his captains were too impatient to follow this advice and set upon the Dutch flagship at about ten that night, when they exchanged broadsides. The battle continued throughout the next day and until the Spanish were forced to withdraw and the Dutch fleet headed across the Pacific towards Ternate.

As a result of this defeat Juan Arias could only bemoan the attacks on the Pacific coast by both the English and the Dutch 'pirates'. In a letter to King Phillip III arguing for the continued Spanish exploration of the Pacific he wrote:

> That in consideration of the great advantage which will accrue to the service of Your Majesty, to the extension of the Catholic Church, and to the increase of our holy faith, from the conversion of the Gentiles of the southern land, which is the principal obligation to which Your Majesty and your crown are pledged, I now earnestly beg to solicit Your Majesty's consideration to that which is here set forth. For the English and Dutch heretics, whom the devil unites for this purpose by every means in his power, most diligently continue the exploration, discovery,
> and colonisation of the principal ports of this large part of the world in the Pacific Ocean, and sow in it the most pernicious poisons of their apostasy, which they put forth with the most pressing anxiety in advance of us, who should put forth the sovereign light of the gospel.

After rounding Cape Hoorn the *Eendracht* sailed north before sailing west across the Pacific at a latitude of 15 degrees South with the aim of finding the Solomon Islands and the land of Terra Australis, a land which Jacob Le Maire and Willem Schouten could claim for the Australia South Company and make their fortunes. They sailed 1600 leagues from Peru and passed numerous small islands without seeing any mainland. Water and provisions were short and the crew were now drinking wine instead of water. Jacob Le Maire wanted to believe that Terra Australis was very near and to continue sailing west. While Schouten was a realist who knew that having come this far and discovered nothing, and with their food and water in short supply they had no choice but to abandon their search. Relations between Le Maire and Schouten were now strained and it was only after pressure from the crew that the *Eendracht* eventually turned north-west for New Guinea and then Ternate. History would have been different if Jacob Le Maire had been able to continue on their course of between 15° and 16° S for they would have reached the coast of Queensland. As a result there was no discovery of Australia by the Australia South Company.

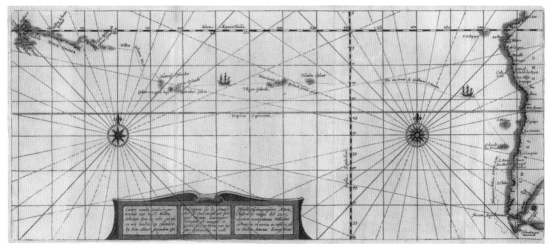

Map of the voyage across the Pacific, Willem Schouten, 1618 (National Library of Australia)

The VOC had somehow learned that Torres had found a route along the south coast of New Guinea and Schouten wanted to try and find this passage however Le Maire and the crew were increasingly uneasy and preferred to take the known route along the north coast towards Ternate. Willem Schouten recorded the reasons for their decision:

> If we continue to sail west we should without doubt fall southward of New Guinea, and if there, no passage or channel is found, then the ship and goods would be lost and all of us must perish, as it would be impossible to return east from there on account of the steady easterly winds which in these parts blow continuously.

After sailing along the north coast of New Guinea, a battered and dispirited *Eendracht* anchored off Fort Oranje on Ternate and beside the *Morgenster* on the evening of 17 September 1617. The following day Jacob Le Maire went ashore with a letter of introduction that his father had written to the Governor of Ternate and was met by the Governor-General of the East Indies, Laurens Reael and Jasper Janson the Governor of Ambon who together comprised the Council of India. The VOC officials were courteous but firm; the Australia South Company was not permitted to trade in the East Indies but having exhausted their supplies they were allowed to sell any surplus ships gear to the VOC to help feed the crew. That same day they sold two of their pinnaces together with most of the naval supplies saved out of the unfortunate *Hoorn* and purchased rice, vinegar, Spanish wine and three tons of ships biscuit. Hoping to further cripple the activities of the Australia South Company the VOC then offered employment to all of the *Eendracht*'s crew, of whom 15 decided that the VOC offered better prospects and sought their release, while 25 remained with the ship.

In a memorandum written to the Lord States of Holland and Westfriesland in 1618 the VOC Directors had stressed that regarding the charter of the Australia South Company, it should be excluded from the southern regions:

> The Dutch East India Company opines that in every case the Australia South Company aforesaid ought to be excluded from the southern parts, situated between the meridian passing through the eastern extremity of Ceylon and the meridian lying a hundred miles eastward of the Solomon Islands; seeing that the Dutch East India Company has repeatedly given orders for discovering and exploring the land of Nueva Guinea and the islands situated east of the same, since, equally by her orders, such discovery was once tried about the year 1606 with the yacht *Duyfken* by skipper Willem Janszoon and subcargo Jan Lodewijs van Rosingijn, who made sundry discoveries on the said coast of Nova Guinea, as is amply set forth in their journals.

The *Eendracht* then sailed for Java and Bantam where everything got worse. They were received by the newly arrived Jan Pieterszoon Coen, who, for his own purposes refused to believe they had found a new passage around South America. During the official hearing against Jacob Le Maire in Bantam, Admiral Joris van Spilbergen, the commander of the Dutch fleet which had preceded them to Ternate and Bantam declared:

> On a voyage of such long duration they had with this vessel discovered no unknown nation, no countries of fresh intercourse, nor anything that might be for the common weal; although they claimed to have found a passage shorter than the usual one, yet this was without any probability, since they had spent on their voyage as far as Ternate fifteen months and three days, and that to (according to their own admission) with a favourable wind and only one ship, which is not called upon to wait for others, as happens in a whole fleet. These claimants to the discovery of a new passage through the South Sea were greatly surprised that the fleet had been so long before them at Ternate.

Jacob Le Maire argued that the reason the voyage took this long was because they had to find a new and unexplored route around South America, where the waters of the Pacific Ocean and the Atlantic Ocean clash in the region of Cape Hoorn. And then they had to search the South Pacific for the 'known but undiscovered' continent of Terra Australis. However, this was clearly a show trial with the outcome already predetermined.

Jan Pieterszoon Coen accused Le Maire and Schouten of violating the VOC charter and declared that the *Eendracht*, its papers and its cargo be seized and declared forfeit. Most importantly, Le Maire's journal which had detailed every day of their voyage was also seized. Le Maire and Schouten were forced to return to the Netherlands together with Admiral Joris van Spilbergen on the *Amsterdam* and for his efforts Coen was to be promoted to Governor-General of the Company in Ambon. A depressed and dispirited Jacob Le Maire died on the voyage back to the Netherlands. Spilbergen wrote that he was 'deeply grieved, since he was a man endowed with remarkable knowledge and experience in matters of navigation'.

Isaac Le Maire was extremely bitter about losing both his son and his ship and blamed his son's death on the actions of the VOC and Jan Pieterszoon Coen in Bantam. Writing to the Gentlemen Seventeen he said:

> You have killed my son, taken my ships, besmirched my name and stole my money. But you can't ignore me. I am a citizen of the Republic and I will act according to the laws of liberty, however much I shall be denied them. Go against me as much as you like, through the States General, through the States of Holland and through all your powerful friends, Isaac le Maire will arise and create something new. I will flourish like before.

Years of litigation followed, the outcome being that Isaac and Jacob Le Maire were comprehensively vindicated and the VOC ordered to pay restoration for the vessel and its cargo to its owners, to meet all costs, and to pay interest since the date of the seizure. As a result of the court case Isaac Le Maire finally gained access to the records of the voyage and in 1622 was able to publish his son's journal, which detailed this first voyage around Cape Hoorn and their search for Terra Australis. However, the court case had taken so long that the Australia South Company was virtually bankrupt and the four-year monopoly originally granted by the States General was almost over. Three years later Isaac Le Maire himself passed away and his tombstone wryly records that of his trading life:

> He had been so richly blessed by God that in thirty years he lost over one and a half million guilders.

12 Hendrick Brouwer and the Brouwer Route, 1610

Between 1602 and 1795 the Dutch East India Company built 1700 large East Indiamen. These ships were built in the VOC shipyards at Amsterdam, Delft, Hoorn, Middleberg, Rotterdam, Enkhuizen, Zeeland and Goeree. The Amsterdam shipyard was to become the world's largest industrial enterprise, with 1500 employees and an average production of three East Indiamen each year.

The VOC shipyard in Amsterdam, Ludolf Backhuizen, 1696

The East Indiamen sailed for the Indies twice a year around Christmas and Easter, although as the number of ships departing for Asia increased the dates of departure were spread out over the year. Sailing orders were established for sailing down the Atlantic and a so-called wagenspoor (cart track) south of the Cape Verde Islands to the equator was marked precisely on the charts. After this the ships sailed in a large arc towards the coast of Brazil and then back towards the Cape of Good Hope. Water, wood and fresh food would be collected at Table Bay before the fleets sailed up the east coast of Africa then across to Madagascar or Mauritius before setting a course to the Sunda Strait between Java and Sumatra. This outward leg proved slow going. Ships were becalmed for long periods, the pitch between the planking melted and provisions rotted beneath the hot sun. Worse, the lack of fresh food and water exposed the crew to the dangers of scurvy and other diseases.

In 1569 the Dutch cartographer Gerard Mercator published a revolutionary new map projection which was an indispensable aid to navigation since it allowed sailors to plot a compass bearing on their map in a straight line. VOC captains and navigators were obliged to use Company charts and it was their professional duty to make notes and sketches of unknown coasts, reefs and other relevant features encountered during the voyage. Captains and navigators handed over their charts to the company cartographers at the end of each voyage and the official charts were then updated in the VOC's hydrographic offices established in Amsterdam and Batavia. In 1617 the VOC appointed Hessel Gerritz as their exclusive mapmaker, a position which he held until his death in 1632. As chief cartographer based in Amsterdam, he studied all the charts and logs prepared by VOC sea captains and produced maps based on their discoveries. The Dutch East India Company also wished to keep important information secret and therefore maps were drawn rather than printed, in order to control production and prevent them from leaking out to competitors.

When leaving the United Provinces the master of each ship was issued a complete set of several dozen vellum charts rolled up in a tin cylinder. These charts were considered to be state secrets and the VOC required the captain of each vessel to sign for them at the beginning and end of each voyage and be responsible for any that were missing. Vellum, which is made from goatskin, was the material of choice for sea charts as it is much more durable than paper and not easily torn, even when wet.

In addition to sailing orders and sea charts, the directors gave each master a trunk containing a large number of navigational tools, which included dividers, an hourglass, a compass, a semi astrolabe, a mariner's astrolabe, a quadrant and a cross-staff. With skill and some luck, according to the weather conditions, the captains and navigators of the VOC vessels would hopefully reach Batavia after a passage of some 23,000 kilometres and eight months.

There were two people in charge of each VOC ship, the captain and the supercargo (superintendent of cargo). The captain was responsible for the ship, the crew, the navigation and for bringing the ship safely to its destination. The supercargo was responsible for ensuring the cargo was safely packed in the holds and protected from damage during the voyage and for all trading activities.

The ship's crew was divided into three eight-hour watches, which were subdivided into messes. Each mess was responsible for a specific set of shipboard tasks including handling the ship, standing watch, cleaning and maintaining their area of the vessel and looking after their sick and injured. The crew ate in messes of seven to nine people and were required to act as orderlies on a weekly roster of fetching food from the galley and washing up. Officers and senior merchants dined at the captain's table which was furnished with pewter plates, spoons, linen and tablecloths. After a few weeks at sea almost the only fresh food was fish. Ship's stores included salted meat, sea biscuits made of flour and water, rice, oats, beans, dried peas, cheese and mustard. Each person received about one and a half litres of water or beer a day. Beer was preferred because after a month or two at sea stored water would be foul smelling and needed to be mixed with wine or arak to make it palatable.

Mornings at 8 o'clock the crew was served grits cooked in butter with dried prunes 'to keep the body open'. The midday meal consisted of green peas or haricot beans with meat, stockfish or bacon in butter sauce. The evening meal was the day's leftovers. In addition, once a week each crewman received half a pound of butter and five pounds of bread or ship's biscuit. Importantly, every day the crew received a small jug of wine or gin and a litre of beer for as long as it could be preserved.

Many of the crew, some recruited off the streets, were in poor health even before the start of the voyage, which meant that many sailors died at sea from a range of illnesses such as dysentery, scurvy, typhus, and pneumonia and the average mortality rate was of the order of 14 percent.

During the long voyage ships would stop at the Cape of Good Hope and anchor in Table Bay to take on water, firewood and fresh meat from the local natives. However it was not until 1652 that the VOC sought to establish a permanent settlement there when Jan van Riebeeck arrived with three ships and 90 artisans to fortify the site as a way station for the VOC trade route between the Netherlands and the East Indies. The primary purpose of this way station, which was to become Cape Town, was to provide fresh provisions for the VOC fleets so as to reduce the amount of sickness and death en route. Within three decades Cape Town had become home to a large community of mainly former VOC employees who decided to settle there after completing their service contracts. These settlers undertook to spend at least twenty years farming the land within the fledgling colony's borders and in exchange they were lent tools, seeds and received tax-exempt status.

The Roaring Forties are the strong westerly winds found in the southern hemisphere between the latitudes of 40 and 50 degrees. These strong west-to-east air currents are caused by the Earth's rotation and air being displaced from the equator towards the South Pole. The large tracts of open ocean south of the 40th parallel are interrupted only by Tasmania, New Zealand, and the southern part of South America, allowing continuous strong winds to develop. The idea for a southern route to the East Indies is believed to have begun with Petrus Plancius, the Dutch minister of religion, mathematician and geographer as he wrote:

> South of the Cape of Good Hope, wind and sea currents are in an easterly direction, one is less troubled by heat, and it is moreover advisable as the longitudinal degrees at this particular latitude are much smaller than around the equator, making the distance shorter.

In December 1610 Hendrick Brouwer departed the United Provinces as commander of a small fleet, including the *Rode Leew* (Red Lion) and the *Gouda*, heading for the East Indies. His orders were to explore a better route to Bantam by making use of the steady westerly winds blowing between the latitudes 35 and 40 degrees South which the Dutch called the Westenwindengogdel (west wind girdle). From the Cape of Good Hope they sailed south until the direction of the wind turned in their favour, then east at these latitudes in cold and wind-driven seas until turning north towards the Sunda Strait and Bantam. The voyage took Brouwer fewer than six months, which was almost half the time taken in the traditional northern route across the Indian Ocean. By taking this route the cooler weather meant that food did not spoil as quickly as on the northern route and VOC ships could reduce the risk of infectious disease and death among the crew. Brouwer wrote a report outlining the many advantages of this new route and recommended it be generally adopted.

This route was sailed again in 1616 by Pieter de Carpentier, the commander of a five-vessel fleet and the captain of the *Trouw*, who wrote in his report:

> The instructions to sail southward to 36 degrees and beyond was thought very good, as indeed it proved to be. And if we had to sail a hundred times to the Indies we should use no other route than this. It ensures the maintenance in good condition of trade goods and provisions, and a healthy crew besides. We have brought, thanks to God, not a single sick man to Bantam.

The VOC directors were suitably impressed. Faster voyages meant quicker profits, while also giving the company a distinct advantage over its competitors. The new route was then included in the official VOC sailing instructions as written below and issued to all vessels:

Article 12

All ships which have refitted at Caap de Bona Esperance or in Table Bay should lay their course further to the east at latitudes of 35, 36, 40 to 44 degrees South, depending where the seamen can find best the west winds because these do not always occur at exact latitudes 35 or 36, but often blow much more to the south and must be sought there.

Article 13

Now after the west winds have been found the ships should sail eastwards for at least 1000 mijlen (around 4000 nautical miles) before turning and laying their course to the north, for because of its convenient position there is nothing to be feared in the Javanese coast, which does not extend more than 7 ½ degrees to the south. If on the other hand one alters course before covering 1000 mijlen, one is running the risk of being driven off course to the shores of Sumatra. Because of the south-easterly winds which blow in that region from April to October inclusive, one is likely to be becalmed there for a long time.

The main problem with the Brouwer Route was working out when to turn north. While navigators were able to ascertain their latitude (distance north or south of the equator) by determining the angle of the sun above the horizon at midday, there was no reliable method for determining longitude (distance east or west of a given point) at sea until the development of the marine chronometer in the eighteenth century. The only method the Dutch captains could use to measure distance and hence longitude was a log-line. The line was knotted at specific intervals and coiled around a reel. At its free end was a triangular board which was thrown overboard at the bow of the vessel. An hourglass was set up by the reel and each hour the rope was hauled in and by counting the number of knots, the speed in knots per hour could be calculated. Assuming there was no current then this would measure the speed of the ship (in knots on the rope) and in combination with the time measured by the sand trickling through an hourglass they could then calculate distance travelled.

The system was full of possible errors relating to the coordination of release of the log-line, the turning of the hourglass, variations in the flow of sand through the hourglass at sea and the coordination of the call of time-up and stopping the log-line. Without there being any islands in the Indian Ocean to use as landmarks, deciding where was the point in the middle of an empty ocean to turn north and head for the Sunda Strait was always going to be problematic. The map entitled Mar da India by Pieter Goos shows four vessels in full sail crossing the Indian Ocean on the Brouwer Route, with the lead vessel about to turn north towards the Sunda Strait between Java and Sumatra. It also shows two vessels making the return voyage from the Sunda Strait towards the Cape of Good Hope.

Spanish silver dollars were still the preferred trade item and spices and other goods coming from across the Indonesian archipelago or from other ports across Asia would be collected and stored in the VOC warehouses in Batavia. When the large East Indiamen were ready to return to the Dutch Republic the ships were loaded in the roadstead.

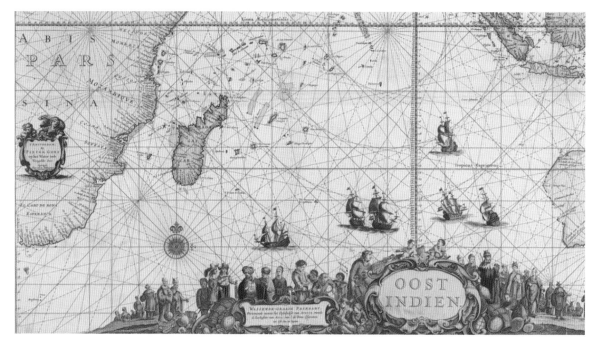

Mar da India, detail, Pieter Goos, 1658 (National Library of Australia)

Heavy ballast goods, such as saltpetre or sugar were placed in the bottom and covered with mats; then came a layer of pepper and other spices in bags, which was also covered. Bales of textiles rested on this lower layer with the more expensive textiles on the top. Spaces between the bundles were filled with loose pepper or chips of sappanwood which was the raw material for making red dye. Raw silk and other valuable goods were stored underneath the quarterdeck.

At the beginning of the seventeenth century ships returned as soon as their holds were loaded, however due to the circumstances of war and piracy it became necessary for several ships to sail in convoy. Sailing instructions were issued that returning fleets should leave Java in September or the end of January to avoid cyclones that developed near the island of Mauritius between January and March. After leaving the Cape of Good Hope the fleet set course in the direction of the island of Saint Helena, which stood out like a beacon in the middle of the Atlantic Ocean. If there was the risk of war with the English or capture by French pirates in the English Channel, the fleet would take the long way home around Scotland to their home ports in the United Provinces.

At the end of the voyage the seamen were discharged with just a small bundle of clothing under their arm. They could only collect their sea chests after these were inspected by the VOC and permitted trade goods auctioned on their behalf. The main cargo was carefully guarded, sorted, inventoried, and stored in the Company warehouses for delivery under contract to regular groups of merchants and any undelivered merchandise would then be sold at auction.

Obviously, Article 13 describing the sailing instructions for the Brouwer Route should have come with a warning explaining the dangers of sailing more than 1000 mijlen eastward and the fact there were the uncharted shores of an entire continent standing in the way. The west coast of Australia stood as a hazard to Dutch ships sailing to Java and an accidental encounter with Terra Australis was inevitable.

13 Dirk Hartog and the Discovery of Eendrachtlandt, 1616

Dirk Hartog was born in Amsterdam around 1583. He grew up in Nieuw Haarlemmersluis within sight of the bustling waterfront and the smoking and packing of North Sea herring at the Haringpakkerstoren, so it is no surprise that he was destined to become a seaman like his father.

View of the herring-packing stores at Nieuw Haarlemmersluis, 1693 (Rijksmuseum)

He first sailed to the East Indies as a steersman for the Dutch East India Company around 1606. The VOC records show he served on the *Enkhuizen* when it ran aground off the island of Halmahera in the Moluccas in 1607, as he filed an official statement on the drowning of a fellow crew member. The records then show that he returned from Bantam to Zeeland on the *Ter Veere* in 1609.

After this service he then sailed in merchant vessels around the Baltic and in 1611 became captain of the small trading vessel named *Dolfijn* carrying cargo under contract to various Amsterdam merchants. This was the same year that he married at the Old Church in Amsterdam and the marriage certificate reads:

> Dirk Hartog, skipper, 28 years of age, living at Nieuw Haarlemmersluis, accompanied by his mother, Griet Jansdr, on one side and Meijngen Abelsdr, 18 years of age, residing at Lijnbaansgracht, accompanied by Abel Albertsz, her father, on the other side.

In 1615 he sold the *Dolfijn* to again enter VOC service and at the age of 35 was appointed captain the *Eendracht* (named the *Unity* after the union of the seven United Provinces) and it would have been a great honour to serve as captain on this ship for what would be its maiden voyage to the East Indies. A VOC fleet of five ships was due to leave the United Provinces in January 1616 consisting of the *Eendracht* (Amsterdam Chamber, 700 tonnes), the *Bantam* (Enkhuizen Chamber, 800 tonnes), the *Trouw* (Amsterdam Chamber, 500 tonnes), the *Gouden Leeuw* (Rotterdam Chamber, 500 tonnes), and the *Westfriesland* (Hoorn Chamber, 800 tonnes). The *Eendracht* belonged to the largest class of ships in the VOC fleet. Solidly built of oak, it was designed to carry large cargoes and the supplies of food, water and equipment for around 200 people while sailing up to eight months from Holland to the East Indies. The *Eendracht* was armed with 32 cannon to defend itself and its valuable cargo of trade goods, which were ten large chests containing 80,000 Spanish silver reales and valued at about 200,000 guilders.

The departure of the *Eendracht* was delayed when the Textel anchorage froze over and the ship became ice-bound. Some of the crew who had been recruited out of the Amsterdam bars and poorhouses with promises of a vast sum of money were now sober and having second thoughts about the voyage. The freeze allowed 21 seamen and eight soldiers to abscond by walking across the ice to their freedom. One senior barber also absconded, which created a problem because the barber had the necessary instruments and skill to quickly amputate a limb, a painful but necessary procedure if you were to be saved from a slow death from infection and then gangrene.

After reaching the Cape of Good Hope the fleet's orders were to sail the Brouwer Route across the southern Indian Ocean. However they soon split up and the *Eendracht* as the slowest vessel was left behind. Obviously, the main difficulty with the Brouwer Route was accurately determining the distance travelled using the log-line and knowing when to turn north towards Java. After two months at sea, on 25 October, the crew heard the cry 'Landt in Zicht' (Land in sight) from the crow's nest. This was a new and unchartered land and it must have been frightening for Dirk Hartog and his crew to observe the fearsome surf washing onto the low cliffs of an unknown coast and realise how lucky they were to have not been cast onto its shores. Unable to land, they carefully sailed over 200 kilometres north along the coast while looking out for treacherous reefs, strong currents and shallow water. After reaching Shark Bay and the northernmost point of what is now called Dirk Hartog Island, they found a safe place to anchor in the lee of the island and row ashore.

This was a new and undiscovered land. Could it be the 'known but undiscovered' land of Terra Australis that philosophers and cartographers had discussed for centuries? Unfortunately the ship's logs describing their thoughts or opinions of this discovery have not survived, but they did spend three days exploring the coast and the nearby islands and determined that it held no treasure, no people, and apparently nothing of commercial value.

It was important to mark this new discovery and Dirk Hartog ordered two of his crewmen to take a large pewter serving plate from the grand cabin, flatten its rim, and inscribe it with details of their arrival, recording the landing date, the name of the ship, its senior crew and details of the onward journey. It seems the two men sent ashore to fix the plate at the top of a barren north-facing cliff, now known as Point Inscription, could not resist adding their own names to the base of this historic inscription as it reads:

> On 25 October 1616, the ship *Eendracht* of Amsterdam arrived here with senior merchant Gillis Mibais of Liege, skipper Dirck Hartog of Amsterdam. 27 October made sail for Bantam. Junior merchant Jan Sins, first steersman Pietr Dook van Bill, Anno 1616.

Sailing north from what is now Shark Bay, Dirk Hartog charted some 400 kilometres of the Western Australian coastline and named it Landt van de Eendracht (the Land of the Eendracht) or Eendrachtlandt (Unity Land). A new piece of Australia could be included in the Tasman Map and Eendrachtlandt began to appear on world maps in place of Terra Australis Incognita.

The Hartog plate (Rijksmuseum)

Dirk Hartog's sailing orders had been to sail with the fleet to Bantam. However, after sailing north from their charting of Eendrachtlandt, he reached the East Indies at the Sape Strait between the islands of Sumbawa and Flores and directly south of the Dutch trading post at Macassar. He was then presented with a dilemma: should he sail west to Java knowing that the rest of his fleet would have arrived in Bantam months before him, or should he sail east to Ambon knowing that his valuable cargo of Spanish silver was needed in the Spice Islands to purchase the latest harvest of cloves and nutmeg and its late arrival would have a serious effect on trade? He decided to sail north to the Dutch trading post at Macassar for much needed supplies of food and water, arriving there on 10 December 1616. Unaware that the VOC had already abandoned their trading post there, sixteen of his crew were killed in a confrontation with locals before he could sail on to Ambon and deliver the chests of Spanish silver dollars to Governor Steven van der Haghen.

The *Eendracht* then spent most of the following year trading nutmeg between Banda, Ambon and Bantam. It departed Bantam in December 1617, fully loaded with a cargo of spices for the United Provinces. After his return to Amsterdam Dirk Hartog left VOC employ and bought another trading ship the *Gelukkige Leeuw* (Lucky Lion) in which he carried cargo to European ports until his premature death in 1621 at only 38 years of age. We do not know exactly what caused his death but it may have been related to financial problems as we know that within two weeks of his burial the *Gelukkige Leeuw* was sold to pay for an outstanding advance.

Dirk Hartog's plate would lie undisturbed on its windswept island for more than 80 years, until the arrival of Willem de Vlamingh's expedition in the ships *Geelvinck*, *Nyptangh* and *Weseltje* in 1696. De Vlamingh had been instructed to search for possible survivors from the wreck of the VOC ship *Ridderschap van Holland*, which had been lost in 1694 with a large cargo of silver. While he was unable to find any trace of the missing ship, his expedition resulted in the naming of Rottnest Island and the Swan River and the mapping of nearly 1500 kilometres of the southern coastline of Western

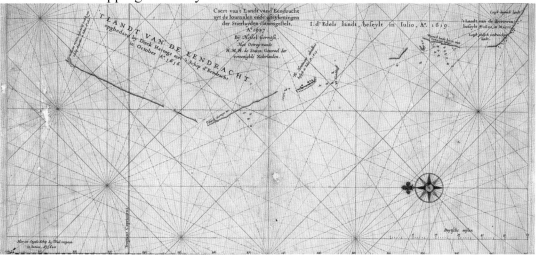

Landt van de Eendracht, Hessel Gerritsz, 1627 (National Library of Australia)

Map of Dirk Hartog Island, Victor Victorsz, 1697 (National Library of Australia)

Australia. This map from their expedition shows the anchorage at the northern part of the island and the location of the Hartog Plate.

In February 1697 De Vlamingh and his crew landed at Dirk Hartog Island and discovered the inscribed plate lying half-buried in the sand beside its now decayed oak post. Paintings of the coast from de Vlamingh's voyage are the oldest known pictorial representation of any part of Australia. To the right on the watercolour of Hartog's roadstead, a pole is shown with a legend next to it: 'Here the pewter plate was found'. Willem de Vlamingh then nailed his own inscribed plate onto a new pole at the spot where the Hartog plate was found, to commemorate his visit to the island.

In March 1697 de Vlamingh delivered the Hartog plate to Batavia as 'proof of the daring spirit of his ancestors'. The following year the plate was taken to the VOC headquarters at East India House in Amsterdam, where it remained until the Company was dissolved in 1795. In 1819 the plate was handed to the Koninklijk Kabinet van Zeldzaamheden (Royal Cabinet of Curiosities) in Den Hague, which became part of the Rijksmuseum in 1883. Today it endures as a powerful icon of shared cultural heritage, symbolising the longstanding maritime connections between the Netherlands and Australia. In 1991 Dirk Hartog Island was included in the Shark Bay World Heritage Area, in recognition of the value of its outstanding natural history, while in

2006 the Cape Inscription area was added to Australia's National Heritage List as a place of national significance.

New maps would have to be made showing the discovery of this new land and the potential hazard to Dutch shipping. The 1627 chart of Landt van de Eendracht by Hessel Gerritsz shows the numerous discoveries of the west coast of Australia by the Dutch ships sailing the Brouwer Route including *Eendracht* (1616), *Mauritius* (1618), *Dordrecht* (1619), *Leeuwin* (1622) and the *Tortelduijff* (1624).

14 Willem Janszoon and the Voyage of the Mauritius, 1618

After his return from the voyage of discovery to Neuva Guinea on the *Duyfken* Willem Janszoon was given command of a much larger vessel, the 350 ton *Westfriesland,* to sail from Ambon to the North Moluccas and trade for spices. Here his ship was defeated in a battle with the Spanish for control of the clove trade and as reported by Captain Saris in Bantam:

> The *Westfriesland* arrived here from Ternate; whence she was beaten by the Spaniards; she was not above half-laden with mace, cloves, and cotton yarn.

Janszoon commanded the *Westfriesland* on its return voyage to Holland; however, the vessel foundered in a heavy gale off Mauritius. He then built a smaller ship from the wreckage and together with his surviving crew sailed it back to Bantam. He finally returned to Holland in 1611 when he was described in a letter from the Zeeland Chamber as a 'very competent and sober man, who has pleased us greatly by his account of trade in the East'. He sailed again to the East Indies at the end of December 1611 and served on several more ships before being given command of Fort Henricus on the island of Solor after its capture from the Portuguese in 1614. Solor was the centre of the sandalwood trade from Timor and the Dutch East India Company hoped to monopolise this trade for themselves and use sandalwood to break into the highly lucrative China market for silk. Jan Pieterszoon Coen reported that;

> No one should be allowed to trade on Timor except at the fort on Solor. It will need a few ships to police the area, but it is worth all of that. With this sandalwood we can force the Chinese to trade us their silk.

Willem Janszoon returned to Holland in 1616 as chief merchant in charge of the *Zeelandia* and then sailed again for the East Indies two years later as the upper merchant of the ship *Mauritius* under the command of Captain Lenaert Jacobs. The painting by Hendrik Cornelisz Vroom shows the *Mauritius* sailing from Textel with the other ships of the fleet at the beginning of this voyage.

Also on board the *Mauritius* was a young soldier who was destined for a bright future in the East Indies. Born in Culemborg in 1593, Anthony van Diemen moved to Amster-

The *Mauritius* sailing out of the Masdiep near Texel, Hendrik Cornelisz Vroom, 1619
(Rijksmuseum)

dam at the age of 23 in hope of making his fortune as a merchant. Unfortunately his business venture with a certain Jan Engels failed and he was declared bankrupt. With his future prospects seriously limited he sought to enlist with the VOC as a means of repaying his creditors. The VOC, however, refused to employ bankrupts, for bankruptcy was considered proof of both commercial and moral delinquency, so he enlisted as an ordinary soldier under the assumed name of Thoisz Meeuwisz van Utrecht. In January 1618 and at the age of 25 he embarked on board the merchant vessel *Mauritius* to start a new life in the East Indies.

On the VOC ships there was an enormous social distance between the ordinary sailors and soldiers who sailed 'before the mast' and the ship's officers and passengers whose quarters were in the ship's stern. Willem Janszoon as the upper merchant would have occupied one of the spacious cabins in the stern, while Thoisz Meeuwisz van Utrecht, as a common soldier, made the voyage confined to the so-called *koedek* (cow's deck), where unable to stand fully upright because of the low ceiling, he was crammed together with 100 companions in a cluttered space full of hammocks, sea-chests, barrels and ropes.

After rounding the Cape of Good Hope the *Mauritius* sailed the Brouwer Route across the Southern Ocean and on 31 July 1618 their lookout sighted unexpected land ahead. Janszoon and the whole ship's crew would have thanked God this encounter had occurred in daylight hours and saved them from shipwreck on this deserted coast. After first sighting land the *Mauritius* probably sailed along a stretch of the coast between Point Cloates and North West Cape until they found an opening in the Ningaloo Reef that would have allowed them to send a boat ashore.

Captain Lenaert Jacobsz gave orders for the *Mauritius* to drop anchor and Willem Janszoon went ashore with a party of soldiers and sailors on to the sandy coastline of North West Cape. The shore party noticed human footprints in the sand and although they did not see any people they were probably observed as they wandered along the beach. After some distance they came upon a freshwater stream which Janszoon named the Willems River and is now called Yardie Creek. The location is shown on the northern part of the 1627 map Landt van de Eendracht as drawn by Hessel Gerritsz and it is more likely the river was named in honour of the assassinated Prince Willem of Orange rather than Willem Janszoon himself.

This was the second time that Willem Janszoon had set foot on the Australian continent. His first landing was twelve years earlier in 1606 on the Cape York Peninsula which he believed was part of New Guinea, and now in 1618 he was on what he believed to be an island somewhere off the Endraacht Land encountered by Dirk Hartog. He would never have imagined that he had discovered a whole continent and that a continuous landmass connected the North West Cape with the Cape York Peninsula. The log of the voyage has not been found but fortunately Janszoon reported his findings in a letter of 6 October 1618 to the Amsterdam Chamber:

> Worshipful Wise Provident Discreet Gentlemen,
> This serves only to inform you that we passed the Cape of Good Hope on 8 June in the ship *Mauritius* with strong westerly winds, so that we did not deem it advisable to call at any land. We sailed 1000 mijlen to the eastward in latitudes 38 degrees south. On 31 July we discovered an island, landed on it and found human footprints. On the west side it extends NNE and SSW; it measures 15 mijlen in length and its northern extremity is in 22 degrees south … from there through God's grace we arrived at Bantam on 22 August.

Some time after the *Mauritius* and Thoisz Meeuwisz van Utrecht arrived in Batavia, the VOC administration in the United Provinces became aware of his false identity and this letter came from Amsterdam to Jan Pieterszoon Coen, the Governor-General of the East Indies:

> Amongst the soldiers who have been sent out to the Indies … there may be some debauched characters, bankrupts, and other people who have grossly forgotten themselves in other respects … We consider it urgently necessary that Your Excellency employ such people only as soldiers and that, without our specific foreknowledge and consent, no such person is advanced to a position of influence in commerce. Under no circumstances are they to be entrusted with our effects, cash and merchandise, lest they deal with our property in the same

way as they have dealt with their own property and that of their parents and friends. One such person is a certain Anthony van Diemen.

This could have marked the end of his career with the Dutch East India Company, but a voyage of many months at sea is a good opportunity to judge someone's character and the young van Diemen arrived with good references from those he worked with on the *Mauritius*. Jan Pieterszoon Coen drafted him into service in his own administration, so that when the letter from Amsterdam arrived Coen had already formed his own opinion of van Diemen and, short of good men, he allowed him to continue in his service. The young van Diemen felt obliged to write this heartfelt letter to the VOC directors in Amsterdam in his own defence:

> I took ship under the name Thoisz Meeuwisz van Utrecht, not because I wanted to hide my true identity and mislead Your Honours, but simply because I feared that in the Indies the name Anthony van Diemen would be better known than the person himself … If Your Honours would only be so kind as to inquire into my previous conduct in life, you will not find any evidence that I have ever been debauched, nor have I indulged in any kind of excess. As God is my witness, Jan Engels has been the sole cause of my ruin and misfortune, and I pray to the Almighty that He may inspire Your Honours to moderate the order you have issued … His Excellency, the Governor-General, is certainly not rash in selecting people, nor does His Excellency extend any favours to persons who do not deserve them. But it seems that Your Honours have had it in for me, and that I am in complete disgrace. Nonetheless, I hope with God's help that, despite everything, my exemplary behaviour and good services will lead to my advancement and promotion. In the meantime, all I ask of Your Honours is to give me as much credit as my deeds shall merit.

Anthony van Diemen did not remain a mere secretary to the Governor-General for long because in 1626 he was named director-general of Commerce. In just over six years he rose from the rank of common soldier to become a director and a Councillor of the Indies, the six-man executive board that with the Governor-General deliberated on all important matters concerning the Company's operations in the East. From this time onwards Anthony van Diemen was to actively contribute to the VOC's decision-making process and his signature began to appear on almost all the executive decisions of the Governor-General and Council. This meant that van Diemen, largely through his connection with Jan Pieterszoon Coen, had now reached the most senior echelons of the Dutch East India Company in Batavia.

After more than ten years in Batavia, Anthony van Diemen became increasingly anxious to return home to the Netherlands. Twice he petitioned the new Governor-General, Jacques Specx, for permission to return home, only to see his requests denied because Specx was reluctant to part with his services. When van Diemen submitted his request for the third time, Specx reluctantly agreed and gave him the prestigious and lucrative commission of admiral of the return fleet, lucrative because the VOC granted a gold medal and bonus payment to the commander of a successful home fleet.

In March 1631 van Diemen and his wife Maria, a well-to-do Batavian widow whom he had married a year earlier sailed on the *Deventer,* the flagship of a fleet of eight vessels richly laden with spices and all kinds of other eastern treasures bound for the United Provinces. The voyage across the Indian Ocean proceeded speedily and in late April the fleet approached the Cape of Good Hope. Here they encountered a series of severe gales and thunderstorms that continued unabated for eleven days. Although none of the ships was lost it was necessary to seek shelter in Table Bay to carry out urgent repairs. The fleet was able to resume its voyage up the Atlantic and they reached the Netherlands with all the ships and their cargo intact, for which Anthony van Diemen would have been rewarded with a large bonus.

After the arrival of the *Mauritius* in 1618 Willem Janszoon remained in the East Indies and in 1619 was awarded a gold chain worth 1000 guilders for his part in capturing four English East India Company vessels which had aided the Sultan of Bantam in an attack against the Dutch after their establishment of a fortified warehouse in Batavia. Near the end of his service he became the Governor of Banda from 1623 to 1627, where he had the job of administering the division of the islands into separate nutmeg plantations to be run by the Dutch planters and overcome a manpower shortage since most of the native Bandanese had been wiped out by Jan Pieterszoon Coen in the Banda massacre. To solve the labour shortage the VOC brought in indentured labourers from Java, Malaya and China. He returned to Batavia in 1627 and soon afterwards was appointed the admiral of a fleet of eight vessels that were sent on a diplomatic mission to India. In December 1628 he made his final voyage from Batavia to the Netherlands on the ship *Prins Willem.*

After almost 30 years of service with the Dutch East India Company, Willem Janszoon made his final report on the state of the East Indies to the Gentlemen Seventeen, the States General and the King, at Den Hague in July 1629. In that period he had risen from an ordinary steersman, to the commander of the voyage that made the first Dutch discovery of the continent of Australia, to the commandant of Fort Henricus, to be the governor of the most valuable part of the Dutch East Indies at Banda, and then to become a vice-admiral and finally admiral.

However, Willem Janszoon will always be remembered as the captain of the brave little *Duyfken,* of being the first European discoverer of Australia and of adding this very first segment of Australia's coast to the Tasman Map.

15 Frederik de Houtman and the Voyage of the Dordrecht, 1619

Frederik de Houtman was experienced in the Indies as he had taken part in the first Dutch expedition to Bantam in 1595 with his brother Cornelis de Houtman as the commander. In their second voyage to the East Indies his brother was killed in Aceh and Frederik de Houtman was imprisoned by the Sultan of Aceh for eighteen months. He spent his time there learning Malay and studying astronomy, until the Sultan set him free after receiving a letter and promises from Prince Maurits the Dutch Stadtholder. After his return to the United Provinces he published a treatise on the constellations of the southern hemisphere. These observations supplemented those made by Keyser on the first Dutch expedition of 1595 and the constellations formed from their observations were published on a celestial globe made by Willem Blaeu in 1603.

De Houtman returned to the East Indies in 1604 with the first VOC war fleet sent to the East Indies and after the capture of the Portuguese fort in Ambon, Steven van der Haghen appointed him as the first VOC governor in 1606. Here he used his knowledge of the Malay language and its people to maintain good relations with the Ambonese leaders and he remained as governor for the next five years until 1611. This was the period of the 'clove wars' with the Spanish in the northern Moluccas around Ternate and Tidore which would have been his main concern while governor.

However he is credited with some good works including using his knowledge of Malay to translate children's catechism and a few simple prayers into the native schools he opened, and when he returned to the United Provinces in 1611 he took some young Ambonese with him to train as schoolmasters. After his return he lived in Alkmaar, where he was a member of the city council from 1614 to 1618. The portrait of him in military uniform and standing next to a globe was probably made during this period.

Frederik de Houtman departed for the East Indies for the third time in December 1618 as the commander of a fleet of eleven ships. During the voyage the fleet was scattered, but the *Dordrecht* and the *Amsterdam* left the Cape together in June 1619 and followed the Brouwer Route for the prescribed 1000 mijlen. As described by de Houtman in his report to the stadtholder, Prince Maurits:

On 8 June 1619 we set sail from Table Bay with a fair wind with the ships *Dordrecht* and

Portrait of Frederick de Houtman as Governor of Ambon, Anonymous, 1618 (Rijksmuseum)

Amsterdam and on 19 July suddenly came upon the Southland of Beach in 32 degrees 20 minutes; we spent a few days there in order to gather some knowledge of it, but a heavy gale prevented us from making a landing, whereupon we set our course for Java which we sighted on 19 August and we arrived safely before Jacatra on 3 September.

It should be noted that de Houtman used the old name of Beach for the mysterious and unknown South Land. He named this coast which was somewhere near present-day Rottnest Island and Perth after Jacob d'Edel, a member of the Council of the Indies who was sailing on the *Amsterdam*, and it appears on the 1627 Hessel Gerritsz map as d'Edels Landt. Sailing up the coast of West Australia, the *Dordrecht* narrowly avoided a group of dangerous reefs at the edge of the continental shelf some 80 kilometres west of Geraldton. The islands formed on the reefs are very flat with an average height of only a few metres. As a warning to other navigators de Houtman named them the Abrolhos reefs from the Portuguese phrase 'abri vossos olhos' or 'keep your eyes open', a common warning for seamen on watch. These reefs would later be known as the Houtman-Abrolhos reefs and as described by de Houtman:

> On the 29th July, deeming ourselves to be in an open sea, we shaped our course north-by-east. At noon we were in 29° 32' S. Lat.; at night about three hours before daybreak, we again unexpectedly came upon a low-lying coast, a level, broken country with reefs all round it. We saw no high land or mainland, so that this shoal is to be carefully avoided as very dangerous to ships that wish to touch at this coast. It is fully ten miles in length, lying in 28° 46'.

Being out of sight of land, these reefs were extremely hazardous for shipping and ten years later in 1629 they would become the graveyard of the *Batavia* and many of its unfortunate passengers and crew. After rounding these reefs the ships sailed north and several days later came upon the coast discovered by Dirk Hartog and the *Eendracht*

Beacon Island (*Batavia*'s graveyard) and the Houtman-Abrolhos reef (Natali Pearson)

in 1616. The red, muddy coast indicated to some of the crew that the land may be gold bearing:

> We are all assured that this land is the land which the ship *Eendracht* discovered ... and no way doubt that all the land they saw is one uninterrupted mainland coast ... This South Land, as far as we could judge, seems to be a very fair coast, but we found it impossible to land on it, nor have we seen any smoke or signs of inhabitants there, but further investigation is wanted on this point ... which according to the surmises of some of us might not unlikely prove to be gold-bearing, a point which may be cleared up in time.

The *Dordrecht* reached Bantam in September 1619, where de Houtman was appointed a member of the Council of the Indies. After Jan Pieterszoon Coen was appointed as Governor-General, based in Batavia. de Houtman replaced him and he again became Governor of the Moluccas based in Ambon from 1621–23.

Jan Pieterszoon Coen had come up with a strategy to gain a VOC monopoly over the clove trade. This involved the transplantation of clove trees from the Spice Islands of North Maluku to Ambon and its surrounding islands in Central Maluku, which the Dutch now controlled. Here the VOC required the obligatory cultivation of clove trees by officially authorised villages. In these villages each head of family had to plant and maintain 100 or more clove trees, and any clove trees that were cultivated without consent were destroyed. Of course the Ambonese had every right to trade the cloves grown on their own lands to whoever they liked. especially as native traders would offer a higher price than the Dutch contract price. The uprooting or burning of clove trees became a form of punishment for those villagers that dared challenge the Dutch monopoly and trade their excess cloves with native traders from Java or Macassar.

The VOC enforced its monopoly in the outer islands by the hongi-tochten system. The 'hongi' were fleets of large kora-kora manned by Dutch soldiers and Ambonese oarsmen, while 'tochten' meant duty rounds. In the case of trouble in the islands, Frederik de Houtman as the Dutch governor of Fort Victoria in Ambon would call up the hongi and dispatched it on its tochten. If the troubles were minor, a few Dutch soldiers travelled with the hongi. However, if the troubles were more serious, the hongis would be attached to a military expedition from Batavia. Even in times of peace, the hongi-tochten fleets were dispatched annually as a show of strength. Consisting of 50 to 100 kora-kora, each manned by 100 men, they created an impressive sight, as with flags and pennants streaming in the wind, they swept along the coast to the sound of drums and cymbals beating out a rhythm for the oarsmen.

De Houtman left Ambon in February 1623, which was convenient because the torture and beheading of the seventeen English traders accused of plotting to capture the Dutch fortress in Ambon occurred in March of that year. In January 1624 he returned to the Netherlands with the return fleet from Batavia on the ship *Leyden* and was honoured with a gold medal from the Dutch East India Company for his service in the East Indies. He settled once more at Alkmaar and lived there until his death and burial in the Great Church on 21 October 1627.

16 John Brooke and the Voyage of the Triall, 1622

In 1620 Captain Humphrey Fitzherbert in the *Royal Exchange* became the first English captain to sail the Brouwer Route to the East Indies. He led an expedition of three ships, the *Royal Exchange* (980 tonnes) the *White Bear* (700 tonnes) and the *Unity* (300 tonnes). After anchoring in Table Bay, Fitzherbert had a chance meeting with Cornelis Kunst, the captain of the VOC vessel *Schiedam* also bound for the Indies. The ships left the Cape together and Cornelis Kunst inadvertently showed the English fleet the right latitudes to sail the Brouwer Route to Java, which they reached in only eight weeks after leaving the Cape of Good Hope.

In 1621 the vessel *Triall* under the command of John Brooke with a crew of 143 left Plymouth bound for the English factory in Bantam. On board was a cargo of trade goods including 500 Spanish silver dollars and some valuable jewellery later referred to as spangles to be given as a gift to the King of Thailand. When the *Triall* reached the Cape of Good Hope they met another English vessel, the *Charles*, which was returning from the East Indies. As there was no one aboard the *Triall* with experience of a voyage to the East Indies, Brooke was able to convince Thomas Bright, a merchant officer from the *Charles* to join them and he was immediately appointed first mate. Brooke's correspondence reads:

> I departed from the Cape of Good Hope the 19th day of March. I ran into the latitude of 39 degrees according to Captain Fitzherbert in the journal which your worships gave me orders to follow.

The *Triall* sighted the coast of Western Australia in daylight on 1 May 1622. Sailing past the tip of North West Cape, John Brooke concluded he had reached an island somewhere off Eendrachtlandt and he should sail north-east to reach Java:

> The 1st day of May I saw land being in the latitude of 22 degrees, which land had been formerly seen by the Flemings and which laye in the cardes N.E. by N. and S.E. by S. from the Straits of Sunda. This island is 18 leagues long and we were all verie joyful at the sight thereof but finding 8 degrees variation by our judgment and Captain Fitzherbert's Journal that he went 10 leagues to the southwards of this Island and being in this variation pestered by N.E. and by E. [winds] and fell [in] with the East end of Java.

The *Triall* continued on this course until five days later disaster struck north of the

Montebello Islands when it ran aground on unknown rocks at night and in fine weather. The ship quickly filled with water and those who could make it to the boats were saved, while the remaining crew were left to their fate. As reported by John Brooke:

> The 25th day (of May) at 11 of the clock in the night – faire and smoothe water – the ship struck. I ran to the poop deck and hove the lead. I found but 3 fathom water … I cried to get them to beare up and tack to the westward, they did their best but the rock being sharp the ship was presently full of water … so seeing the ship full of water and the winds increasing I made all the means to save … as many … as I could … The boats put off at 4 in the morning and half an hour after the fore part of the ship fell in pieces! Ten men were saved in the skiff and thirty six in the long boat.

His freshly hired first mate Thomas Bright told a different story when he described the actions of his captain after their collision with the rocks:

> but like a Judas (while I was turning my back in the great cabin) he lowered himself privately into the skiff with only nine men and his son, and then stood for the Strait of Sunda that instant without care and seeing the lamentable end of a ship, the time she split, or respect of any man's life …
>
>   It did seem strange to me that Brookes so cunningly excused the neglect of the Company's letters, spangles and money. The money's he has confessed to having transferred to me. Yet for nigh two hours he did nothing but convey from his cabin to his skiff both letters, spangles and money in his trunk.

When the *Triall* started to break up Bright managed to launch the longboat and save another 36 members of the crew. They waited off from the *Triall* during the night until the vessel began to sink. As they rowed away they could hear the grief-laden cries of their drowning shipmates above the roar of the waves pounding against the stricken ship. Ahead of the men in the skiff and the longboat was a 1000 nautical mile voyage in their open boats towards Java.

Both boats separately attempted to find water and food on the nearby Montebello Islands and then sailed for Batavia. In July 1622 and after three months at sea the skiff with ten shipwrecked Englishmen arrived in Batavia and three days later the other 36 men reached there in the longboat. Without food it takes six weeks before you die because the body will first consume its own resources that is any excess fat and then muscle, before starvation finally affects the vital organs and death is imminent. The survivors must have been able to catch fish to eat during the voyage and to prepare the sail to catch as much water as possible from rain showers moving across the tropical seas. According to the report written to the directors of the VOC on 6 September:

> On the 5th of July there arrived here a boat with ten men forming part of the crew of an English ship, named the *Triall*, and on the 8th her longboat with 36 men. They state that they have

lost and abandoned their ship with 97 men and the cargo she had taken in, on certain rocks situated in Latitude 20° 10' South, in the longitude of the western extremity of Java … The said ship *Triall* ran on these rocks in the night-time in fine weather, without having seen land, and since the heavy swells caused the ship to run aground directly, so that it got filled with water, the 46 persons aforementioned put off from her in the greatest disorder with the boat and pinnace each separately, leaving 97 persons in the ship whose fate is known to God alone. The boat and pinnace aforesaid arrived here each separately, without knowing of each other.

According to John Brooke the sunken rocks were exactly south of the western extremity of Java. Two VOC ships, the *Haringh* and *Hasewint*, were fitted out to sail south, locate the rocks and map this dangerous hazard to VOC shipping and their sailing instructions were as follows:

Inasmuch as Our Masters (the Heeren Majores) earnestly enjoin us to dispatch hence certain yachts for the purpose of making discovery of the South-land; and since moreover experience has taught, by great perils incurred by sundry of our ships – but specially by the late miscarrying of the English ship *Triall* on the said coast – the urgent necessity of obtaining a full and accurate knowledge of the true bearing and conformation of the said land, that further accidents may henceforth be prevented as much as possible; besides this, seeing that it is highly desirable that an investigation should be made to ascertain whether the regions or any part of the same are inhabited, and whether any trade might with them be established … As according to the statements of Jan Huygen van Linschoten and the opinion of sundry other persons, certain parts of this Southland are likely to yield gold, a point into which you will inquire as carefully as possible.

It is important to note that apart from locating the Triall Rocks the VOC was interested in investigating whether the South Land was inhabited and what trade possibilities it would offer. However, other priorities prevented the vessels from sailing and it is believed that John Brooke, to disguise his own fault for the wreck, falsified his journal to show that the wreck site was on the route he had been instructed to take, which was many miles west of the true position. The position of the Triall Rocks remained a perplexing mystery for three centuries even after several attempts to determine their exact position. The Triall Rocks continued to be marked on charts, but gradually sailors began to doubt their existence. In 1705 the captain of the *Jane* wrote in his journal:

Hove to, according to custom, on account of the Trial Rocks (if they exist), for although they are reported to extend 20 league in length I was informed by the Commodore of the Dutch Ships … that he had never heard of these rocks being seen. He went on to correctly surmise that 'If they exist they must lie much farther east than in the route toward Java Head'.

In 1818 the British brig *Greyhound*, captained by Lieutenant Ritchie, encountered some rocks north and east of the Montebello Islands which were published on various maps as Ritchie's Reef or the Greyhound Shoals. After examining the records and

Bright's letter countering Brookes' likely falsehoods, historian Ida Lee concluded in 1934 that what was then known as Ritchie's Reef was probably the site of the Triall Rocks. In the 1960s Eric Christiansen, a diver and amateur historian, reached the same conclusion that Greyhound Rocks, Ritchie's Reef and Triall Rocks were possibly the same thing. This was confirmed in 1969 after divers led by Eric Christiansen discovered a shipwreck at this site which contained artefacts of the period and is believed to be the *Triall*. Consequently when Captain John Brooke landed on the Montebello Islands in search of water he can be described as the first Englishmen to reach Australia.

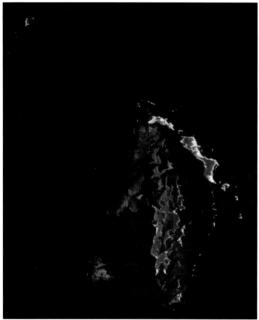

Triall Rocks located to the north-west of the Montebello Islands (NASA Image)

The declining English presence in the Moluccas finally ended after the Amboyna massacre in 1623. The Dutch commander in Ambon arrested seventeen English traders living in and around Ambon and accused them of plotting to capture the Dutch fortress, without attempting to explain how this could be possible without naval support and only a few swords and muskets between them. Methodical torture of the English traders continued until their tormentors produced a confession, which was all the justification the Dutch needed for the executioner's axe. Pen and paper were thrust into one of the cells and William Griggs was allowed to write a final and poignant message before his beheading:

We, through torment, were constrained to speake that which we never meant nor once imagined; the which we take upon our deaths and salvation, that tortured with the extreme torment of fire and water, that flesh and blood could not endure … And so farewell. Written in the dark.

The English East India Company had begun with only enough capital for each voyage and since a willingness to invest in further voyages depended on the success of previous ones, this ad hoc system bred uncertainty and delay. It also caused conflict between those investors who needed their investment back after each voyage and those with a longer term outlook willing to invest in the future of the Company. Consequently the 'race for spices' had been won by the Dutch, and after the expulsion of the English from Rhun and Ambon the English presence in the East Indies was reduced to a few trade representatives operating from Bantam and Macassar.

The English East India Company had retained some sort of legal claim to the island of Rhun, since in 1616 the islanders signed a document given to them by Nathaniel Courthope accepting James I of England as sovereign of the island. Under the 1667 Treaty of Breda the English signed away their rights to Rhun in exchange for the island of Manhattan. This was the real estate deal of the millennium and few would have believed a small trading village on the island of Manhattan was destined to become the modern metropolis of New York and the once valuable nutmeg-growing island of Rhun would sink into obscurity.

Trade was at a standstill, debts were spiralling out of control, and the Company warehouses on the Thames lay almost empty. In 1657 Sir William Cockayne, the Governor of the English East India Company, called a meeting to explain the Company's financial position. The Company was headed towards bankruptcy and there was little hope of any reversal of its fortunes. The heroic voyages and the loss of hundreds of English seamen had been for nothing, as the Dutch East India Company had gained an almost complete monopoly over trade from the East Indies. Sir William Cockayne proposed the closure of the Company and the liquidation of all its remaining assets, including its factories in Bantam and Macassar.

Shocked by this news, Oliver Cromwell and his Council of State asked the Governor and his Council to present alternative proposals. Within twelve days Cromwell agreed to a new charter for the Company of Merchants Trading into the East Indies. It was reborn as a modern joint-stock company and instead of financing each voyage independently its capital would now be permanent. If it was to compete against the Dutch East India Company it needed a similar financial structure and within months London investors had subscribed over £786,000 in new capital. The future of the English East India Company was now going to be in India, and in particular Calcutta.

17 Jan Carstensz and the Voyage of the Pera and Arnhem, 1623

After the ill-fated voyage of Jacob Le Maire and Willem Schouten in search of Terra Australis, the Dutch East India Company demanded of the States General that the Australische Zuid Compagnie (Australia South Company) should under all circumstances be entirely excluded from the southern regions. After making this demand the VOC found it necessary to back their words by sending an expedition south in search of trading opportunities and the entrance to the strait they heard had been navigated by Luis Vaz de Torres in 1606.

In 1623 the VOC sent a second expedition of two ships to Nova Guinea, the *Pera* under the command of Jan Carstensz and the *Arnhem* under the command of Dirck Meliszoon. We are fortunate that the log of the *Pera* survives for it describes their voyage in detail. The ships sailed from Ambon with orders to extend Willem Janszoon's earlier survey and hopefully find the entrance to a strait that would provide a route east towards to the Pacific Ocean. The instructions of the new Governor-General, Pieter de Carpentier, were framed in very practical terms:

> Examine the coast in order to ascertain whether or not it is inhabited, the nature of the land and the people, their towns and inhabited villages, the division of their kingdoms, their religion and their policy, their wars, their rivers, the shape of their vessels, their fisheries, commodities and the manufactures, but specially to inform yourselves what minerals, such as gold, tin, iron, lead and copper, what precious stones, pearls, vegetables, animals and fruits these lands yield and produce.
>
> For the purpose of making a trade we have given orders for various articles to be put on board your ships, such as ironmongery, cloths, coat-stuffs and linen, which you will show and try to dispose of to such natives as you may meet with, always diligently noting what articles are found to be most in demand, what quantities might be disposed of, and what might be obtained in exchange for them, we furthermore hand you samples of gold, silver, copper, iron, lead and pearls, that you may inquire whether these articles are known to the natives, and might be obtained there in any considerable quantity.

Jan Carstensz was born in Emden in East Friesland and like so many before him he was attracted by the opportunities offered by the VOC. Having arrived in Bantam as an undermerchant on board the *Trouw*, he served for the next two years as a merchant on the nutmeg island of Pulau Ai in the Banda Islands before he was promoted to the position of uppermerchant.

The Carstensz expedition followed the same route along the south coast of Nova Guinea as the *Duyfken*. Here the central mountains of Papua reach to almost 5000 metres above sea level and are always covered in cloud. However at a certain time during the voyage, the clouds suddenly cleared and the crew of the *Pera* had this amazing sight, for above them they could see mountain peaks covered in snow, which Jan Carstensz marked on his chart and in his log as a sneeberg (snow mountain):

> We were about one mijl distance from the low-lying land in 5 or 6 fathoms, when at a distance of about 10 mijlen by estimation into the interior we saw a very high mountain-range in many places white with snow, which we thought a very singular sight, being so near the equator.

No doubt these observations drew many jokes and much hilarity in the inns and households of Batavia and Carstensz would have been accused of suffering from 'tropic fever' for whoever heard of snow at the equator. But he was later proved correct for there is a tropical glacier on top of the highest mountain in Papua which at 4884 metres the Dutch named Carstensz Top in his honour.

It had been seventeen years since the voyage of the *Duyfken* and if the Carstensz expedition had access to the journals of Willem Janszoon they would have known that at least eight of the *Duyfken* crew had been killed by natives on the south coast of Papua. Regardless of this fact, Dirck Meliszoon, the captain of the *Arnhem*, led a party ashore and as described by Jan Carstensz:

> This same day the captain of the yacht *Arnhem*, Dirck Meliszoon without knowledge of myself, or the supercargo, or steersman of the said yacht, inadvisedly went ashore to the open beach in the pinnace taking with him fifteen persons, both officers and common sailors; and no more than four muskets, for the purpose of fishing with a seine net; there was great disorder in landing, the men going off in different directions, until at last a number black savages came running from the wood, who first seized and tore to pieces assistant named Jan Willemsz van den Briel who happened to be unarmed, after which they slew with arrows, spears and with oars which they had snatched from the pinnace, no less than nine of our own men, who were unable to defend themselves, at the same time wounding the remaining seven (among them the captain). These last seven men at last returning on board in a very sorry plight with the pinnace and one oar, the captain loudly lamenting his lack of prudence and entreating pardon for the fault he had committed.

They described the natives as tall black men with curly heads of hair, with a bone through a large hole in their nose, stark naked, not even covering their privates and whose arms were arrows, bows, clubs, spears and the like. Dirck Meliszoon died the following day after suffering what was described as grievous pains. After consulting with his council Carstensz selected Willem Joosten van Colster, the second mate, as the new captain of the *Pera*.

The reference on the Hessel Gerritsz map of 1622 to 'the yacht of Quiros' indicates that the Dutch had come into information that revealed the voyage of Torres, who after being abandoned by Quiros at Espiritu Santo had sailed westward amongst many islands, reefs, dry banks and shallow waters for full 34 days, through what later became known as the Torres Strait. The Carstensz expedition had been instructed to find the entrance to this strait and follow its eastern extension as far as possible.

When they reached the shallow bight marked on the Duyfken Map the longboat was despatched from the *Pera* with the mate, twelve men and provisions for four days to explore the open water, presumably north of High Island. This was the most important part of the expedition because the discovery of this passage could provide a route to the Pacific. However the longboat returned after just one day with the news that they had found only shoals, mudbanks and shallow water where the strait might be:

> We were here in 9° 6' S, Lat., about 125 miles east of Aru, and according to the chart we had with us and the estimation of the skippers and steersmen, no more than 2 miles from Nova Guinea, so that the space between us and Nova Guinea seems to be a bight to which on account of its shallows we have given the name of drooge bocht [shallow bight] in the new chart

The expedition continued south and reached the low lying coastline of the Cape York Peninsula as discovered by the *Duyfken*. Sailing past Cape Keerweer, they made their first contact with the Australian Aborigines. We are fortunate that from the Carstensz account of the voyage we have the first surviving European description of any part of the land or people of Australia:

> In the morning of the 12th the wind was S.E with good weather; at sunrise we saw the land of Nova Guinea, showing itself as a low-lying coast without hills or mountains.
>
> On the morning of the 18th we saw persons on the beach and the captain of the *Pera* gave orders to row to the land with two pinnaces … in the afternoon when the pinnaces returned, we were informed by the skipper that as soon as he had landed with his men, a large number of blacks, some of them armed and others unarmed, had made up to them; these blacks showed no fear and were so bold, as to touch the muskets of our men and to try to take them off their shoulders … our men accordingly diverted their attention by showing them iron and beads, and spying advantage, seized one of the blacks by a string which he

wore around his neck, and carried him off to the pinnace; the blacks who remained on the beach, set up dreadful howls and made violent gestures … as regards their customs and the nature of the country, Your Worships will in time be able to get information from the black man we have got hold of.

Unfortunately there is no further record of what happened to this unfortunate Aboriginal man. The expedition reached the southernmost part of their voyage and a river they named the Staten River, after the States General of the United Provinces. Accompanied by some crew members, Carstensz went inland and observed that the land 'was flooded in several places and in appearance not very different from Waterland in Holland, so that we concluded that further inland there are large waterways and lakes'. Having found no stone they could use to mark the end of their voyage the crew of the *Pera* nailed a wooden tablet to a tree, which read:

> On the 24 April 1623 there arrived here two yachts dispatched by their High Mightiness the States General. We have accordingly named the aforesaid river, the Staten River in the new chart. (17 degrees 8 minutes south)

There had been problems with the vessel *Arnhem*, initially with its rudder, then it nearly founded in heavy seas, and later collided with the *Pera* which Jan Carstensz complained was due to poor seamanship. At some point on their return voyage up the coast Willem Joosten van Colster and the *Arnhem* abruptly decided to leave the expedition and take a more direct route back to Ambon, and as described by Carstensz:

> In order to wait for the *Arnhem* which was only a howitzer's shot astern of us; in the evening, having come to anchor, we hung out a lantern, that the *Arnhem* might keep clear of us in dropping anchor, but this proved to be useless, for on purpose and with malice forethought she sailed away from us against her instructions and our resolution, and seems to have set her course for Aru (to have a good time of it there), but we shall learn in time whether she has managed to reach it.

After the ships became separated the *Pera* continued on its northerly course along Cape York. On the afternoon of 11 May, Carstensz describes sailing past a large river, where he believed the men of the *Duyfken* went up with a boat in 1606 and where one of them was killed by the spears of the blacks. He also describes how in their two landings along this northern coast the Aboriginals had been more hostile than those they encountered to the south:

> The aboriginals seem much more acquainted with muskets, of which they would seem to have experienced the fatal effect when in 1606 the men of the *Duyfken* made a landing here … I went ashore myself with the skipper, and found upwards of 200 savages standing on the beach, making a violent noise, threatening to throw their arrows at us, and evidently full of

suspicion; for, though we threw out to them pieces of iron and other things, they refused to come to parley, and used every possible means to wound one of our men and get him into their power; we were accordingly compelled to frighten them by firing one or two shots at them, by which one of the blacks was hit in the breast.

By this time the second expedition had seen enough of Cape York and in May Jan Carstensz wrote a report which would influence any further exploration of Australia:

> The land between 13 and 17 degrees is an arid and poor tract without any fruit tree or anything else useful to man; it is low and monotonous without mountain, wooded in some places with bush and little oily trees; there is little fresh water and what there is can only be collected from pits specially dug; there are also no points or inlets … In general the men are barbarians all much alike in build and features, pitch black and entirely naked, with a knotted net on head and neck for keeping their food in and what they mainly live on (as far as we have seen) were certain roots which they dig out from the earth … we saw many and different huts made of dry hay; also a great number of dogs, herons and waterfowl and other wild fowl and also very excellent fish which can easily be caught in a net; they have no knowledge at all of gold, silver, tin, iron, lead and copper; even nutmegs, cloves and pepper which had been shown to them several times on the voyage and made no impression on them.
>
> In our judgement this is the most arid and barren region that could be found anywhere on earth. The inhabitants too, are the most wretched and poorest creatures that I have ever seen in my age or time.

The *Arnhem* on its return to Ambon made a significant discovery of new lands on the western side of the Gulf of Carpentaria which they named Arnhemslandt. They first sighted land at a point they called De Caep Mauritius which is a southern point of Groote Eyland and then named De Caep Hollandia at the present Cape Arnhem. North of this they named Speult Eyland after the VOC governor in Ambon. Meanwhile the *Pera* retraced its route back to Banda and Ambon, where Jan Carstensz recorded in his log:

> In the evening of 8 June we came to anchor before the castle of Ambon, having herewith brought our voyage to a safe conclusion by the merciful protection of God Almighty, who may vouchsafe to grant prosperity and success in all their good undertakings to their High Mightiness the States General, to his excellency the Prince of Orange, to the Lords Managers of the Dutch East India Company and to the Worshipful Lord General and his Governors.

The 1658 map of the East Indies by Arnold Colom shows the coastline mapped by the *Pera* of Papua and the Cape York Peninsula including the sneeberg or glacier observed in the mountains of Central Papua and the shallow bight they explored without finding any entrance to the Torres Strait.

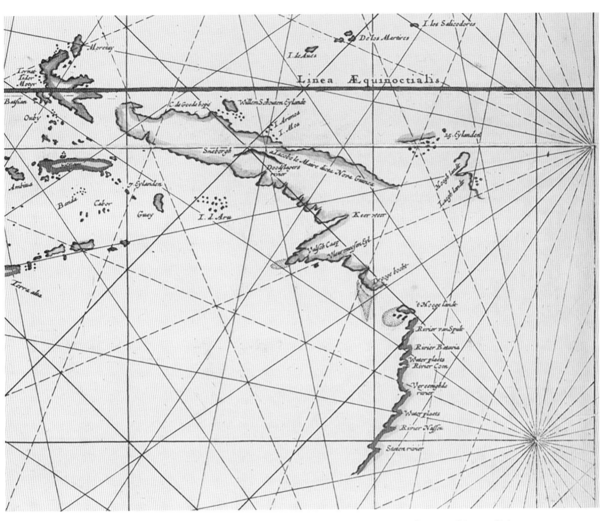

Map of the East Indies, detail, Arnold Colom, 1658 (National Library of Australia)

The VOC considered the results of the expedition as disappointing. After the return of the yachts *Pera* and *Arnhem* to Banda and Ambon a letter from Isaac de Brune, Governor of Banda, to the Governor-General, Pieter de Carpentier, on 16 May 1623 reads:

> They have not done much worth mentioning, for at the place where the chart they had with them, led them to expect an open passage, they did not find any such passage.

For the Dutch East India Company there seemed to be no justification to further explore the southern reaches of what they had named as Nova Guinea and it was another thirteen years before they commissioned a third expedition.

18 Jan Pieterszoon Coen and the Voyage of the Gallias, 1627

On his return to the Netherlands in 1624 Jan Pieterszoon Coen became head of the VOC chamber in Hoorn and one of the Gentlemen Seventeen on the Board of the Dutch East India Company, where he was responsible for establishing new policies. New policies which would bring even more riches to the VOC. Only one year later he was reappointed as Governor-General of the East Indies, but his departure was hindered by an English blockade of Dutch ships as a consequence of the Amboyna massacre. It was in March 1627 that he finally sailed from Texel with the ships *Gallias*, *Utrecht* and *Texel* for his second term as Governor-General of the East Indies, with his wife Eva Ment, their newborn child and Eva's brother and sister.

On the voyage across the Southern Ocean the rudder of the *Gallias* broke in high seas and it was separated from the other ships before it could be repaired. It was then storm-driven eastwards and on 5 September they unexpectantly encountered Eendrachtlandt as discovered by Dirk Hartog. The steersman's chart showed no land, there was no land in sight, but there were obvious breakers on the reefs ahead. After this dangerous encounter the *Gallias* safely arrived in Batavia and Jan Pieterszoon Coen wrote a letter of warning to the directors of the VOC:

> On 5 September in latitude 28 ½ degrees we chanced upon the land of Eendracht. We were less than half a mile distance from the breakers before perceiving the same, without being able to see land. If we had come to this place in the night-time we would have been in a thousand perils with our ship and crew. In the charts the reckonings of our steersmen were still 300 and 350 miles from any land … We would request your worships to direct attention to this point, and have such indications made on the sea charts as experts should find to be advisable; a matter of the highest importance, which if not properly attended to involves grievous peril to ships and crews (which God in his mercy avert).

It was during his second term in Batavia that Jan Pieterszoon Coen successfully developed the intra-Asian trade and he wrote of his plans to the directors of the VOC in his usual forthright manner:

> Gujarati textiles must be traded for pepper and gold on the shores of Sumatra: Pepper from Bantam for textiles from the coast of Coromandel, Chinese goods and gold for sandalwood, pepper and reales, silver can be got from Japan for Chinese goods, the textiles from the Coromandel coast for spices, pieces of eight from Arabia for spices and other small goods, making sure that one compensates the other, and that all is done in ships without money from the Netherlands. Your worships have the principal spices already so what is stopping it then? Only a few ships and a little water to work the pumps? Are there more ships in the world than in the Netherlands? Is there a lack of water there to prime the pumps? (I mean with this, send enough money, until the marvellous native trade has been reformed)

'All is done in ships without money from the Netherlands' was the key part of this trading equation and Jan Pieterszoon Coen delivered even greater profits to the VOC. From its headquarters in Batavia he oversaw a vast commercial empire that spread across Asia from India to Japan. Shipping was subject to the rhythm of the monsoons. In May and June ships sailed from Batavia to China and Japan, between July and September to India and Ceylon, and between November and February to the Spice Islands. All goods and commodities were consolidated in Batavia before the annual fleet now consisting of up to ten fully loaded East Indiamen left to return to Holland in convoy between November and February. Only 50 years after the establishment of Batavia the Dutch East India Company was the richest private company the world had ever seen, owning 150 merchant ships and 40 warships, with 50,000 employees and an army of 10,000 soldiers and sailors to defend their interests. Incredibly, the Company was able to return an average annual dividend of 18 percent for the next 200 years, due to the policy followed by its directors of reinvesting much of their substantial profits back into the business. The painting by Adam Willaerts shows the East Indiamen of the return fleet anchored off Batavia. To the left and right of the main canal are Fort Batavia and the spice warehouses, while goods which have been stored in Batavia are coming on boats down the main canal to be loaded on the East Indiamen of the return fleet.

Jan Pieterszoon Coen ruled his realm with an iron fist and he remained in Batavia until his death at the age of 42:

> He has gone to rest in the Lord after he had suffered for a considerable time from the flux, but only slightly ill, suddenly dying of a heart failure, some would say of a spasm … On that date his wife was in child-bed with a young daughter, four days old; how such an affliction that has been your Honours can only imagine.

His reign as 'King Coen' had ended and two days later Jacques Specx was provi-

Asian and Dutch ships at anchor off Fort Batavia, 1649, Adam Willaerts
(Netherlands Maritime Museum)

sionally elected Governor-General at Batavia. A statue built by the Dutch Colonial Government in Coen's honour in Batavia was destroyed in 1945 by nationalists during the struggle for Indonesian independence. However a memorial still exists in Jakarta on the site of where Jan Pieterszoon Coen was buried near the former Dutch Stadhuis and inside what is now the Wayang Museum, it reads:

> In this place stood from 1640 to 1730 the Old Dutch Church or Cross-Church and from 1736 to 1808 the New Dutch Church. In these churches and the grounds around them – the Dutch churchyard – the founder of Batavia Jan Pieterszoon Coen found his place of rest in 1634, as did the 18 Governors-General mentioned here as well as a great number of high officials of the Compagnie and many of their spouses and family members.

Coen's lasting legacy was the Dutch monopoly over the growth of nutmeg and cloves in the Spice Islands which he established by force of arms, and the deaths,

Memorial to Jan Pieterszoon Coen in Jakarta (Ian Burnet)

exile or enslavement of thousands of islanders. A statue stands in the town square of Hoorn in honour of its most famous son, but whatever honours and reputation as an empire-builder Jan Pieterszoon Coen enjoyed during his lifetime, these were always accompanied by charges of barbarity and inhumanity. His statue in Hoorn has always been the subject of controversy, it has been torn down at least once, and a new clause was subsequently added to the words on the memorial plinth:

> This statue is controversial. According to critics, Coen's violent mercantilism in the East Indian Archipelago does not deserve to be honoured.

Surprisingly, Jan Pieterszoon Coen is still remembered on the Cape York Peninsula by the Coen River, so named by the Carstensz expedition, and by the town of Coen which is found on the upper reaches of that river.

19 Francois Thijssen and the Voyage of the Gulden Zeepaard, 1627

The *Gulden Zeepaard*, captained by François Thijssen, was fitted out by the Middleburg Chamber of the Dutch East India Company and sailed from Vlissingen for Batavia on 22 May 1626. The ship carried a crew of 158 people including 56 soldiers and was part of a fleet of nine ships under the command of Admiral Wijbrandt Schrans. The most senior Dutch official on board the *Gulden Zeepaard* was Pieter Nuyts, who was born in the town of Middelburg in Zeeland and gained a Doctorate of Philosophy at the University of Leiden before joining the VOC. As a member of the Council of the Indies he was on his way to take up the position of Governor of Formosa and Ambassador designate to Japan. However the *Golden Zeepard* did not reach Batavia until 10 April 1627, almost a year after leaving the Netherlands and long after the other vessels of the fleet. So what happened along the way?

The ship followed the Roaring Forties so far south that it almost managed to miss Australia altogether and they first sighted the Australian coast near Cape Leeuwin at the most southern point of Western Australia. The *Gulden Zeepaard* was a long way off course and there must have been a formal decision by the ship's council to keep sailing east and explore this new land. François Thijssen kept sailing for another 1800 kilometres, in sight of the flat-topped cliffs of the Great Australian Bight, and made an accurate map of the southern coast. It was impossible for them to find a protected anchorage below these cliffs where they could go ashore until in January 1627 they reached some islands near Ceduna in South Australia which they named Saint François and Saint Pieter after the first names of Thijssen and Nuyts. The chart that Thijssen sent back to the Netherlands named the land he discovered as Landt van Pieter Nuyts, which was a mark of respect for the highest ranking VOC representative on the voyage. The extension of their voyage provided valuable information on the south coast of the South Land but there was also a resulting loss of life as 28 of the passengers and crew died from scurvy during this long voyage. There are no surviving ship's logs or records of the voyage and when the French explorer D'Entrecasteaux visited the same area 165 years later he wrote:

> It is not surprising that Nuyts has given us no details of this barren coast; for its aspect is so uniform, that the most fruitful imagination could find nothing to say of it.

The choice of Pieter Nuyts as the Governor of Formosa and Ambassador designate to Japan was unfortunate, as his lack of diplomatic skills led to the Japanese describing him as 'a typical arrogant western bully who slighted Japanese trading rights and trod on the rights of the native inhabitants'. Nuyts also acquired some notoriety while Governor of Formosa for apparently taking local women to his chamber and having a translator hide under the bed to interpret his pillow-talk and sexual urgings. Because of these and other failings he was eventually recalled to Batavia and then returned to the Netherlands.

The extension of the southern coastline towards the east opened a potentially valuable passage into the South Pacific by following the westerly trade winds of the Roaring Forties. Written fifteen years later, Anthony van Diemen's instructions to Abel Tasman show the VOC's interest in a route directly across the Southern Ocean to South America.

> Should it prove such a route practicable; which God in his mercy grant, the Company will have opportunities, owing to the said route, to snatch rich booty from the Castilians in the West Indies, who will never dream of such a thing.

The map produced by Hessel Gerritsz in 1628 is the first to show a recognisable outline of a large part of Australia based on the discoveries of Dirk Hartog, Willem Janszoon, Frederik de Houtman, François Thijssen and others. Only twelve years after Hartog's discovery of Eendrachtlandt in 1616, segments of the western and southern parts of the Australian continent had been mapped by Dutch navigators and a recognisable coast of western Australia emerges from the Indian Ocean to be added to the Tasman Map.

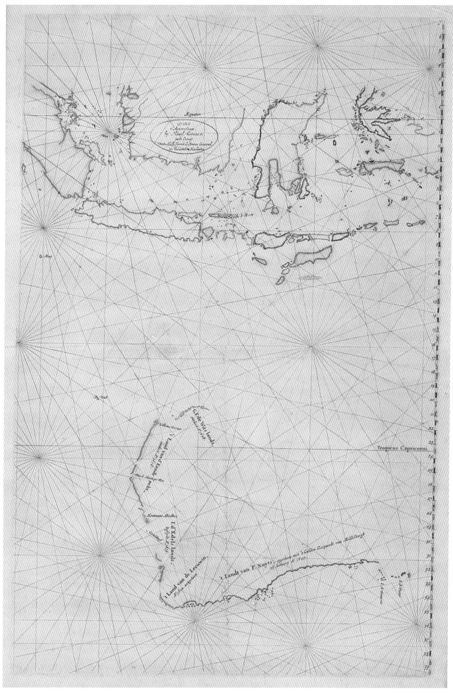

Map of the Malay Archipelago, Hessel Gerritsz, 1628 (National Library of Australia)

20 François Pelsaert and the Wreck of the Batavia, 1629

In October 1628 a fleet of five ships left Amsterdam bound for Batavia. The commander of this fleet was Jacques Specx, a Councillor of the East Indies and later governor-general. It would be the maiden voyage for a recently completed East Indiaman named the *Batavia* which was the pride of the fleet. One of the largest vessels of its day, displacing 1200 tons and measuring 160 feet from stem to stern, it carried 340 people and all the supplies necessary for a six-month voyage. Built with a double oaken hull, she had four decks, three masts and included 30 guns to protect her valuable cargo. For ballast she carried 175 huge sandstone blocks, already carved and decorated, which would form an impressive 25 foot high stone gateway for Kasteel Batavia.

Ariaen Jacobsz, a skilled and experienced captain, was given command. The senior merchant was François Pelsaert, a gifted and well-educated man who had served the VOC since 1618 in Batavia, India and Persia. In their wisdom the VOC always had two masters on the one ship, who could report on the deeds (and usually misdeeds) of each other. Unfortunately, these two men had a difficult history for Pelsaert had returned from India to the Netherlands as a senior merchant on the ship *Dordrecht* captained by none other than Ariaen Jacobsz. The men may not have taken an instant dislike to each other but after Pelsaert, the faithful company man, officially reported the captain for indulging in forbidden private trade there was always going to be bad blood between them.

As senior merchant, François Pelsaert was the commercial agent responsible for ensuring the voyage would be profitable for the directors of the Dutch East India Company and for securing the trading currency of eleven chests of silver bullion and silver dollars worth millions in current value, as well as a casket of jewels, including a giant agate stone standing in a silver gilt frame studded with several jewels and known as the Boudaen Jewel. For this voyage the VOC had hired a deputy merchant named Jeronimus Cornelisz who was being sent to Batavia. A very strange man, he was a former apothecary who had presented himself well to the directors but turned out to be a psychopath needing to leave the Netherlands in a hurry because of his association with immorality, heresy and satanism.

Another reason for conflict between the captain and the senior merchant was Madam Boudewijn van der Mijl. A renowned beauty travelling to join her husband in Batavia with her maid Zwaantje Hendrix, she had become an object of desire and after she refused the advances of Jacobsz he had taken up with her maid while she nursed an increasingly ill François Pelsaert. When the fleet reached the Cape of Good Hope a quarrel broke out between Pelsaert and Jacobsz. For the second time the senior merchant had to reprimand his own captain, this time for his drunken behaviour with Zwaantje in front of the other VOC captains in port. He wrote this report to his superiors in Amsterdam:

> At the Cape of Good Hope the Captain and Jeronimus, taking Zwaantje, went ashore without my knowledge when I had gone inland in search of beasts. Further more they behaved themselves on the yacht *Sardem,* and after that on the ship *Bueren,* in a very unseemly manner, with words as well as deeds so that the captains of these ships felt very obliged to complain about this.

During the Indian Ocean crossing the *Batavia* lost touch with the other ships of the fleet and following the Brouwer Route they had to make their own decision as when to turn north. Obviously they did not heed the words of Frederik de Houtman, who as a warning to other navigators named the Houtman-Abrolhos reefs from the Portuguese phrase *abri vossos olhos* or 'keep your eyes open', a common warning for seamen on watch. For on the night of 4 June 1629, with Ariaen Jacobsz in charge of the night watch, the *Batavia* ran aground on these same reefs. This was a tragedy of huge proportions. It was the maiden voyage of the *Batavia,* a ship that embodied the pride and power of the Dutch East India Company, a ship with 340 people on board and a cargo of silver and jewels worth millions of guilders. As described by François Pelsaert in his journal:

> On the fourth of June [1629], it being Whitmonday, with a light, clear full moon, about two hours before daybreak … I felt the ship's rudder strike the rocks with a violent horrible shock. Upon which the ship's course was forthwith checked by the rocks … I rushed on deck, and found all the sails atop; the wind south-west; our course during the night had been north-east by north, and we were now lying amidst thick foam. Still, at the moment, the breakers round the ship were not violent, but shortly after the sea was heard to run upon us with great vehemence on all sides … When day broke, we found ourselves surrounded by shoals … I saw no land that I thought would remain above water at high tide, except an island, which by estimation was fully three miles from the ship. I therefore sent the skipper to two small islets, in order to ascertain whether our men and part of our cargo could be landed there. About 9 o'clock the skipper returned, informing me that it was well-nigh impossible to get through the shoals, the pinnace running aground in one place, and the water being several fathoms deep in another. As far as he could judge, the islets would remain above water at high tide. Therefore, moved by the loud lamentations raised on board by women, children, sick people, and faint-hearted men, we thought it best first to land the greater part of our people there.

In an attempt to refloat the *Batavia* the mainmast was cut down and the guns were thrown overboard, but the ship was firmly stuck on the reef and with breakers crashing around them there was a danger that it would break up. The ship's sloop managed to transfer the greater part of the crew and passengers, about 180 people, to the larger islet with sufficient food but little water.

The more than 70 men, mostly soldiers and sailors, who remained on the *Batavia* had raided the ship's stores of wine and spirits and were engaged in a last drunken orgy before the vessel would probably break up and sink. The drunken men broke into chests in the great cabin and dressed in the plumed hats and brocades of the 'gentlemen' while conducting a grotesque and desperate final festival. These men had abandoned any hope of survival and as a consequence any respect for authority, and Pelsaert writes:

> Our goodwill and diligence were impeded by the godless unruly troops of soldiers as well as sailors, and their likes whom I could not keep out of the hold on account of the liquor or wine, so that one could not get there, and in the meantime the entire hold became flooded.

In fact the *Batavia* held together for another nine days before she finally tipped into the breakers and those remaining on board, who were probably unable to swim, either drowned or as is the case of Jeronimus Cornelisz managed to float ashore on the wreckage.

Ariaen Jacobsz, François Pelsaert and the ship's senior officers had based themselves on the small islet which was closest to the *Batavia* while they moved people and supplies off the wreck. Pelsaert and Jacobsz knew that their only chance of rescue was to try to sail for Batavia in the longboat, an open boat 30 feet long, sloop rigged and with leeboards in the Dutch fashion. To tell the others of this plan was out of the question, and loaded with 45 people they sailed away at night from the small islet which then became known as Traitor's Island. The initial plan was to search for water but they found little on this dry coast. Pelsaert describes their desperate situation in his journal:

> Seeing that we were now more than 100 miles from those we had left on the island rocks and that up to now we had not found water enough to assist them all, but only so much as would afford two mutchkins daily to ourselves, we were compelled to resolve to do our best in order with God's help to continue our voyage to Batavia as expeditiously as possible, that the Honourable Lord Governor-General might order measures to be taken for the succour of those we had left behind.

They then faced the ordeal of sailing 1800 kilometres in an overloaded open boat without sufficient food or water. It was the sailing skills of Ariaen Jacobsz and the other seamen that brought 45 people including Zwaantje Hendrix and another woman with her baby safely to the Sunda Strait, where they were rescued by a VOC ship and finally reached Batavia on 7 July. Once in the Kasteel Batavia, François Pelsaert confirms that

Ariaen Jacobsz was on the night watch when the *Batavia* ran onto the reefs of the Hout-man-Abrolhos. Jan Pieterszoon Coen would have remembered his own close encounter with a reef off Eendrachtlandt only two years earlier and his warning to the directors of the VOC:

> In the charts the reckonings of our steersmen were still 300 and 350 miles from any land … We would request your worships to direct attention to this point, and have such indications made on the sea charts as experts should find to be advisable; a matter of the highest importance, which if not properly attended to involves grievous peril to ships and crews (which God in his mercy avert).

For his actions Ariaen Jacobsz is flung into a cell and his fate was sealed as the charges against him read:

> Because Ariaen Jacobsz, captain of the wrecked ship *Batavia*, is notorious through allowing himself to be blown away by pure neglect; and also because through his doings a gross evil and public assault has taken place on the same ship of the widow of the late Boudewijn van der Mijl. It has been decided by his Hon. [Coen] and the Council to arrest the mentioned captain and bring him to trial here in order that he may answer those accusations made to his detriment.

A rescue ship needed to be sent as soon as possible and Jan Pieterszoon Coen provided the pinnace *Sardam*, with 25 crew, to rescue the survivors and a team of divers to attempt the salvage of the chests of silver and the casket of precious jewels. Pelsaert departed Batavia on 15 July with the following instructions:

> We thought it proper to discharge in all haste the pinnace *Sardam* and to dispatch her thither to rescue the people in time, to secure as much money and goods of the lost ship as possible and to bring them here. You shall therefore set sail tomorrow in the name of God, and shall hasten your journey with all possible diligence in order to arrive most speedily at the place where you have lost the ship and left the people, being as has been said before, at the latitude 28 ½ degrees southern latitude, called Houtman's Shoals. After you have arrived you shall try and find as many people, money and goods as possible.
>
> Signed by Jan Pieterszoon Coen, Antonio van Diemen and Pieter Valk – Kasteel Batavia.

The *Sardam* had difficulty of finding the wreck site amongst the maze of reefs but on 17 September they sighted East Wallabi Island:

> At daybreak we again weighed anchor with a northerly wind; we were now still about 2 miles from the high island and made for it. When at noon we had got near the island we saw smoke rising up from a long island, two miles to westward of the wreck and also from another islet, close to the wreck, at which we were all of us greatly rejoiced, hoping to find the greater part or almost all the people alive. Therefore, when we had come to anchor, I went in a boat to the highest island, which was quite close to us, taking with me a cask of water, a cask of bread, and a small keg of wine; when I had got there I did not see any one, at which

we were greatly astonished.

Jeronimus Cornelisz, the deputy supercargo, was the last of the *Batavia*'s survivors to reach land when he washed ashore exhausted and half-drowned. As the highest ranked Company official amongst the shipwreck survivors he soon established his authority. He recruited some of the men as his personal guard and they were able to collect and store all the weapons in order to centralise their control over the other survivors. He and his co-conspirators or mutineers then decided that with so many people their water and provisions would soon become scarce and that some, especially the old, the sick and the young, should be eliminated as soon as possible. On the pretence of distributing the survivors more evenly among the small islands, Cornelisz separated groups of passengers and many were murdered as they landed. Pelsaert subsequently determined that after his departure from the wreck site some 120 people had met a terrible death at the hands of Jeronimus Cornelisz and his followers. This group also used their control to force Madam Boudewijn van der Mijl and the younger women to stay with them for their personal pleasure. The preacher, Gijsbert Bastiaensz, had seen his whole family butchered, except for his eldest daughter who had been taken by one of Cornelisz's deputies and he wrote:

> So we all of us together expected to be murdered at any moment, and we besought God continuously for merciful relief … O cruelty! O atrocity of atrocities! They proved themselves to be nothing more than highwaymen. Murderers who are on the roads often take their belongings from people, but they sometimes leave them their lives; but these have taken both, goods and blood.

Cornelisz particularly wanted to get rid of a group of soldiers who had grouped around a natural leader called Wiebbe Hayes and he had them dropped on West Wallabi Island without food or weapons. Contrary to his expectations they found natural wells filled with fresh water and were able to live off seabirds and small marsupials. The soldiers erected a walled enclosure of stone and after successfully defending themselves against attacks by the Cornelisz mutineers had recently been able to capture Jeronimus Cornelisz himself. On sighting the arrival of the *Sardam,* Wiebbe Hayes paddled as fast as he could to reach the vessel and inform François Pelsaert of the horrors that had transpired since he had departed from Traitor's Island.

From his interrogations and their own confessions Pelsaert learned that Cornelisz and his men had drowned, murdered and brought to death with all manner of cruelty, more than 120 persons, men, women and children. The principal murderers were Jeronimus Cornelisz, Lenet Michaelsz van Os, Mattys Beer, Jan Hendricxsz, Allert Janssen,

The murderers attacking the other survivors on the island, Jan Jansz, 1647
(Australian National Maritime Museum)

Rutger Fredricx, Jan Pelgrom de Bye, Wouter Loos and Andries Jonas. Pelsaert wrote in his journal:

> Such a scoundrel, the cause of so many disasters and of the shedding of human blood – and still he had the intention to go on … I examined him in the presence of the Sardam's council, and asked him why he allowed the devil to lead him so far astray from all human feeling, to do that which had never been so cruelly perpetrated among Christians, without any real hunger or need of thirst, but solely out of bloodthirstiness.

François Pelsaert quickly dealt with the conspirators and the ship's council sentenced eight of the murderers to be hanged on makeshift gallows erected on Seal Island. Pelsaert read out Cornelisz' sentence, which was the maximum penalty available under Dutch law:

> We, the undersigned persons of the Council … in order to turn us from the wrath of God

and to cleanse the name of Christianity of such an unheard of villain, have sentenced the foresaid Jeronimus Cornelisz that he shall be taken a place prepared to execute justice, and there first cut off both hands, and after that punish him on a gallows with a cord until death follows.

It was decided that two young men, Wouter Loos and Jan Pelgrom de By, who were only seventeen years old, should be provided with food and arms and be marooned on the mainland near the mouth of the Murchison River. They were never seen again but might be considered Australia's first European residents. In the instructions given to them they were ordered to collect as much material as possible about the country and its people:

> Whereto you are being given by the Commander some toys, as well as knives, beads, bells and small mirrors of which you shall give to the blacks … Having become known to them, if they will then take you into their villages to their chief men, have courage to go with them willingly. Men's luck is found in strange places; if God guards you, then you will not suffer any damage from them, but on the contrary, because they have never seen any white men, they will honour you with all friendship.

The other important task was to salvage the money chests that had sunk with the *Batavia*. The divers had already done their work and ten of the eleven chests were recovered. The eleventh chest was found but was wedged amongst the rocks and could not be brought to the surface. For Pelsaert this was an immense relief for the recovery of the money chests would hopefully save his reputation. The yacht *Sardam* sailed from these luckless and ill-fated islands on 15 November and returned to Batavia on 5 December together with what could be salvaged from the wreck and as written by Anthony van Diemen:

> The 5th of this month returns here to anchor from the Southland the yacht *Sardam*, bringing with them 74 souls from the wrecked ship *Batavia* together with 10 chests of cash, amongst them the chest No. 33 with 9 sacks of ducats. The chest with jewels to the value of 58,000 guilders and some wrought silverwork … Thanks to the Almighty for this, as we would not have expected it to come out so well.

An interesting sidelight of the survivors' stay on West Wallabi Island was their reliance on wallabies for food and they had plenty of time to examine the habits of these unusual creatures, from which we have the first detailed description of these uniquely Australian marsupials:

> Besides, we found in these islands large numbers of a species of cats, which are very strange creatures; they are about the size of a hare, their head resembling the head of a civet-cat; the forepaws are very short, about the length of a finger, on which the animal has five small

nails or fingers, resembling those of a monkey's forepaw. Its two hind-legs, on the contrary, are upwards of half an ell in length, and it walks on these only, on the flat of the heavy part of the leg, so that it does not run fast. Its tail is very long, like that of a long-tailed monkey; if it eats, it sits on its hind-legs, and clutches its food with its forepaws, just like a squirrel or monkey. Their manner of generation or procreation is exceedingly strange and highly worth observing. Below the belly the female carries a pouch, into which you may put your hand; inside this pouch are her nipples, and we have found that the young ones grow up in this pouch with the nipples in their mouths. We have seen some young ones lying there, which were only the size of a bean, though at the same time perfectly proportioned, so that it seems certain that they grow there out of the nipples of the mammae, from which they draw their food, until they are grown up and are able to walk. Still, they keep creeping into the pouch even when they have become very large, and the mother runs off with them, when they are hunted.

When François Pelsaert returned to Batavia with the survivors his reception was not particularly enthusiastic. Ariaen Jacobsz had been put to death but somehow Pelsaert was also held responsible for the wreck of the *Batavia* and the subsequent deaths of so many people. His career with the VOC was effectively over and he did not get the position of councillor, which had been promised when he left Amsterdam. Mentally and physically broken, his life ended only one year later, without him ever returning to the Netherlands.

21 Anthony van Diemen as Governor-General, 1636

Anthony van Diemen's return to the Netherlands from Batavia in 1631 was short lived because almost immediately the VOC began pressuring him to re-enter their service. In March 1632 they invited him to attend a board meeting held in the Zeeland town of Middelburg. At this meeting the directors told van Diemen they had decided to recall Jacques Specx from Batavia because they were not entirely satisfied with his performance as governor-general. Specx would be replaced with Hendrik Brouwer, the same person who had pioneered the southerly route to the East Indies twenty years earlier. The directors then asked van Diemen whether he would be prepared to return to the Indies as director-general on the understanding he would succeed Hendrick Brouwer as governor-general upon the expiration of his three-year term.

This was an offer too good to refuse and in November that year van Diemen left the Netherlands on the flagship *Amsterdam* as commander of a fleet of three vessels sailing for Batavia together with his wife Maria and a few of their relatives. In the journal van Diemen kept on this voyage, he carefully recorded the weather conditions encountered, the squadron's position and all occurrences of significance. He described in detail the inauspicious start of the voyage. For several weeks the ships battled contrary gale-force winds in the North Sea, forcing them to seek shelter first in Zeeland and later at the Isle of Wight. It was not until mid-February 1633 that weather conditions had improved sufficiently for the fleet to head out into the Atlantic Ocean. For the rest of the voyage they enjoyed favourable winds and the fleet sailed rapidly down the Atlantic, passing the Cape of Good Hope in mid-May before heading south into the Indian Ocean. Conscious of how he had almost been shipwrecked on his first voyage across the Southern Ocean eighteen years earlier, van Diemen offered a reward of four pieces of eight (about ten guilders) to the first sailor aboard his fleet to sight new land, a reward that was to be increased to six pieces of eight if the discovery was made after nightfall. And, indeed, on 20 June 1633 an island came into view that did not appear on any of their charts. Clearly fascinated by this discovery, van Diemen spent some time circumnavigating this uninhabited volcanic island and making sketches of it in his journal. Van Diemen could claim to have discovered this remote island in the southern Indian Ocean and he named it after his flagship *Amsterdam*, a name which the now French-controlled island bears to this day.

In Batavia, Anthony van Diemen continued his good work and Governor-General Brouwer wrote in his report to the directors in January 1635 that van Diemen's help was invaluable:

> The afore-mentioned Mr van Diemen is very industrious, extremely observant, an enemy of sloth and indolence, friendly, honourable, respectable, and effectively able to manage all things, so that Your Honours have in him a servant of distinction.

Anthony van Diemen as Governor-General, Dirk Jongman (Rijksmuseum)

Accordingly, when Brouwer's three-year term ended he stepped down as governor-general to be succeeded by Anthony van Diemen, who was formally sworn in on the first day of January 1636. The following nine years that he served as governor-general were extremely important for the commercial success of the Dutch East India Company. He devoted much of his energy to expanding the power of the VOC throughout South-East Asia and under his rule they were able to defeat the Portuguese both in Sri Lanka and in Malacca.

In 1635 France entered the Thirty Years War against Spain and blocked the overland supply lines which allowed Spain to resupply their Army of Flanders in the southern provinces. The Spanish were forced to resupply their army by sea through Dunkirk and in the following years Spanish fleets had managed to reach Dunkirk without being spotted by Dutch naval squadrons. However, in 1639 a Dutch fleet commanded by Admiral Maarten Tromp sighted in the English Channel a Spanish fleet consisting of 77 galleons with 13,000 troops which was attempting to reach Dunkirk. Tromp's fleet of twelve ships waited for Admiral De Witt to arrive with five more ships before attacking on 17 September. Despite his numerical inferiority Tromp got the upper hand in a running fight which lasted into the night. The next day Commodore Joost Banckert arrived to reinforce the Dutch with twelve more ships and fighting continued until the Spanish were decisively defeated in what was to become known as the Battle of the Downs.

This crushing defeat and the inability to support their army forced Spain to relinquish any idea of the re-conquest of the United Provinces. Tromp's epic victory removed any Spanish naval threat to the Netherlands and earned the Hollanders the reputation of being the leading naval power in Europe. This important change in the balance of power meant that the United Provinces could now deploy their ships from fighting the Spanish in Europe to fighting the Portuguese in Asia.

In 1635 King Rajasingha, the ruler of the Kandian Kingdom of Sri Lanka, invited the Dutch East India Company to join with him to force the Portuguese off the island. On the promise of a monopoly over the cinnamon trade, Anthony van Diemen and the Council of the Indies in Batavia agreed to comply with this request and in 1637 they sent four ships to the island. On 4 January 1638 a decisive sea engagement took place between Portuguese and Dutch naval forces in which the Portuguese fleet was decimated. Following that victory Admiral Adam Westerwolt decided to attack the Portuguese fort at Batticaloa on the east coast of Sri Lanka and together with strong Singhalese forces he conquered the fort on 18 May. Admiral Westerwolt, in the name of the States General, his Highness Prince Frederik Hendrik and the Dutch East India Company, then signed a new treaty with King Rajasingha. After concluding this alliance the Dutch drove the Portuguese from the ports of Negombo and Galle in the south of the island which then gave them access to valuable cinnamon producing hinterlands and for the next eighteen years Galle would remain the centre of Dutch power in Sri Lanka.

The VOC still needed to preserve their self-declared monopoly over the clove trade in the Moluccas and in 1638 Anthony van Diemen led a large-scale naval expedition to the Spice Islands, and through a combination of military force and shrewd negotiation he succeeded in extending Dutch control over the clove islands. However, minor trade still continued outside the Dutch monopoly and cloves were being smuggled to Macassar, Manila and Portuguese Timor, because these markets were offering twice the price that the Dutch were.

Ambon and its surrounding islands, Haruku, Saparua and Nusa Laut, were now the only ones where the Dutch allowed cloves to grow in any quantity. These islands produced an estimated annual crop of two million kilograms of cloves, there being about 500,000 trees, each easily producing four kilograms of cloves. The Dutch East India

Company was able to sell cloves in Amsterdam for 25 times the contract price paid in Ambon and attempted to balance production with world demand in order to keep prices high. Sometimes drastic measures needed to be taken and the most fragrant scent would spread over all of Amsterdam as the VOC was burning a huge quantity of cloves to reduce an oversupply on the market.

It was in 1640 that Anthony van Diemen and the Council of the Indies made the decision to capture Malacca on the Malay Peninsula and he wrote:

> We have from time to time seriously considered the capture of Malacca from the Portuguese, our hereditary enemies, not only for the expansion of trade, but to strengthen our influence and prestige over the neighbouring monarchs and princes.

A Dutch delegation was sent from Batavia to the Sultan of Johor to enlist his support. The heir to the lost throne of Malacca was soon fully committed to support the VOC in their plans to capture the city and he signed a document etched on gold paper allying himself with the Dutch East India Company. Their written agreement called for their mutual cooperation for the conquest of Malacca and the removal of their common enemy, the Portuguese. It was also agreed that on upon the successful capture of Malacca, its town and fortress would be controlled by the VOC, while all the surrounding territory would be controlled by the Sultan of Johor. Importantly, the treaty required each party to respect the other's religion, a condition inserted by the Sultan who had endured the Portuguese intolerance of Islam and the expulsion of Muslim traders from Malacca.

The VOC amassed forces off Batavia in readiness for their third attempt to capture Portuguese Malacca. The fort in Malacca known as *A Famosa* was immensely strong with thick walls and defensive bastions. Considered impregnable, it had over 100 heavy cannon and an ample supply of gunpowder to defend itself. After the arrival of the Dutch fleet off Malacca in June 1640, a half-moon formation of twelve ships and six boats blockaded the town and an almost continuous artillery duel commenced between the protagonists. The Dutch estimated they fired 40,000 cannon balls against the fort but were still unable to force an entry through its massive walls. At the end of July a fleet of 40 boats and 1500 men sent by the Sultan of Johore arrived and their combined forces attempted to storm the fortress by land. There was still no way to force an entry through its massive walls and the Dutch were forced to lay siege to the fort in what was to become a war of attrition. The siege lasted five months and twelve days before the Portuguese surrendered. The toll was enormous and it was estimated that 8000 citizens and soldiers of Malacca died from injuries or starvation, as well as 1500 Dutch soldiers and their allies from Johor.

The news of the final capture of Malacca was received with jubilation at Company headquarters in Batavia and a report reads:

> Thus falls into our hands this important fortress generally recognised as impregnable, with all its cannon and war materials. Henceforth it will be under the rule of the States General of the Free United Netherlands and his Royal Highness the Prince of Orange. Further it will be considered private territory and a dominion of the United East India Company.

After the capture of Malacca, Anthony van Diemen was only prevented from capturing Goa and the headquarters of the tottering Portuguese Estado da India by the signing of a ten-year Portuguese–Dutch truce. He reluctantly obeyed his orders from the Gentlemen Seventeen but looked forward to its expiration and the renewal of the war against 'that perfidious nation', writing:

> The Portuguese in Goa are completely powerless, so that it seems the right time has come to throw them out of Asia altogether, which would be an incredible advantage for the Company.

Having driven the Portuguese out of Sri Lanka and Malacca and succeeding in building a Dutch seaborne empire across Asia, Anthony van Diemen could now turn his attention to the exploration of the lands south of the East Indies. The unexpected encounter with a perceived island off the coast of Eendrachtlandt 30 years earlier by the young 'Thoisz Meeuwisz van Utrecht', also known as Anthony van Diemen, may have begun his interest in exploring the South Land.

By this time the Dutch had assembled an intriguing jigsaw puzzle of the land or lands to the south of Java. The west coast of Cape York had been mapped but was this part of Nova Guinea or of the South Land? Parts of the west coast of Western Australia had been charted and named Eendrachtlandt, the south coast of Western Australia had been charted between Cape Leeuwin and the Nuyts Archipelago off South Australia and named Nuytsland. Were these discoveries a series of islands or were they joined together into a single continent?

22 Gerrit Pool and the Voyage of the Klein Amsterdam and the Wessel, 1636

Upon becoming Governor-General, van Diemen wasted little time in organising the first voyage of exploration he would send to the South Land. On 19 February 1636, just a few weeks after he had been sworn in he issued a set of detailed instructions to Commander Gerrit Pool, whom he had appointed to lead the expedition:

In as much as for a long time past the 'Heeren Majores' have been very constantly recommending to us the discovery of the South-land, and still continue to do so, and we have frequently discussed the matter with Hendrick Brouwer even before his departure, therefore it has been resolved and determined in the Council of India that you shall be employed with the yachts *Klein Amsterdam* and *Wessel* in the said discovery of the lands east of Banda and of the South-land extending to westward. The men of the yachts *Pera* and *Arnhem* have, as before mentioned, sailed along this coast from about 4 degrees to 17 degrees 8 minutes, and have landed at various places, where they found nothing but barren coasts and lands, and utterly barbarian, cruel, wild natives, who surprised nine of our men fishing, and assassinated the same. The various strands, rivers, bays, points and the trend of this coast you will gather from the chart aforesaid.

From the farthest point they discovered, which as before mentioned, is in Lat.17° 8' South, you will skirt the coast as far as Houtmans-Abrolhos in 28 and 29 degrees, and farther still, if your provisions hold out, if the condition of your crews will allow of it, and if your Yachts are proof against the rough seas that prevail in the Southern Ocean in 33 and 34 degrees; after which you will return to Batavia through Sunda Strait, trying in passing to touch at the Triall Rocks, that further information about this rock and its situation may in this way be obtained …

Commander Francisco Pelsaert, having in 1629 put ashore there two Dutch delinquents, who had in due form of justice been sentenced to forfeit their lives, you will grant passage to the said persons, if they should be alive to show themselves and should they request you to be brought hither.

It would be a thing highly desirable for ships bound from the Netherlands to the East Indies, if on the coast of the South-land between 26 and 28 degrees a fitting place for obtaining refreshments and fresh water could be discovered, seeing that mainly about that latitude scorbut [scurvy] and other disorders begin to show themselves, at times carrying off numbers of men even before they reach Batavia.

Done in Kasteel Batavia, this 19th of February, A.D. 1636.

(Signed)

Anthony van Diemen, Philip Lucasz, Artus Gysels and Jan van der Burch.

Van Diemen's aim was to follow the voyage made by the vessels *Pera* and *Arnhem* over a decade earlier by continuing the survey of the coast westward from the Gulf of Carpentaria. The interest of the directors of the VOC in the stranded *Batavia* criminals was in the hope they would have acquired valuable information about the resources of the red continent and its inhabitants. Captains were told to search for these two men in instructions for later voyages but nothing seems to have been heard of them. However, in 1697 the Dutch explorer Willem de Vlamingh found a well-made clay hut by Wittecarra Spring, built in a different style to those usually found in the area that could have been constructed by the abandoned Dutchmen.

After leaving Banda, Gerrit Pool reached the south coast of Papua whereupon he followed along the coast in a south-easterly direction as done by the prior expeditions. On 29 April when Pool had reached the mouth of a substantial river he decided to make landfall, a decision that was to have the most disastrous consequences both for himself and for the expedition he was leading. Despite the tragedies of the two previous expeditions on the Papuan coast and the specific warning from the Council of the Indies in his sailing orders, Gerrit Pool headed for the shore in the boat of the *Klein Amsterdam*. He landed on the beach with ten men, three of whom were armed with muskets, and they proceeded towards a hut situated on the shore when a large crowd of warriors suddenly appeared out of the forest. The ship's merchant Pieter Pietersz recorded in his journal the events that followed:

> Unexpectedly, as many as one hundred savages emerged from the forest and rushed towards the landing party. They were black of skin, like the Kaffirs of Angola; they were taller, bigger and of more powerful build than the Europeans; they had long, black hair that reached over their shoulders; they were completely naked, except that their private parts were more or less covered. Their weapons consisted of throwing spears, assegais with iron tips and

bows and arrows. Even though the musketeers fired at them, they continued to rush forward like mad people, uttering frightful screams. The spears, assegais and arrows fell like hail upon the little group so that they were forced to seek refuge in the boat. Turning around, Commander Pool tried to reach the boat, but on account of the loose sand on the beach he tripped two or three times, allowing one of the savages to catch up with him and stab him in the back with an assegai. The same happened to Merchant Schiller, of the yacht *Wessel*. After he had been hit, Pool cried out to his people: 'Go, go, save yourselves!' But these were the last words he uttered, for the savages were now upon him. One of them took away his sabre and used it to hack him into pieces, whereupon others took hold of these pieces and ran off into the forest.

Later in the day, the ship's council met in order to review these dramatic events and to decide on a course of action. At this meeting, it was resolved that merchant Pieter Pietersz would take over command of the expedition and that the river where the incident had occurred be known as 'Moordenaars Rivier' (Murderer's River). Though the council decided to continue their voyage, the death of Pool and the others was a severe blow to the prospects of a successful expedition. The loss so early in the voyage of the expedition's commander, of the man best able to motivate the crews, must have been extremely demoralising for those who remained.

The *Klein Amsterdam* and *Wessel*, now under the command of Pieter Pietersz, resumed their course along the south New Guinea coast. A few days later, on 6 May, the two ships decided to turn west and make for the Aru Islands which seemed to be a popular port of call for Dutch ships. After briefly exploring this island group (or to have a good time of it there?), they sailed south towards the Gulf of Carpentaria. However, all attempts to beat south were frustrated by strong gales which drove the little ships towards Arnhem Land. On 13 July, when the two ships had reached the latitude of 11 degrees, land was sighted to both the east and the west. They had reached what is now known as the Dundas Strait, with the Cobourg Peninsula to the east and Melville Island to the west. Sailing along the east and north coast of what is now known as Melville Island, Pietersz saw land that he described as chiefly level, thickly covered with trees, and with a sandy beach. But even though Pietersz made landfall at several places, it proved impossible to make contact with the indigenous people. There was no sign of human habitation, except for the great clouds of smoke further inland, which Pietersz saw billowing in many places. Still, there were no fruit trees, houses, vessels or natives and the land seemed to be quite wild.

On 21 June, when the expedition had reached the north-western point of Melville Island, Pietersz again called a ship's council. At this meeting it was decided that the lands be known as Van Diemen's Land, a name that today survives in the name of Cape van Diemen for Melville Island's north-western point and the Van Diemen Gulf for the waters enclosed by the Cobourg Peninsula and Melville Island. At this point he decided:

> To abandon further investigation in the east and to explore the newly discovered Van Die-men's Land, also called Arnhem or Speult-land and after one had explored this and obtained the necessary knowledge to set course again northward to get accurate information about the islands of Timor and Timor Laut [Tanimbar].

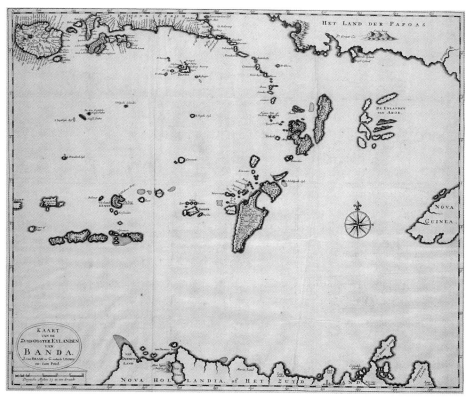

Map showing Nova Hollandia and the Zuyt Land, 1724, François Valentyn
(Koninklijke Bibliotheek)

These were new discoveries; however, Pietersz had no idea that the hinterland of the Coburg Peninsula belonged to a continent, and he was ignorant of the insular character of Melville Island. It was further decided that, in view of the manifest wildness and barrenness of the country, the impossibility or unwillingness to make contact with its people and with dwindling provisions, there was no alternative but to discontinue the expedition. Accordingly, on 22 June, Pietersz set a north-westerly course towards Timor and after briefly reconnoitring the Timor coast he returned to Fort Nassau in the Banda Islands, where he arrived on 7 July 1636 before proceeding to Ambon and Batavia.

In Batavia, van Diemen was understandably disappointed with the results of this voyage. From a commercial point of view the expedition had been an abject failure. Nothing of value to the Company had been discovered and the voyage had not yielded any new trading opportunities; no new products had been discovered; no gold or silver mines had been found. From a geographical standpoint the results had been minimal as the expedition had failed to explore the full extent of the Gulf of Carpentaria or sail as far south as the Houtman-Abrolhos. These failures were probably related to a lack of leadership after the tragic death of Gerrit Pool, meaning that none of van Diemen's expectations had been achieved other than the discovery of a small part of the north Australian coast that would eventually be added to the Tasman Map.

23 Abel Tasman and the Voyage of the Heemskerck and Zeehaen, Van Diemen's Land, 1642

Abel Janszoon Tasman was born in 1603 at Lutjegast near Groningen in the northern Netherlands. From when he was a young boy listening to heroic tales of the 'Sea-Beggars', those romantic heroes who began the liberation of the Northern Provinces from Spanish control, he was destined for a life at sea. The Sea Beggars were Dutch privateers or pirates, led by a succession of daring leaders, who plundered Spanish shipping. They sought refuge in English ports where they were able to refit, replenish their stores and share sea stories with their fellow English pirates who were supported by Queen Elizabeth. However, in 1572 the Queen abruptly refused to admit the Sea Beggars to her harbours. No longer having a refuge, they made a daring attack upon the port of Brielle in the southern Netherlands, which they captured by surprise on 1 April 1572. Encouraged by this success and no longer Sea Beggars but now Protestant Rebels, they then seized Vlissingen at the mouth of the Scheldt River which allows access to the port of Antwerp. The sudden capture of these two Spanish-controlled ports prompted the Northern Provinces to join in a general revolt against the Spanish and is regarded as the beginning of Dutch independence.

Abel Tasman's name first appears in the Amsterdam city records with the proclamation of his second marriage, in December 1631, to Jannetje Tjaerts aged 21, which describes him as a common sailor and widower. His first record of service with the Dutch East India Company was as first mate of the *Weesp* sailing from Batavia to Ambon in 1634 and then returning with a cargo of cloves and nutmeg. Later that year and now captain of the *Mocha*, he was patrolling the seas around Ambon and engaging in skirmishes with Moluccans attempting to smuggle cloves to the port of Macassar. The VOC records show that during a visit ashore to barter for supplies, two of Tasman's men

The plaque erected by the Tasmanian government in honour of Abel Tasman at Lutjegast

were killed and three others wounded by natives on the island of Ceram. Thus from his early years with the VOC Abel Tasman had risen from a common sailor to the captain of a trading vessel as a result of his skills learned at sea and his ability to take command.

Having been absent from the Netherlands and his wife for four years he returned to Amsterdam in late 1636 as senior officer on the *Banda* which sailed from Batavia loaded with valuable spices from the Moluccas. It was after his return that the Company ruled that senior officers would be permitted to take their wives to Batavia if they signed a ten-year contract. This suited Tasman and he returned to Batavia in April 1638 as skipper of the *Engel* accompanied by his wife and daughter.

This elegant seventeenth-century portrait of the Tasman family is believed to have been painted in 1637 by Dutch artist Jacob Gerritsz Cuyp before the family left for Batavia. It portrays Abel Tasman with his second wife, Jannetje Tjaerts, and his daughter from his first marriage, Claesgen. The arrangement of the three figures is symbolic. Abel Tasman points towards a globe and the East Indies, as if introducing himself to the viewer as an experienced sailing captain, while his wife passes an apple to her stepdaughter, representing the transfer of knowledge from maturity to youth.

The following year Tasman sailed from Batavia as part of an expedition in search of two islands believed to abound in silver and gold lying east of Japan. These islands did

Abel Tasman and family, Jacob Gerritsz Cuyp, 1637 (National Library of Australia)

not exist, nothing was found, and the expedition returned to Batavia in 1640 ravaged by scurvy. Tasman then made a trading voyage as captain of the *Oostcappel* with a fleet sailing to Formosa, to Cambodia and then to Formosa again. On the second voyage to Formosa his three vessels were savaged by storms, Tasman and his ship survived, even with a broken mast and a hold full of water, but the rest of the fleet was never seen again.

Anthony van Diemen had maintained his interest in the concept of Terra Australis and he asked Francois Visscher, the Compagnie's chief geographer and cartographer in the Indies, to draw up plans for a voyage of discovery to the Southern Ocean. Visscher's proposal dated 22 January 1642, stated:

> An expedition should leave Batavia about the middle of August in order to take advantage of the long summer days in the southern latitudes. The ships should proceed to Mauritius, where water, firewood, and other necessities could be taken on, thence south to the parallels of 51 to 54 degrees latitude and then steer east till they reach the longitude of the east end of

Nova Guinea or of the Solomon Islands. They should then turn north and return to Batavia by the north coast of these islands.

On 1 August 1642 Anthony van Diemen and the Council of the East Indies formally signed the resolution to send an expedition in search of Terra Australis Incognita or the 'Known but Undiscovered South Land':

> Since our predecessors the Lords Governor-General Jan Pieterszoon Coen (deceased), Pieter de Carpentier, Henrick Brouwer and ourselves, pending their administration and ours, have been greatly inclined to forward the navigation to the partly known and still unexplored South and East land, in order to the direct discovery of the same, and to the consequent opening up of important countries or leastwise of convenient routes to well-known opulent markets, in such fashion that the same might in due time be used for the improvement and increase of the Company's general prosperity.
>
> Nevertheless up to this time no Christian kings, princes or commonwealth have seriously endeavoured to make timely discovery of the remaining unknown part of the terrestrial globe, although there are good reasons to suppose that it contains many excellent and fertile regions, seeing that it lies in the frigid, temperate and torrid zones, so that it must needs compromise well-populated districts in favourable climates and under propitious skies … there must be similar fertile and rich regions south of the Equator, of which matter we have conspicuous examples and clear proofs in the gold and silver bearing provinces of Peru, Chile, Monomtapa or Sofala … so that it may be confidently expected that the expense and trouble that must be bestowed in the eventual discovery of so large a portion of the world, will be rewarded with certain fruits of material profit and immortal fame.

From this document it seems the Dutch now believed in a south-land which was the seemingly worthless Eendrachtlandt discovered by Dirk Hartog and others, and an east-land which was the fabulously wealthy Terra Australis which some believed had almost been discovered by Quiros and Le Maire. If van Diemen had wanted to continue exploration of the South Land he would have extended the voyage of François Thijssen and the *Gulden Zeepaard* along the south coast of Australia and discovered Bass Strait and the east coast of Australia. However, if there were riches to be found in the known but undiscovered Terra Australis then Anthony van Diemen wanted to be the man to do it and his idea to organise a major voyage of discovery towards the Pacific and the contribution it made to geographical knowledge would become his most enduring legacy.

Abel Tasman was named as commander of this new expedition and was able to choose from among the ablest seafarers in the Batavia roadstead to man his two vessels, the flagship *Heemskerck* with 60 crew and an armed transport ship the *Zeehaen* with 50 crew. François Visscher who had planned the voyage was appointed pilot-major and commander of the *Zeehaen*. Isaac Gilsemans was appointed merchant or supercargo and sailed on that same vessel. Tasman began his journal of their voyage with these words:

Journal or description drawn up by me, Abel Janszoon Tasman, of a voyage made from the town of Batavia in East India for the discovery of the unknown south land in the year of our Lord 1642, the 14th of August. May God Almighty vouchsafe His blessing on this work. Amen

In August 1642 the *Heemskerck* and the *Zeehaen* passed through the Sunda Strait and headed west into the Indian Ocean and towards Mauritius, where the ships came to anchor off Fort Frederick Hendrik on 5 September. Here repairs were carried out to the ships' riggings and hulls in preparation for the long voyage ahead. While this work was in progress, Tasman sent parties of men ashore to fetch water, cut wood and hunt the abundant feral goats and pigs, to supplement their food supply.

With all these tasks completed, the expedition set sail on 8 October and headed far south to explore the uncharted Southern Ocean. Again their instructions from Batavia were quite specific:

> Set sail from Mauritius, shaping your course with the trade-wind nearly southward … until you get into the western trade-wind, with which you will sail until you come upon the unknown South-land, or as far as South Latitude 52 or 54 degrees inclusive; and if in this latitude you should not discover any land, you will set your course due east, and sail on until you get into the longitude of the eastern point of Nova Guinea or the Solomon Islands, situated in about 220 degrees longitude, or until you should meet with land; and when this is the case, whether in the beginning or afterwards when you have sailed more to the eastwards, you will sail further east to get a better passage from the Indian Ocean and to prepare the way by which to find … a short passage to Chile.

The South latitude of 52 or 54 degrees is significant because it is equivalent to that of the Strait of Magellan. The discovery of a southerly route to Chile was important because there were rumours that that the citizens in Chile and Peru wanted to free themselves from the Spanish trading monopoly and were interested in direct trade with the Dutch in the East Indies, which would mean that the main trading currency, Spanish silver dollars, could come directly across the Pacific without first being shipped to Europe and then on to the East Indies.

The small fleet sailed as far south as 49 degrees where they experienced, recurrent fog, constant high seas, periodic storms, plus squalls of hail and snow. Making the situation even worse were the giant pursuing waves. Every time one of these slammed into the port or starboard quarter they lifted the stern of the vessels, which would roll heavily like lumbering elephants amid a churning mass of white foam. At the same time a bitterly cold spray rose from the bow of the vessel chilling the bones of the already soaked crewmen on deck. According to the Tasman journal:

> We had a storm from the west with hail and snow, and ran on before the wind with our fore-

sail barely halfway up the mast; the sea ran very high and our men began to suffer badly from the severe cold.

The ship's council decided to move north where they expected conditions were more moderate. On 7 November 1642, François Visscher confirmed this decision with written advice to Abel Tasman:

> We should stay at the 44 degrees south Latitude, until we have passed the 150th degree of Longitude, and then run north as far as the 40th degree south Latitude, remaining there with an easterly course, until we have reached the 220th degree Longitude.

The *Heemskerck* and the *Zeehaen* were sailing far south of the voyage that the *Gulden Zeepaard* had taken along the Australian Bight, where the southern coast was almost always visible in the distance. They were sailing where no men had sailed before and with no knowledge of what hazards lay before them. You can imagine the trepidation that Tasman and the crew felt as the cold winds and waves of the Roaring Forties pushed them into completely uncharted seas. Their long nights would have been full of the nightmares of being suddenly dashed against unknown rocky shores before being plunged into freezing waters to die a cold and lonely death. On 17 November Tasman writes that:

> In the morning before the serving of breakfast we saw a good deal of rockweed and manna-grass drifting by. Therefore I had the flag flown whereupon the officers of the *Zeehaen* came aboard our ship. I convened the council and at the meeting we considered the instructions from the Governor-General and Councillors of India concerning sightings and being aware of land, shoals, blind rocks, etc. Members of the council were questioned on the merits of observing such signs of land by keeping a man constantly at the masthead to keep a lookout for land, shoals, blind rocks, and other dangers and we also discussed what should be fixed as a reward for sightings. So the council approved the plan to have a man constantly on the look-out and the man who first sights land, shoals, blind rocks, etc., shall be rewarded with three reals of eight and a canne of arrack.

The rockweed might be a sign they were close to land and four weeks later, in the late afternoon of 24 November, and thankfully still in daylight, they sighted distant mountains. An overnight storm could dash them onto this unknown coast and they prudently decided to run out to sea until the next day:

> We were on a latitude of 42 degree 25 minutes and a longitude of 163 degrees 31 minutes, the course was held northeast and we sailed thirty miles; the wind from the south-west, later from the south with a gentle topsail breeze; in the afternoon about 4 o'clock we saw land to the north-east of us some 10 miles away; it was very high-lying land; towards the evening we saw again three high mountains in the east-south-east and in the north-east also two mountains which were not as high as those in the south … it was unanimously resolved to

run out to sea at the expiration of three sand glasses, to keep doing so for the space of ten sand glasses, and after this to make for the land again.

The land they sighted was the west coast of Tasmania near Macquarie Harbour. Before them were mountains clothed with dark forest and those they sighted were subsequently named Mount Heemskerck and Mount Zeehaen in their honour by the British explorer Mathew Flinders. On 25 November Tasman's journal records:

> This land being the first land we have met with in the South Sea and as it has not yet been known to any European we called it Anthony van Diemen's Land, in honour of the Governor-General, our illustrious master, who sent us out to make this discovery. The islands round about, as many as were known to us, we have named after the Honourable Councillors of India.

These islands on the south coast of Tasmania still have the names of De Wit, Sweers and Maatsuyker, the members of the Council of the Indies who had signed their sailing orders. The fleet rounded the most southern part of Van Diemen's Land and on 29 November the expedition approached what looked like a likely anchorage. The journal records:

> In the evening about 5 o'clock we came before a bay which seemed likely to afford a good anchorage, upon which we resolved with our ship's council to run into it, as may be seen from today's resolution; we had nearly got into the bay when there arose so strong a gale that we were obliged to take in sail and to run out to sea again under reduced sail, seeing that it was impossible to come to anchor in such a storm; in the evening we resolved to stand out to sea during the night under reduced sail to avoid being thrown on a lee-shore by the violence of the wind.

Storm Bay has retained the name given by Abel Tasman and by daybreak they found they were far offshore. After rounding South Cape (Cape Pillar) and Tasman Island they sailed north-west and on 1 December entered a wide sheltered bay they named Frederick Hendrik Bay after Prince Frederick of Nassau, the head of the Dutch Republic:

> In the afternoon we hoisted the white flag upon which our friends of the *Zeehaen* came on board of us, with whom we resolved that it would be best and most expedient, wind and weather permitting, to touch at the land the sooner the better, both to get better acquainted with its condition and to attempt to procure refreshments for our own behalf … about one hour after sunset we dropped anchor in a good harbour, in 22 fathom, white and grey fine sand, a naturally drying bottom; for all which it behoves us to thank God Almighty with grateful hearts.

The expedition had been at sea for 55 days since they left Mauritius and in the morning of 2 December two boats went ashore to search for water, firewood and what else may be available there. Visscher was in charge of the pinnace from the *Heemskerck,* and was accompanied by the cock-boat from the *Zeehaen*. Both boats had musketeers on board, and the rowers were armed with pikes and side arms. They were gone the whole day and in the evening they delivered an account of their exploration to the ship's council:

> The land was high, level and covered with vegetation (not cultivated, but growing naturally by the will of God). There was good timber but the water they found wasn't deep enough to fill barrels, because the watercourse was so shallow that the water could be dipped with bowls only. This was impracticable in view of the amount of water they needed to bring aboard.

They did not see any native people during their visit but they heard sounds resembling a trumpet or a little gong, which they thought came from humans but which could equally have been bird sounds. They did, however, note physical evidence of the presence of people:

> They saw two trees about 2 to 2 ½ fathoms thick and measuring 60 to 65 feet to the lowest branches and the bark of those trees was peeled off and they were notched with flint stones (to climb up and rob the nests of birds above) to form steps five feet apart, so that our men presumed that the people here must be very big or that they avail themselves of some practical means to climb the trees. In one of these trees these carved steps were very fresh and green as if they had been cut less than four days before.
>
> That the footprints of certain animals observed on the ground were not unlike the paws of a tiger; they also brought back some excrement, presumed to be from quadrupeds, as well as a small quantity of fine gum that had dripped from the trees and resembled gum-lac …
>
> That the land was mostly covered with trees, spaced well apart, so that one may pass everywhere and look far ahead, such that one could see any natives or wild beasts unhindered by thick scrub and undergrowth, which should allow exploration.

This was fertile land, the first fertile land the Dutch had seen in the South Land, and certainly much different to what they had found on the Cape York Peninsula or on the coasts of Western Australia. It was here on 3 December that Abel Tasman decided to take possession of this new country for the United Provinces and he sent the sloop to make a landing in what is now called North Bay. His instructions from Batavia stated specifically that 'in populated lands, or which have undoubtedly lords, the consent of the people or king shall be necessary in the taking of occupation or possession'. In this case Tasman could hardly claim the land was uninhabited even though there had been no encounters with the local population. He describes the landing:

> When we were close inshore in a small inlet west-south-west of the ships, the surf was so rough that we could not land; there was danger that our sloop would be smashed to pieces. We let the carpenter swim alone to the shore with the pole and the Prince flag and we waited with the longboat facing the wind. The pole and the flag were planted in the earth, in the middle of the bay, near four high, recognisable trees in the shape of a half-moon … we rowed our boat as close to the shore as we dared, and the carpenter swam back to the longboat through the surf. His task thus completed we rowed back towards the ship, leaving a touching memorial to posterity and to the inhabitants of this land (although they did not show themselves we suspected that some were not far from where we were and scrutinised our movements and doings with watchful eyes).

On 4 December the small fleet left what is now Blackman's Bay and began sailing north along the east coast of Tasmania where they passed Maria Island which they named after van Diemen's wife, Schouten Island which they named after the ill-fated Councillor of the Indies, Joost Schouten, and what appeared to be another island which they named Vanderlins Island but is actually the southern part of the Freycinet Peninsula.

In 1606 the Dutch had landed on the most northern point of Australia at Cape York and here in 1642 they had reached the most southern point when they rounded Van Diemen's Land. But what lay in between? Should Tasman decide to sail north to explore the east coast of this new land? Having just claimed this new land for the VOC this would seem a logical decision, but they had their instructions to sail to 220 degrees longitude before turning north. Sailing up the east coast of Tasmania they ran into headwinds and Tasman decided to turn and sail on an easterly course across what is now the Tasman Sea:

> At this point the land fell off to the north-west so that we could no longer steer near the coast here, seeing that the wind was almost ahead. We therefore convened the council and the second mates, with whom after due deliberation we resolved, and subsequently called out to the officers of the *Zeehaen* that pursuant to the resolution of the 11th ultimo we should direct our course due east, and on the said course run on to the full longitude of 195 degrees or the Solomon Islands. At noon we then shaped our course due east for the purpose of making further discoveries.

Tasman left Van Diemen's Land without having personally stepped ashore, without having met its people, or knowing if it was an island. It is interesting to speculate that if he had decided to explore the east coast of Australia, then the whole continent would have become known as Hollandia Nova and history would have been very different.

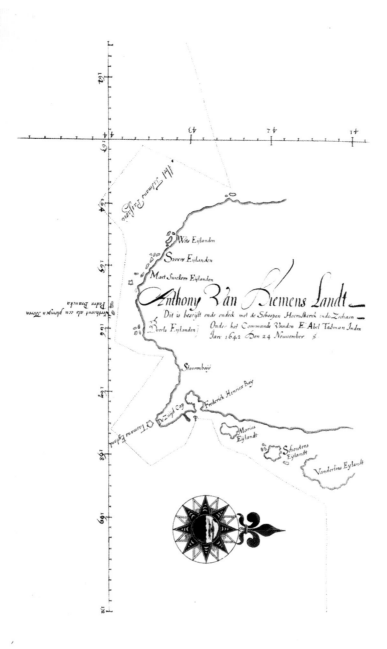

Map of Tasman's passage around Van Diemen's Land,
1642, François Visscher (Algemeen Rijksarchief)

24 Abel Tasman, the Heemskerck and the Zeehaen, New Zealand, 1643

With strong westerly winds and mostly under clear skies the *Heemskerck* and the *Zeehaen* continued sailing east and on 12 December Tasman wrote in his journal:

> The heavy swells still continuing from the south-west, so there is no mainland to be expected here to the southward.

These heavy swells made it a rough but rapid voyage across what would later be named the Tasman Sea and on 13 December 1642 large high land came into view as they approached the west coast of the South Island of New Zealand, somewhere near Cape Foulwind:

> Towards noon we saw a large, high lying land, bearing south-east of us at about 15 miles distance. We turned our course to the south-east, making straight for this land, fired a gun and in the afternoon hoisted the white flag, upon which the officers of the *Zeehaen* came on board of us, with whom we resolved to touch at the said land as quickly as possible.

However, because of heavy swells they could not find anywhere that was safe to land on this unprotected coast. Tasman named the territory Staten Landt after the land Cornelis Schouten and Jacob Le Maire had sighted in 1616 to the east of Tierra del Fuego and Cape Hoorn. The 1570 map of Abraham Ortelius had shown a continuous landmass across the Southern Ocean and Tasman speculated that the coast he encountered may be the west coast of a great landmass stretching from South America across the Pacific – truly the fabled Terra Australis he had been sent to discover.

> To this land we have given the name Staten Landt, in honour of Their High Mightinesses the States General since it could be quite possible that this land was connected with Staten Landt, although this is not certain. This land looks like being a very beautiful land and we

trust that this is the mainland coast of the unknown south land.

During the next few days Tasman sailed north-west looking for a safe anchorage in the hope of obtaining fresh water and food. On 18 December he entered a sheltered inlet (presently Golden Bay). Shortly after anchoring, two Maori canoes appeared, heavily manned with natives that Tasman described as being of ordinary height, but strong of voice and build, varying in colour between brown and yellow, with black hair which they wore in the manner of the Japanese tied at the crown of their heads. Tasman stated that these people had refused repeated invitations to come on board, so that it was difficult to know their disposition:

> The men in the two canoes began to call out to us in a rough, hollow voice, but we could not understand a word of what they said. We however called out to them in answer, upon which they repeated their cries several times, but came no nearer than a stone shot; they also blew several times on an instrument of which the sound was like that of a Moorish trumpet.

The next day the *Zeehaen* launched the ship's boat to bring the quartermaster across to the *Heemskerck*. However when the boat returned to the *Zeehaen* it was unexpectedly attacked by several Maori canoes and four of the seven crew were killed:

> They struck the *Zeehaen*'s small boat with their stem on the side, dashed over that same violently, whereupon the foremost in this canoe of rogues, pushed the quartermaster Cornelis Ioppen in the neck several times with a long blunt pike so fiercely, that he had to fall overboard, whereupon the rest of them set to with short thick pieces of wood … and their paddles, overpowering the small boat, in which violence three of the *Zeehaen*'s people killed, and the fourth through heavy blows was mortally injured … After this monstrous deed and detestable thing, the murders let the small boat drift, having pulled one of the dead into their canoe, and drowned another. We and those of the *Zeehaen* on seeing this shot hard with muskets and cannon, but although we did not indeed hit them, they nevertheless hastened back and paddled for land out of shooting range.

Tasman named the inlet *Moordenaarsbaai* (Murderers Bay) and quickly concluded that nothing good could be accomplished here. Sailing east into what they named Zeehaens Bight, Tasman noticed that the tide came from the south-east which indicated there could well be a passage which he planned to investigate. However, persistent easterly winds for several days prevented him from examining this further and possibly discovering the Cook Strait. On 31 December the fleet turned north and followed the coast in a north-westerly direction until on 4 January 1643 he reached a cape which he named after van Diemen's wife, Cape Maria van Diemen. Realising that he had now reached the end of this previously unknown landmass, Tasman, with Visscher's

DE MOORDENA ARS BAAY
Vertoont zich aldus, als gy daer in op 15 vadem ten anker legt.

A. *Onze Scheepen*. B. *De Praeuwen die om ons boort quaemen*.
C. *Zeehaens Praeutien dat naer ons boort quam Scheppen, en van de inwoonders des Lands vermeestert wiert, doch door ons schieten wederom verlaeten*.
D. *De vertooning van hunne Praeuwen, en het fatzoen van't Volk*.

The murders at Murderers Bay, Frederick Ottens (National Library of Australia)

agreement, resolved to set a north-easterly course which he undertook to maintain until they reached the approximate longitude of eastern New Guinea and the Solomon Islands. Accordingly, on 7 January 1643 the fleet headed out into the South Pacific.

It should be noted that later in the same year a Dutch expedition under Hendrik Brouwer confirmed that Staten Landt off Tierra del Fuego and named by Jacob Le Maire was in fact an island and some time after this Tasman's Staten Landt was renamed Nova Zeelandia after the Dutch province of Zeeland.

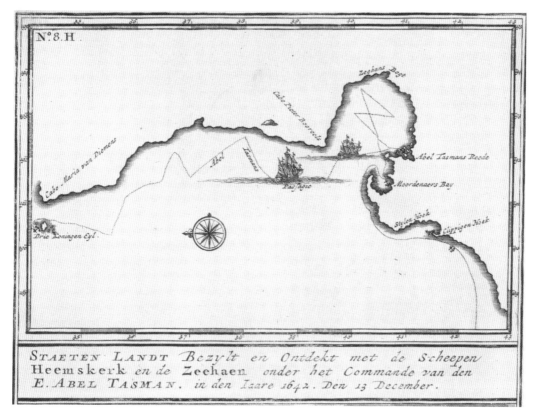

Map of Tasman's passage along Staten Landt, Frederick Ottens
(National Library of Australia)

Tasman's plan was to call for water and supplies at Le Maire's islands of Hoorn and Cocos and thence to sail by way of the Solomon Islands for New Guinea. For two weeks he headed in a north-easterly direction until, on 21 January, the Tonga Islands which had been discovered by Willem Schouten and Jacob Le Maire 27 years earlier came into view. Here Tasman managed to establish friendly contact with the local people who came aboard his ships to trade and who assisted him in obtaining much-needed water, fruits, meat and various other foods. For many of his crew this was the first time they were able to go ashore since leaving Mauritius and they enjoyed the luxury of being able to walk around on dry land and observe the islanders. At one stage an expedition ashore was able to collect eight casks of water and was provided with four live hogs and a number of fowls, coconuts and bananas to supplement their meagre rations.

On 1 February, after bidding farewell to the local chiefs, Tasman resumed his voyage. Suspecting he was at a longitude far to the east of the Solomon Islands, he now set a north-westerly course which he maintained for several days until, on 6 February, he reached another unknown group of islands (the Fiji archipelago).

Here Tasman on several occasions came perilously close to shipwreck on account of the maze of shallows and coral reefs within which they had become entrapped and it was only with great difficulty that he navigated a passage through them:

> Seeing that we could clear neither the reef straight ahead nor another which lay to the north of us we observed to leeward a small space about two ships' lengths wide where there were no breakers; for this we made since there was no other way of escape; we passed between rocks in four fathom, though not without great anxiety.

Resuming his north-westerly course, Tasman was plagued by prolonged calms and persistent westerlies. Then with heavy rain, poor visibility and the possibility of the winds driving them onto a lee shore, the results of their expedition seemed to be at risk. Their position relative to the Solomon Islands and New Guinea was unsure and Tasman requested the opinions of all his senior officers in writing. They all said they should sail north to 5 or 6 degrees from the equator and the following is the response from the Isaac Gilsemans:

> My judgment in this matter is as follows: since we are at present in Latitude 15° 55' south, Longitude 194° 24', and the weather here about this time of the year would seem to be very variable, while in this region of the world we are as it were at the mercy of winds blowing from all the four quarters, and we do not know how near we have sailed to the land of Nova Guinea … it is therefore my opinion, regard being had to the roughness of the weather and to the possibility that we may be nearer to the said land than we suspect, to the fact that we do not know its trend in this latitude and what bays, inlets, bights, shoals and the like there may be in and about it, to the risk that with these northerly winds we may by storm or rough weather be cast and driven on a lee-shore, which would grievously endanger both ship and cargo; it is therefore, I repeat, my opinion that we ought to steer our course north-north-west to the known part of Nova Guinea about as far as 4 or 5° Southern Latitude, and by so doing avoid all perils as much as possible. Given on board the flute-ship the *Zeehaen* this 15th of February, 1643.
>
> Signed,
>
> Your devoted servant,
>
> I. Gilsemans

It took more than five weeks to finally to reach the latitude of 5 degrees South along which, he knew, the Solomon Islands were positioned. If they could find an island recognised by Isaac Le Maire and Willem Schouten when they sailed this route in 1616, then they could follow their passage through the islands. When on 22 March they sighted the atoll of Ontong Java, a group of small coral islands that form part of the Solomon Archipelago, Tasman was then able to follow the passage. Sailing west they arrived at the north coast of what is today known as New Britain. In the belief that New Britain and New Guinea formed a continuous landmass, Tasman followed the north coasts until on 15 May they reached the western extremity of Nova Guinea.

According to their instructions the vessels should now sail south around Nova Guinea into the Gulf of Carpentaria and chart the north coast of Australia as far as Willems River. This was too much to ask and Tasman called a ship's council on 24 May. At this meeting, attended by Visscher and all the officers of the *Heemskerck* and *Zeehaen* they agreed that it was too late in the monsoon season to sail south towards the Gulf of Carpentaria and decided to set course for the Moluccan island of Ceram and then head directly to Batavia. Accordingly, Tasman sailed through the more familiar waters of the Indonesian archipelago to Batavia where, on 15 June 1643, his ships safely came to anchor and the final entry in his journal was:

> In the morning at daybreak I went to Batavia in the pinnace. God be praised and thanked for this happy voyage. Amen.

It was a remarkable voyage as only six men had been lost to illness and another four killed by natives in New Zealand. Tasman had managed to circumnavigate Australia without ever seeing the mainland, but he had discovered new lands at Van Diemen's Land and Staten Land. Even though this voyage had not yielded any immediate material advantage to the Company, van Diemen was mostly pleased with its outcome. He rebuked Tasman for not giving him more details about 'the appearance and the nature of the newly-discovered lands and their peoples' but, at the same time, he praised him for his 'extraordinary efforts and diligence'. In recognition of these efforts van Diemen awarded Tasman, Visscher, the officers and crews two months extra pay. It seems that van Diemen would have liked Tasman to be more 'adventurous', but he had been given a very detailed set of instructions to follow.

Tasman seemed determined to do everything exactly as he had been instructed and not to take any risks with his vessels or crew. The ship's council consisted of seven people, the captains, navigators and ship's mates of both the *Heemskerck* and the *Zeehaen*. Tasman made a point of discussing all important decisions with them and at times asked their opinion in writing:

> In the council shall be discussed and resolved all matters which affect the progress of the voyage and the execution of our instructions; in cases of an equality of votes the commander shall have the casting vote … save that in matters which affects the navigation, what course

to take, what discoveries to make etc, the chief pilot shall have the casting vote … the resolutions must be carried by a majority, put down in writing and signed and executed effectively for the service of the Company.

There was some difference of opinion with Isaac Gilsemans of the *Zeehaen*, whose calculation of the longitude of the west coast of van Diemen's Land was different from that of Tasman and Visscher on the flagship *Heemskerck*. This is an example of Tasman clearly imposing his authority:

> Towards noon I had the upper standard flown, whereupon the *Zeehaen* came at once astern of us and we called out to her men that Mr Gilsemans should come on board. Mr Gilsemans without delay came across to our ship and I declared to him the reasons which are mentioned in the following subjoined note. Mr Gilsemans was asked to take these instructions to the *Zeehaen* and show the same to the skipper Gerrit Janszoon, and also direct the attention of their steersmen in accordance with its purport:
>
> That the officers of the flute ship *Zeehaen* shall in their daily registers describe this land which yesterday we have seen and been near in the longitude of $163^\circ 50'$ E., as we calculated on the average. We shall take this figure as firm and therefore reckon further longitudes from the above-mentioned figure. He who before this had reckoned the longitude of 160° or more, will henceforth have to take this land for his starting point. In order to prevent all faults, as far as possible, all officers and mates shall now make reckonings from this land discovered. I find this to be proper and any charts which should be made by anybody shall lay down that land in the averaged longitude which is the aforementioned figure of 163° $50'$ E.

The Tasman voyage had made several important contribution to geographical knowledge. Tasman had found a passage from the Indian Ocean to the Pacific Ocean along the southern latitudes. He had discovered Tasmania and New Zealand as well as the Fiji Islands. Most importantly, by broadly circumnavigating the South Land he had delineated its maximum extent and had taken a giant step towards answering one of the great geographical questions of the time. Tasman's discovery of Staten Landt and the possibility that it could be the west coast of the fabled Terra Australis was hugely significant. Was this where Anthony van Diemen would find his gold and silver mines? It was possible, but the deaths of four of his crew at Murderers Bay did not indicate the natives would be friendly. It was another 130 years before James Cook in the *Endeavour* circumnavigated New Zealand and determined that it was two islands, separated by what is now known as the Cook Strait.

In his second voyage in 1773, Cook and HMS *Resolution* criss-crossed the vast swathes of the southern Pacific Ocean for months in search of Terra Australis. All they found was endless water but they crossed the Antarctic Circle three times and in January 1774 reached as far south as $71^\circ 10'$ where they were blocked by solid sea ice. Terra

Australis, the 'known but undiscovered' southern land mass remained undiscovered, but Cook believed that there was a tract of land near the Pole, which was the source of most of the sea ice which is spread over the Southern Ocean. He called the existence of such a polar continent probable and wrote in his journal that it is more than likely that he had seen part of it. The Antarctic continent is twice the size of Australia and as predicted by Aristotle and Ptolemy it is this southern landmass which keeps the earth happily spinning on its axis.

25 Abel Tasman and the Voyage of the Limmen, Zeemeeuw and de Bracq, 1644

As far as Anthony van Diemen was concerned there was still unfinished business to take care of. According to the original instructions to the Tasman expedition, they should have sailed south to the Gulf of Carpentaria and explored the north coast of the South Land as far as Willems River. There were questions that still needed to be answered. Was the South Land a complex of islands or one vast continent? Was there a passage undiscovered by the Dutch between New Guinea and Australia? Was the Gulf of Carpentaria the entrance to a large gulf that would stretch towards the south or east and provide a more direct route to the Pacific Ocean?

There were some reservations about Tasman the explorer for having failed to fully establish the nature of the lands and peoples he encountered in his first expedition. However, the following year he and Visscher were given command of a second expedition with three smaller ships, the *Limmen*, *Zeemeeuw* and *de Bracq,* to explore Australia's northern coastline. Their instructions from the Council of the Indies were to explore the unknown coasts of the South Land together with the channels and islands presumably lying between them:

> Both by word of mouth and through the perusal of Journals, Charts and other writings, it is in the main well-known to you, how the successive Governors of India, at the express command of our Lords and Masters the Heeren XVII, have, in order for the aggrandisement, enlargement and improvement of the Dutch East India Company's standing and trade in the East, at divers times diligently endeavoured to make timely discovery of the vast country of Nova Guinea and of other unknown Eastern and Southern regions; to wit, that four several voyages have up to now with scant success been made for this desired discovery.
>
> In sailing along the coast you will have all the bays and inlets you may meet with, diligently examined, and keep a sharp lookout for the discovery of channels or openings that might afford a passage into the South Sea, since we may surmise that such passage must be looked

for to the northward than to the southward, considering the breadth of the South-Land between 28 and 32 or 33 degrees.

In case you should discover channels leading to the South Sea, or should find the South-Land to consist of islands, you will endeavour to pass through or between the same, diligently observing the mouths and outlets, and then returning again through the same passage in order to proceed with your discovery along the northside.

In the castle of Batavia, this 29th of January 1644. Signed Antonio van Diemen, Cornelis van der Lijn, Joan Maetsuijcker, Justus Schouten and Salomon Sweers

On 30 January 1644 the expedition left Batavia for the Banda Islands with three small vessels, thought more able to explore the passages they hoped to find. Tasman and Visscher sailed on the 120-ton yacht *Limmen* with a crew of 45 sailors and eleven marines. Captain Dirck Haen and the merchant Isaac Gilsemans sailed on the 100-ton yacht *Zeemeew*, with a crew of 35 sailors and six marines. The *de Bracq*, a small shallow-draft vessel with Captain Jasper Jansz Koos and fourteen men completed the expedition fleet.

Almost 40 years earlier, the Dutch had heard indirectly from the Spanish on Ternate that Torres had sailed along the south coast of New Guinea on his voyage from Vanuatu to Manila. Tasman was instructed to follow the New Guinea coast to the shallow bight chartered both by Willem Janszoon in 1606 and Jan Carstensz in 1623, and to send the *de Bracq* into this bay to determine whether there was a passage between Nova Guinea and the South Land, their instructions read:

Cautiously cross the shallow bay situated there before sending off the galiot *de Bracq* into the bay for the space of two or three days, with the object of finding out within this vast bay any eventual passage to the South Sea.

If Tasman was to find a passage, he was to sail through it and investigate whether Van Diemen's Land was attached to the South Land. In other words find and explore the east coast of the South Land. This was the most important part of Tasman's voyage and if he had been able to find a passage through the Torres Strait then it would have changed the history of Australia.

Unfortunately Tasman did not find the entrance into the Torres Strait and it is thought he did not try very hard to do so. Perhaps it was the persistent shoals, combined with the prevailing easterly winds and currents, that made him decide that a voyage from west to east through any strait would be almost impossible. Since Tasman's journal of this voyage has been lost, we can only speculate as to the reasons for his failure to find what is now called the Endeavour Strait, which is south of Prince of Wales Island or what the Dutch called High Island.

The fleet now proceeded down the west coast of Cape York Peninsula past Cape Keerweer and then Staten River which was the furthest point reached by the Carstensz expedition in 1623. From here the VOC thought there might be a passage south that would lead to Van Diemen's Land. Sailing along uncharted shores, Tasman followed the coast of the Gulf of Carpentaria as it turned west naming various islands and inlets, but without finding any passage to the south.

The fleet then proceeded along the west coast of the Gulf of Carpentaria passing between Groote Eylandt and the mainland until they reached the coast that Willem Colster had explored in the *Arnhem* in 1623. Sailing along the north coast of Arnhem Land, Tasman reached the region known today as the Cobourg Peninsula and Melville Island, which had been explored by Pieter Pietersz in 1636. Proceeding further west Tasman failed to notice the Clarence Strait, an oversight that led him to suppose that Melville Island was a peninsula and the present Dundas Strait was thought to be the entrance to a closed bay which had been named Van Diemen's Bay.

Tasman continued to chart what was the continuous north and west coast of the South Land, until he reached Eendrachtland at latitude 23° just south of the North West Cape and approximately eighteen miles past Willems River. Faced with dwindling supplies of water and food, the ship's council decided against proceeding to the Houtman Abrolhos and returned to Batavia where on 4 August 1644 his three ships came to anchor.

Where did members of Tasman's second expedition land on the north and north-west coast and what were the results of their encounters with the natives? We shall never know as the journal of this voyage has been lost; however, the Tasman Map of 1645 shows points at which they anchored and could possibly have gone ashore. In a letter to the VOC directors of 23 December 1644 van Diemen assessed the results of the voyage as follows:

> The pinnaces … set sail from Banda on 29 February and followed the coast without finding passage between the partly explored Nova Guinea and Eendrachtland. They sailed as far as latitude 22 2/3 degrees and longitude 119 degrees but found no through channel between the half known Nova Guinea and the known land of the Eendracht but only found a great spacious gulf or bay as the chart and journals show. They did not discover anything important, but only found wretched naked beachcombers without rice or other valuable produce and in many places wicked men, as your Honours will be able to learn more fully and in detail in the Batavia report … Meanwhile this great and until now unknown Southland has been circumnavigated by the aforesaid Tasman on two voyages and the land is estimated to be 2000 miljen on the charts which we send along to Your Honours to show.

Tasman's orders were to fill in the gaps between the coastlines separately discovered and named between 1606 and 1636 and look for any passages to the south or east. During the voyage he surveyed a continuous northern coastline extending from the Gulf of Carpentaria to the North West Cape. Following this voyage the lands of Carpentaria,

Arnhems Landt, Baii van Diemen, De Wit Landt, Eendrachtlandt, De Edels Landt, Landt van de Leuwin and Nuyts Landt were all joined together into the half of one continent which the Dutch declared as Hollandia Nova, as shown on this 1658 map by Pieter Goos. The existence of Torres Strait was however still an open question.

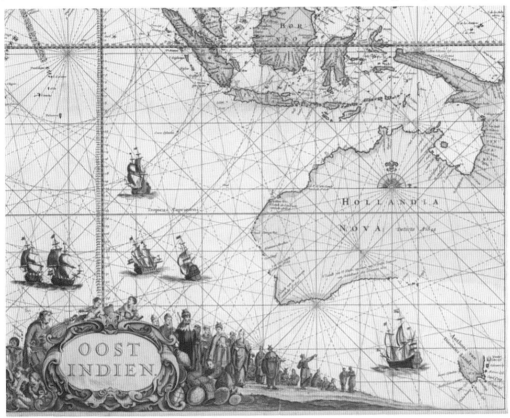

Mar da India, detail, 1658, Pieter Goos (National Library of Australia)

On his return to Batavia the VOC rewarded Tasman with the rank of commander and he was also made a member of the Council of Justice. He continued his voyages and in 1647 he commanded a trading fleet to Siam. In 1648 he led a fleet of eight ships on an unsuccessful attempt to capture a Spanish silver-ship in the Philippines. By 1653 Tasman had retired in Batavia and become a wealthy merchant. He owned 288 acres of town land and captained a small cargo ship of which he was a part-owner. When making his will on 10 April 1657 he described himself as ill but not bedridden and he died in October 1659.

Having found no easy passage to Terra Australis or Staten Landt, van Diemen was now determined to find the gold mines in the newly declared Hollandia Nova and in a letter to the directors of the VOC he wrote:

It seems hardly credible that nothing of value is to be found in such a vast landmass …
Your Honours can rest assured that I will soon have occasion to investigate everything more
closely; that I will put men on the ground, and have them explore some distance in the
interior. And when I do this, I will use people more vigilant and more courageous than those
who have been employed up to now. The exploration of new lands is not the kind of work
you can entrust to just anyone.

It was unfortunate for the Dutch that most of their discoveries were of the most barren
parts of the Australian coastline and the Company directors in the Netherlands were not
at all amused when they learned of van Diemen's further plans. Lacking the vision of
their governor-general in Batavia, they had over the past few years become increasingly
alarmed by his program of geographical discovery. Even though the directors greatly
respected van Diemen for the excellent financial results he had obtained, his latest
plans regarding the further discovery and exploration of Nova Hollandia caused them
to lose patience. In September 1645 the Heeren XVII, disappointed by the results of
Tasman's voyages, wrote to Anthony van Diemen instructing him to desist from further
exploration of the South Land:

We see that Your Excellency has again taken up the exploration of the coasts of Nova
Guinea in the hope of discovering gold and silver mines there. We do not expect great things
from the continuation of such explorations, which more and more burden on the Company's
resources, since they require an increase in ships and sailors. Enough lands have already
been discovered for the Company to carry on its trade, provided the latter is attended by
success. We do not consider it part of our task to seek out gold- and silver mines for the
Company, and having found such to try to derive profit from the same; such things involve
a good deal more, demanding excessive expenditure and a large number of hands … These
plans of Your Excellency aim somewhat beyond our mark. The gold and silver mines that
will best serve the Company's prospects, have already been found, which we deem to be our
trade over the whole of the Indies

In his nine years as governor-general Anthony van Diemen had been hugely
successful in expanding the power and the commercial success of the VOC as well
as extending the knowledge of the South Land as far as Tasmania and New Zealand.
Fortunately he did not have to suffer the humiliation of reading these instructions from
the Company directors as he died in Batavia in April 1645 and it can be said that the idea
of further Dutch exploration of Australia died with him.

Memorial at Anthony van Diemen's burial site in Jakarta (Ian Burnet)

The major voyages of discovery initiated by Anthony van Diemen, their contribution to geographical knowledge and to the Tasman Map would be his enduring legacy. Significantly, the Tasman Map would remain unchanged for the next 125 years until 1770 when the British explorer Lieutenant James Cook charted the east coast of Nova Hollandia and named it New South Wales.

26 The Amsterdam City Hall and the Tasman Map

The crushing Dutch defeat of the Spanish fleet attempting to resupply their Army of Flanders in 1639 forced Spain to relinquish ideas of the re-conquest of the United Provinces. Admiral Tromp's epic victory removed any Spanish naval threat to the United Provinces and earned the Dutch the reputation of being the leading naval power in Europe. This change in the balance of power meant that there would eventually have to be a peace treaty. The 1641 truce between Spain and the Seven United Provinces was ratified in 1648 as the Treaty of Münster (also known in Europe as the treaty of Westphalia). The treaty was hugely important as it ended 80 years of religious war between Protestant and Catholics, guaranteed the independence of the Dutch Republic and created the new nation of the Netherlands.

The Dutch East India Company was now at the peak of its mercantile and naval power. It had expelled its Spanish, Portuguese and English rivals from the East Indies and the profits from its monopoly over the spice trade could now flow uninterrupted to its investors. The new nation was rich. A period of unprecedented prosperity dawned for the young republic which was to go down in history as the Dutch Golden Age. Artists no longer worked exclusively for the Church and the aristocracy, as a thriving middle class demanded paintings of themselves, their patrons and the world around them with an unprecedented realism. In a period of less than 50 years they were responsible for hundreds of thousands of paintings and it was the wealth coming from the VOC and the East Indies, and the profits which flowed into private homes that financed much of this art. Today, the best known painters of the Dutch Golden Age are the period's most dominant figures such as Rembrandt, the Delft master of genre Johannes Vermeer and Frans Hals who infused new life into portraiture.

Dutch architecture was also taken to a new height in the Golden Age. Cities expanded greatly as the economy thrived and new town halls, weighouses and warehouses were built. Amsterdam commenced building a new ring of canals such as the Herengracht, Keizersgracht and the Prinsengracht. Merchants who had made their fortune built themselves new houses along these canals. Houses which were built in the architectural style of the city with gabled roofs, shuttered windows and ornamented façades that befitted their owners' new status. These merchants also felt a need to fill their new houses with expensive furniture, porcelain, silverware and of course the paintings that characterise the Dutch Golden Age. An example of these is the Van Loon House on the Keizersgracht, which is now a museum and open to the public. Willem van Loon was a co-founder of the VOC and his grandson became mayor of Amsterdam. Built in 1672, it is a real home as the Van Loon family still inhabit the upper floors.

The Netherlands made to plans to celebrate their hard-won independence by building a new Amsterdam City Hall. The structure was built facing the landing wharfs along the Damrak, which at that time would have been busy with ships. This remarkable building which was constructed on 13,659 wooden piles at a cost 8.5 million guilders, was completed in 1655 and still dominates the Dam Square. The relatively simple exterior of the hall is strikingly different to the exuberant Baroque style of the interior, with its huge allegorical paintings and marble reliefs derived from the Bible and Classical mythology. At the centre of the building is the high-ceilinged Burgerzaal, which is a rare example for this period of a large non-religious architectural space. On top of the building is a large domed cupola, topped by a weathervane in the form of a cog ship, which is the symbol of Amsterdam.

Painting of the Amsterdam City Hall, 1672, Gerrit Berckheyde
(Rijksmuseum)

   Access to the Groote Burgerzaal is up a flight of marble stairs from the main
entrance to the palace and then through an imposing set of bronze gates. From there you
can admire the vastness of the hall, with a marble statue of Atlas holding up the world,
six huge chandeliers hanging from the ceiling, and the three marble maps making up
the floor.

The Groote Burgerzaal, Jean-Christophe Benoist (Wikimedia Commons)

   When the new city hall was completed, a large world map in two hemispheres
composed of marble and copper was laid on its floor to celebrate the trade supremacy
of the Dutch East India Company and the Dutch West India Company. Intended to
impress visitors, the floor was a symbol in stone of the extension of Dutch sea power
across the world. The Eastern hemisphere details the regions explored by VOC ships
including the exploration of Hollandia Nova and the results of Tasman's voyages. This
cartographical work of art was badly damaged over time by people walking over the
floor and the two hemispheres were later filled in with plain marble slabs lacking any
pictorial representation. However, while this important cartographical monument was
lost to posterity, we have an image and a description from 1663:

   One sees here in the centre, on the floor of the Burgerzaal, two half spheres, bisected
   at the axis and a celestial hemisphere, of which each at the centre line or diameter is a
   length of approximately two-and-twenty and in its circumference approximately six-
   and-sixty feet. On the one terrestrial hemisphere, towards the east in the Burgerzaal,
   the contours of the outermost limits of the three parts of the world, to wit Europe,

Asia and Africa, as also even the islands, promontories, rivers and oceans, and parts of Hollandia Nova are shown very ingeniously by red and other coloured inlaid stone.

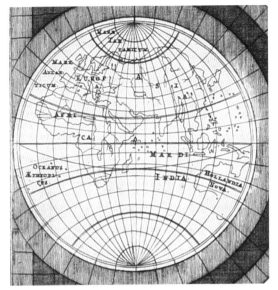

Le Pave de la Grande Salle des Bougeios, detail

In 1746 the Amsterdam government commissioned Jacob Martenesz to execute a new world map of two hemispheres in marble to replace those of 1655. For reasons unknown the work was not used as intended and remained forgotten in a storeroom of the City Hall. It was not until 1953 that the forgotten marble maps were finally installed in their intended place in the Groote Burgerzaal. The eastern hemisphere shows Nova Hollandia, including Terra Concordia (Eendrachslandt) and Terra Diemensis (Van Diemens Landt) all based on the 1644 Tasman Map.

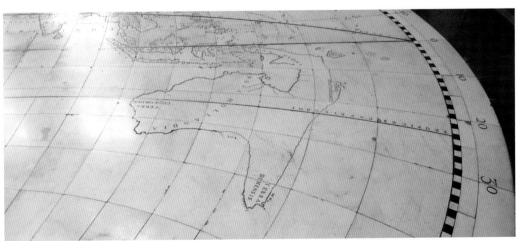

The Marble Map of Nova Hollandia (Ian Burnet)

In 1795 French armies occupied the Dutch Republic, bringing with them many patriots who had previously fled to France and the ideas of the French Revolution – freedom, equality and fraternity. In 1806, Napoleon Bonaparte installed his younger brother Luis Bonaparte as King of Holland. The new king converted the City Hall into his palace from which he ruled Holland until his abdication in 1810 and the Dam Palace is still used today by the Dutch Royal Family for official occasions.

27 The Mitchell Library, the Tasman Huydecoper Journal and the Bonaparte Tasman Map

The government of Batavia was required to make six copies of all important documents to send to the headquarters of the Dutch East India Company and to be deposited with each of the six chambers. Accordingly the Tasman Journal of 1642–43 and 1644, and the Tasman Map of 1642–43 and 1644 would have been forwarded to Amsterdam and into the official files. Our knowledge of the famous voyage of 1642–43 depends principally on two manuscripts, both of which were official copies from that written by Tasman himself.

One of these copies, known as the Tasman Journal, is held by the Netherlands National Archives in The Hague and gives a full account of the voyage. It is a copy of the journal of Tasman's flagship, the *Heemskerck*, and although not in Tasman's hand it has been signed by him. This manuscript is profusely illustrated and these have been copied into the text from now-lost originals made by Isaac Gilsemans.

The other copy of Tasman's 1642–43 journal is held by the Mitchell Library in Sydney and it is thought to have been made for Salomon Sweers, a member of the Council of the Indies in Batavia and one of those who signed the instructions for both of Tasman's voyages. Again, it has been copied by a scribe but appears to have been prepared under the direction of Isaac Gilsemans as the date, month and year are written on each page in his distinctive handwriting.

There is evidence that this journal was originally held by the Sweers family since it has marginal annotations which reveal a preoccupation with Salomon Sweers as an individual. For example, at the point where Van Diemen's Land is discovered a marginal note says that Tasman named islands after members of the Council of the Indies but only Sweers is mentioned by name. Also the binding of the journal has been initialled with the letters CS, which could be those of his nephew Cornelis Sweers or possibly refer to Collection Sweers.

This copy is known as the Huydecoper Tasman Journal, since it was in the possession of the Huydecoper family (Huydecoper van Maarsseveen en Nigtevecht) from about 1844 until 1925 when it was offered to the Mitchell Library by the Dutch bookseller Martinus Nijhoff. The founding member of the family, Joan Huydecoper, one of the initial investors in the Dutch East India Company, became a patron of the arts during the Dutch Golden Age and is described as being the first person to buy a Rembrandt painting. The Huydecoper copy does not have the illustrations corresponding to the copy in the Netherlands State Archives copy but does contain drawings of the Tasmanian coast and two charts of the west coast of New Zealand attributed to François Visscher.

The journal of Tasman's second 1644 voyage has been lost and no copies are known to exist. It appears that a copy of Tasman's 1644 journal was intended to be included in the Huydecoper Tasman Journal as the title of the volume indicates that both voyages are included and there is extra space in the back of the volume, but regretfully it was never included. This means that the primary record we have of the second voyage is the Bonaparte Tasman Map which is held in the Mitchell Library.

This map is a record of both first and second voyages and is thought to have been prepared for presentation to the directors of the VOC in Amsterdam, since it shows the coat of arms of the City of Amsterdam, those same directors who less than a year later decided to abandon any further exploration of Nova Hollandia. Research indicates that both the Huydecoper Tasman Journal and the Bonaparte Tasman Map were compiled in Batavia under the direction of Isaac Gilsemans as his handwriting is found in the journal and on the map.

This ornate manuscript map has been drawn on delicate Japanese paper and was clearly produced for display. It bears, just below the Tropic of Capricorn, the arms of the City of Amsterdam, showing the three crosses of St Andrew below the date 1644. This indicates that the Tasman Map was prepared for display by the Amsterdam Chamber of the Dutch East India Company and the inscription over Western Australia reads:

> Company's New Netherland. In the east the great land of Nova Guinea with the first known South Land and being one land and all joined together as can be seen by the dotted track by the yachts *Limmen*, *Zeemeeuw* and the *quel d'Bracq*. Anno 1644

The inscription in the top right-hand corner, above the line of the equator (Lingne Esquinocsiallis) translates as:

> These lands were discovered by the Company's explorers except for the northern part of New Guinea and the west of Java. This work thus put together from different writings

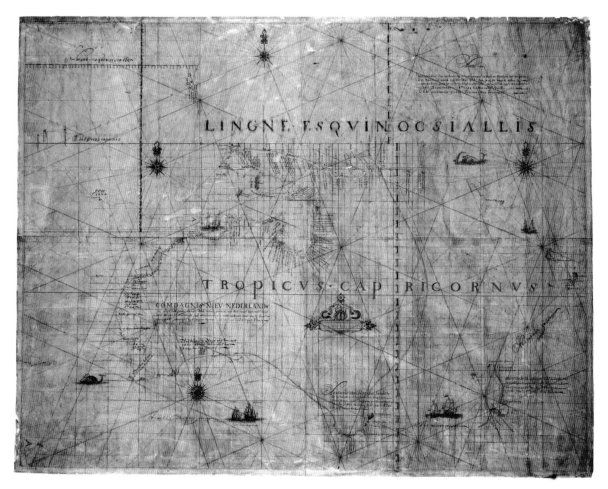

The Bonaparte Tasman Map (Mitchell Library)

as well as from personal observation by Abel Jansen Tasman, AD 1644, by order of his Excellency the Governor-General Antonio van Diemen.

The official VOC mapmaker and keeper of maps from 1638 until his death in 1673 was Joan Blaeu. After his death the Blaeu firm remained the official mapmakers of the VOC until Isaac de Graff was appointed in 1705. Johannes van Keulen was the official cartographer for the VOC from 1714 and was followed by his son Gerard, his grandson Johannes II and his great-grandson Gerard Hulst. It is not known when the van Keulen firm acquired the Bonaparte Tasman Map but it was probably after the bankruptcy and collapse of the Dutch East India Company in 1799. When Gerard Hulst van Keulen, the last of the van Keulens, died in 1801 his widow operated the business until her death. Jacob Swart then became proprietor and continued trading under the van Keulen name. The existence of the map was reported in 1860 by Jacob Swart when he wrote that:

> Among my manuscript maps of early Dutch seamen and hydrographers there is a chart on which Tasman's two voyages to and around New Holland are shown … This map, now about two centuries old … is compiled with care and almost a kind of luxurious indulgence, as well as neatly and in much detail … Perhaps it was compiled under the very eyes of Tasman.

After Jacob Swart's death in 1866 the 200-year history of the van Keulen firm was over and their possessions were sold at auction. The successful bidder for these items was the Frederik Muller Company. The map remained in their possession until 1891 when it was listed as item 2154 in the Muller sales catalogue prepared in French and named *Géographie cartographie-voyages*. This caught the attention of Prince Roland Bonaparte, the grand-nephew of Napoleon Bonaparte and the president of the Geographical Society of France, who purchased the map.

The amazing story of how the Mitchell Library acquired the Bonaparte Tasman Map begins in the most unlikely of places. The Aboriginal camp near the Ooldea Siding on the East–West Railway is in the South Australian portion of the Nullarbor Plain and is one of the most remote parts of Australia. It was here that Daisy Bates the anthropologist and welfare worker lived amongst the desert Aborigines for twenty years and was described as 'the most isolated white woman in the world'. In 1926 she was reading *Round the World*, a 1904 travel memoir by James Park Thomson who was the founder and president of the Queensland branch of the Royal Geographical Society of Australasia. In his book he mentions visiting the president of the Geographical Society of France, Prince Roland Bonaparte, in his grand mansion in Paris. The Prince's library contained 200,000 volumes and Thomson describes it as the most beautiful and elaborately equipped library he had ever seen. Among its numerous treasures, Thomson was able to view the Bonaparte Tasman Map:

> In the cartographical section of the library is preserved one the rarest and most valuable specimens of cartography in the world. This, I may mention, is nothing less than Tasman's original manuscript map of Australia, which I had the privilege of inspecting very closely. It is framed in an especially prominent place, where it occupies a position of honour. The illustrious owner very naturally attaches the greatest importance and value to this unique map, which he pointed to with pride as 'The first map of your great country Australia'.

Prince Roland explained that after his death he wished for the map to be given to the Australian people. Apparently Prince Roland would have liked to present the map to Australia himself but he told Thomson that he was terrified of snakes and that the mere thought of them made him shudder. Thomson unsuccessfully tried to reassure him that it was highly unlikely he would ever see a snake if he did make the trip to an Australian city.

By the time Daisy Bates had read Thomson's memoir in 1926 it was already more than twenty years since Thomson's visit and Prince Roland Bonaparte had died two years earlier. From her isolated post she wrote to the principal librarian of the State Library of New South Wales, William Herbert Ifould, recounting the story told by Thomson and urging him to investigate the location of the map and if possible secure it for the library. Ifould was a great collector and after pursuing her lead he discovered that the map was now in the possession of Bonaparte's only child, Princess Marie Bonaparte.

Princess Marie knew of her father's intentions and her husband Prince George of Greece wanted to come out to Australia and present the map himself. This was not going to happen for a few years and Ifould was concerned that, by the time the planned trip occurred, Prince George may hand it over to Commonwealth authorities. Ifould then requested Lord Chelmsford, the Agent-General of New South Wales in London, to pursue the matter with Princess Marie in Paris and asked to be warned of any imminent visit to Australia by the Prince and Princess.

Lord Chelmsford, who had opened the Mitchell Library when he was Governor of New South Wales, had a real commitment to the Library and after seven years of secret negotiations the Tasman Bonaparte Map was finally secured by William Ifould for the Mitchell Library in 1933.

28 The Mitchell Library and the Tasman Map Mosaic

The Mitchell Library is one of the many historic buildings along Macquarie Street in Sydney and is of cultural significance not just for New South Wales, but for the nation. Built over a period of 50 years, its neoclassical facade forms a majestic streetscape best seen from across the road in front of the southern entrance to the Botanic Gardens.

David Scott Mitchell (1836–1907) was born in Australia. He was among the first intake of students at the University of Sydney and one of its first graduates. From 1887 until his death twenty years later he became increasingly obsessed with collecting material that related to the history of Australia and the Pacific. By the late nineteenth century the terrace house in Darlinghurst Road, Sydney, where he lived was packed with books in every room and every hallway. The book dealer Fred Wymark describes Mitchell and his house overflowing with books and notes that he 'started collecting books and at last the collection collected him and held him in such a grip that he became part of his own collection'.

An example of his collecting zeal is his acquisition of the Australiana collection of his friend and fellow collector, Alfred Lee, whose holdings included Joseph Banks's journal of his voyage with the *Endeavour* and a series of twenty letters from Governor Phillip to Joseph Banks. Over many years Mitchell had unsuccessfully tried to convince Alfred Lee to sell him these items, especially the Banks journal, and he finally solved the problem by purchasing Lee's entire collection.

Towards the end of his life Mitchell offered his immense and unrivalled personal collection of Australiana to the people of New South Wales. A condition of his offer was that a new building be erected to house his collection which consisted of 40,000 books as well as a similarly large number of manuscripts, journals, diaries, letters, maps, pictures, coins and medals, all related to the early history of Australia. These were formally offered to the Trustees of the Public Library in 1898, together with a large endowment of £70,000, and the conditions in his will stated:

I give and bequeath to the Trustees of the Public Library of New South Wales all my books, pictures, engravings, coins, tokens, medals and manuscripts … upon the trust and condition that the same shall be called and known as 'The Mitchell Library' and shall be permanently arranged and kept for use in a special wing or set of rooms dedicated for that purpose.

Mitchell's bequest is one of the nation's greatest cultural benefactions because it made a substantial public collection available to whoever wished to consult original sources. After his death in 1907 the *Government Gazette* issued an official recognition of his bequest stating that David Scott Mitchell was

One of the greatest benefactors this State has known of in recent years. A large-hearted citizen, to whose memory is due an everlasting debt of gratitude for the noble work he had undertaken in gathering together all available literature associated with Australia, and especially with New South Wales, and in making provision that the magnificent collection should, for all time, on his death become the property of the people of his native state.

The construction of the Mitchell Library began in 1906 according to the plans and vision of the Government Architect, W.L. Vernon. The initial library now forms the western part of the building facing Macquarie Street and housed the library reading rooms, work area and galleries. In 1929 an extension known as the Dixson Galleries was built on the south side of that building to provide storage and gallery space for the extensive collection of historical paintings presented to the library by Sir William Dixson. In 1939 work began on the north-facing central portion of the building, which includes the main reading room, the beautiful portico entrance and the ornate vestibule where the reproduction of the Bonaparte Tasman Map in mosaic marble fills the entire floor. The Mitchell Library building was at last completed in 1964 when work finished on the addition to the south-east corner.

Importantly, subsequent architects had followed the original vision and design elements of W.L. Vernon and integrated the buildings by using the same honey-coloured Sydney sandstone and retaining the same nineteenth-century neoclassical façade in the style of the Italian Renaissance. The northern facade is especially magnificent and the design is highlighted by the large portico entrance to the building, supported by eight fluted columns with Ionic capitals.

Commissioned by William Ifould, the marble mosaic map was intended to celebrate Abel Tasman and the early Dutch discoveries of Australia, just as these voyages were celebrated in marble and copper on the floor of the Groote Burgerzaal in Amsterdam. Work was commenced in 1939 by the Melocco Brothers of Annandale who as master

Mitchell Llibrary-State Library of NSW

SIMON FIELDHOUSE

North facade of the Mitchell Library, drawn by Simon Fieldhouse

craftsmen took eighteen months and employed an incalculable degree of skill, knowledge and patience to create one of the most impressive mosaic floors in the world. After its completion Michael Stoker wrote of the vestibule that:

> In the years to come a million feet will cross this floor. They who pass this threshold to the sanctum beyond seek knowledge of man and life, past, present and future. May it never escape their attention that here beneath their feet is History.

The magnificent marble mosaic replica of the Tasman Map fills the vestibule floor. Wombeyan russet marble was selected as being hard wearing and of a tone resembling the varnished paper of the original map. The surface consists of slabs of marble 20 mm thick, joined only where lines occur on the map and fastened together with coloured cement. The map has a border of green and cream terrazzo and over the entire map a tracery of fine brass lines radiate to all points of the compass.

The surrounding mosaic floor has a wave pattern in which are set the coat of arms of the House of Nassau, images of Tasman's ships, cherubs blowing the winds, nautical instruments and traditional mapmakers' motifs in brass filigree work.

The title above the mosaic map reads 'A reproduction of Tasman's Map from the original in the Mitchell Library' and the arms beneath the map are from the Royal

The Mitchell Library vestibule and the Tasman Map Mosaic

Netherlands House of Nassau whose motto *Concordia re parvae crescent* translates as 'Small things are increased by unity'.

An inset map in the upper left-hand corner is drawn to half the scale of the main map and shows the initial course of the Tasman's voyage from Batavia to Mauritius. This explains why Java is shown twice. The tracks of Abel Tasman's 1642 voyage with the ships *Heemskerck* and *Zeehaen* are shown crossing the Southern Ocean and the description over Van Diemen's Land reads:

This is sailed and discovered with the ships *Heemskerck* and *Zeehaen* under command of the honourable Abel Tasman in the year A.D. 1642, the 24 November.

The map shows the *Heemskerk* and the *Zeehan* crossing the Tasman Sea towards New Zealand and here it is written:

The Coat of Arms of the House of Nassau

The *Heemskerck* and *Zeehaen*

Statenlandt, this is sailed and discovered with the ships *Heemskerck* and *Zeehaen* under the command of the honourable Abel Tasman in the year AD 1642, the 13 December.

From New Zealand the map plots the continuation of their voyage to Fiji, Tonga and then finally returning to Java along the north coast of New Guinea, showing that Tasman had managed to circumnavigate Australia without actually sighting its mainland.

The yachts *Limmen*, *Zeemeeuw* and *d'Bracq* of Tasman's second voyage are outlined in the bay now known as Joseph Bonaparte Gulf and the track of Tasman's 1644 voyage along the north and west coasts of Australia is shown as far as Dirk Hartog's discovery of Landt van Eendracht in 1616. From here the remaining coast of Western Australia is partly delineated by the accidental discoveries made by other Dutch ships when sailing from the Cape of Good Hope to Java between 1616 and 1636.

It is intriguing to speculate that the Bonaparte Tasman Map and the Huydecoper Tasman Journal may have both been compiled in Batavia in late 1644 or early 1645 under Abel Tasman's personal supervision. According to Paul Brunton, the Curator Emeritus at the Mitchell Library, it is certainly extraordinary that these two key documents relating to Tasman's voyages were acquired by the Mitchell Library from different sources at around the same time. It would be even more extraordinary if these documents had been compiled together in Batavia under Abel Tasman's watch and are now reunited at the Mitchell Library after almost 400 years of separation.

Author's Note

My time working in the Mitchell Library Reading Room began in 2008 when I was researching and writing the book *Spice Islands.* During this period I crossed the vestibule of the Mitchell Library on a daily basis and would always stop to admire the magnificent marble mosaic Tasman Map.

I would marvel at the length of these voyages halfway around the world, the sense of excitement and apprehension as the passengers and crew left the Netherlands, the deprivations of many months at sea, the lives lost to scurvy, pneumonia and shipwreck, the tragedy of the wreck of the *Batavia*, the desperate voyages to safety in an open boat, the sightings of unknown lands, attacks by cannibals – all stories which are part of the Tasman Map.

It certainly never escaped my attention that here beneath my feet was history and the idea of writing a book about the map formed at this time, as in 2009 I applied to the Library Council for a research fellowship to study the history of the Tasman Map. I love maps and the title of my proposed project read:

> The Tasman Map: A research project involving the voyages of Abel Tasman, the history of the Bonaparte Tasman map, its acquisition by the Mitchell Library and its marble mosaic replica.

It was envisaged that the results of the research would be published in book form and the project summary read:

> Every visitor who passes through the vestibule of the Mitchell Library stops to admire the magnificent marble mosaic replica of the Tasman Map. It is proposed to write a history of the map and the creation of its replica.
>
> The history would involve three related stories. The first is the story of the Dutch East Indies Company, Abel Tasman, and his two voyages of exploration to Australia. The second is the story of the 1644 compilation map and how it eventually found its way into the hands of Prince Roland Bonaparte. The third is the story of how the Mitchell Library was able to acquire the map, the decision to build the marble mosaic replica and the process of its construction by master craftsmen.
>
> This story would bring new recognition to an icon of Australian history and its masterful acquisition by the Mitchell Library.

The fellowship was granted to one of the other candidates but the idea remained. I continued to use the Mitchell Library for the research and writing of three subsequent books until almost ten years later, when I decided it was time to start researching and writing what I then imagined to be a biography of the Tasman Map, including details of most of the voyages that contributed to this first map of the north, west and south coasts of Australia. I also realised that it would be more meaningful to add context to this story by including the related events that were happening both in the Netherlands and in the East Indies.

Most people would imagine that the early Dutch exploration of Australia took place over a period of hundreds of years. What is surprising is that all these voyages took place within a period of only 38 years, before the directors of the Dutch East India Company wrote to Anthony van Diemen to tell him that there was no longer any commercial interest in Nova Hollandia and that:

> These plans of Your Excellency aim somewhat beyond our mark. The gold and silver mines that will best serve the Company's prospects, have already been found, which we deem to be our trade over the whole of the Indies.

Van Diemen's and Tasman's greatest legacy is the two final voyages of exploration leading to the compilation of the Bonaparte Tasman Map. It is they who would have presided over its preparation in Batavia in 1644, probably for presentation to those same directors of the Dutch East India Company who in 1645 decided to abandon any further exploration of Nova Hollandia.

Bibliography

Akveld, Leo and Jacobs, Els, eds, *The Colourful World of the VOC,* Bussum, Thoth Publishers, 2002

Anderson, Grahame, *The Merchant of the Zeehaen: Isaac Gilsemans and the Voyages of Abel Tasman,* Wellington, Te Papa Press, 2001

Beaglehole, J.C., *The Discovery of New Zealand,* Wellington, Department of Internal Affairs, 1939

Birmingham, Nick, 'The Australische Compagnie and the Other Eendracht of 1616', *The Great Circle,* Volume 38, 2016

Burnet, Ian, *East Indies,* Kenthurst, Rosenberg Publishing, 2013

Burnet, Ian, *Spice Islands,* Kenthurst, Rosenberg Publishing, 2011

Dash, Mike, *Batavia's Graveyard,* London, Weidenfeld & Nicolson 2002

Drake-Brockman, Henrietta, *Voyage to Disaster,* Nedlands, University of Western Australia Press, 1995

Duivenvoorde, Wendy van, 'The Dutch Seaman Dirk Hartog and his ship Eendracht', *The Great Circle,* Volume 38, 2016

Duyker, Edward, *The Discovery of Tasmania,* Hobart, Saint David Parkes Publishing, 1992

Eisler, William, *The Furthest Shore: Images of Terra Australis,* Cambridge, Cambridge University Press, 1995

Estensen, Miriam, *Discovery: The Quest for the Great South Land,* Sydney, Allen & Unwin, 1999

Fitzsimons, Peter, *Batavia,* Sydney, Random House, 1995

Gaastra, Femme, *The Dutch East India Company,* Zutphen, Walburg Pers, 2003

Heath, Byron, *Discovering the Great South Land,* Rosenberg Publishing, 2005

Heeres, J.E, *Abel Janszoon Tasman's Journal,* Project Gutenberg, 2003

Heeres, J.E., *Abel Janszoon Tasman: His Life and Voyages,* Amsterdam, 1899

Heeres, J.E., *The Part Borne by the Dutch in the Discovery of Australia 1606–1765,* Project Gutenberg, 1970

Henderson, James, *Sent Forth a Dove: Discovery of the Duyfken,* Nedlands, University of Western Australia Press, 1999

Hogenhoff, Carsten Berg, *Sweers Island Unveiled,* Oslo, Hogenhoff Forlag, 2006

Hooker, Brian, 'New Light on the Origin of the Tasman-Bonaparte Map', *The Globe,* 78, 2015

Hooker, Brian, 'Abel Tasman's Journal of his Voyage of Discovery, 1642–43', Online, 2006

Hornig, Ab and Cor, Emke, *The Ships of Abel Tasman,* Hilversum, Verloren, 2000

Jacobs, Els, *In Pursuit of Pepper and Tea,* Zutphen, Walburg Pers, 1991

Kenny, John, *Before the First Fleet,* Kenthurst, Kangaroo Press 2013

Kraan, Alfons van der, 'Anthony van Diemen: From Bankrupt to Governor-General', *The Great Circle,* Volume 26, 2004

Kraan, Alfons van der, 'Anthony van Diemen: Patron of Discovery and Exploration', *The Great Circle,* Volume 27, 2005

Le Maire, Jacob, *Mirror of the Australian Navigation by Jacob Le Maire,* Sydney, Hordern House, 1999

Leys, Simon, *The Wreck of the Batavia,* New York, Thunder's Mouth, 2006

Major R.H., *Early Voyages to Terra Australia now called Australis,* Adelaide, Australian Heritage Press, 1963

Mawer, G.A., Incognita, *The Invention and Discovery of Terra Australis*, Melbourne, Australian Scholarly Publishing, 2013

McHugh, Evan, *1606: An Epic Adventure*, Sydney, University of New South Wales Press, 2006

Murdoch, Priscilla, *Duyfken and the First Discoveries of Australia*, Sydney, Antipodean Publishers, 1974

Mutch T.D., *The First Discovery of Australia*, Royal Australian Historical Society, 1942

O'Flahertie, Susan, *Celebrating 100 Years of the Mitchell Library*, Edgecliff, Focus Publishing, 2000

Roegholt, Richter, *A Short History of Amsterdam*, Bekking & Blitz, 2004

Schilder, Gunter, *Australia Unveiled: The Share of the Dutch Navigators in the Discovery of Australia*, Theatrum Orbis Terrarum, Amsterdam, 1976

Schilder, Gunter, *New Holland: The Dutch Discoveries – Terra Australis to Australia*, Oxford University Press, 1995

Sharp. A., *The Discovery of Australia*, London, Oxford University Press, 1963

Sharp. A., *The Voyages of Abel Janszoon Tasman*, Oxford, Clarendon Press, 1968

Shaw, Lindsey and Wilkins, Dr Wendy, *Dutch Connections*, Australian National Maritime Museum, 2006

Shorto, Russell, *Amsterdam*, Abacus, 2001

Sigmond, J.P and Zuiderbaan, L.H., *Dutch Discoveries of Australia: Shipwrecks, Treasures and Early Voyages off the West Coast*, Adelaide, Rigby, 1979

Stevens, Harm, *Dutch Enterprise and the VOC*, Zutphen, Walburg Pers, 1998

Thomson, James Park, *Round the World*, Brisbane, Outridge Printing, 1904

Weider, F.C., *Monumenta Cartographica*, The Hague, Martinus Nijhoff, Volume 4, 1990

Woods, Martin, *Mapping Our World: Terra Incognita to Australia*, National Library of Australia 2013

Zanden, Harry van, *1606: Discovery of Australia*, Perth, Rio Bay Enterprises, 1997

Index